TRIO SSS ESC E-146

An Introduction to American Indian Studies

Sovereignty, Culture, and Representation

Edited by

Gabriel S. Estrada
Palomar College

PEARSON

Custom
Publishing

Cover photograph courtesy of Alexandra Harris, 2003. Kumeyaay Cultural Repatriation Committee Solstice Celebration, 2003. Bernice Paipa (Santa Ysabel Indian Reservation) dances to bird songs with baby Anthony Pinto, grandson of Ewliaapaayp tribal elder Tony Pinto. Anthony is from Jamul Indian Village.

Printed in the United States of America

10 9 8 7 6

ISBN 0-536-83658-2

2004420192

AP/JS

Please visit our web site at *www.pearsoncustom.com*

PEARSON CUSTOM PUBLISHING
75 Arlington Street, Suite 300, Boston, MA 02116
A Pearson Education Company

Contents

Introduction

Gabriel S. Estrada

Only a generation ago, Native Americans were routinely told at higher institutions of learning that they could not objectively study their own culture, and therefore had little to contribute to the field of American Indian Studies. The generation before that faced the harsher realities of assimilation through universities and boarding schools. For generations, Non-Indians who had interest in serving Native American communities were left with few intellectual models based upon the articulations of Native Americans themselves. Sometimes, history repeats itself in subtle or obvious ways. This year, a core group of Native American scholars joined together to formulate a plan to standardize American Indian studies so that the divisive patterns of past educational failures could not so readily reappear. I was sent by the Palomar College American Indian Studies Department to participate and contribute to that American Indian Studies Consortium (AISC) discussion held at Arizona State University. The resulting preamble is one preliminary result of that meeting. The preamble generally reflects philosophical motivations for why we at Palomar have written and anthologized our own text this year. Instead of relying upon other texts that were unable to stress the importance of sovereignty politics, a connection to Indian country, and respect for Indigenous intellectual achievements, we wrote our own text that could better reach those goals as reflected in the AISC Preamble:

CONSTITUTION OF THE AMERICAN INDIAN STUDIES CONSORTIUM (AISC) PREAMBLE

AISC supports the development of Native Studies as an academic discipline whose main goals shall support the cultural knowledge of tribal communities through elder consultation.

AISC shall support the infusion of traditional tribal knowledge into AIS courses, teaching methods, research, and in-service to Native communities.

AISC shall support efforts that address the effects of colonization upon tribal people and our tribal communities.

AISC shall defend tribal sovereignty through research creative activities, teaching, and community service.

AISC invites all people interested in Native Studies, to participate in the intellectual development of Native Studies departments and programs. AISC advocates and promotes the hiring of and intellectual participation of Native scholars in academia and in Native Studies programs and departments.

AISC supports the coordination and cooperation with Native Nations, Native urban communities, and other Native organizations toward the development of future directions, increased communication, effective research, and policy analysis. These issues include education, culture, arts, language and literatures, community, and economic empowerment for American Indians, Alaska Natives, and Native Hawaiians.

AISC promotes guidance to Native Studies programs that educate students and professionals engaged in Native studies, Native policy, and indigenous community issues.

AISC maintains a special interest to support and develop effective leadership throughout Indian country and in the communities of Alaskan Natives, and Native Hawaiians.

AISC will demonstrate the importance of outreach and service to the tribal community.

AISC will invite on a periodic basis Native elders to evaluate and provide guidance and advice to the organization and program.

AISC is an organization of individuals.

The last point about "individuality" is important, especially among Palomar American Indian Studies faculty as we all have differing experiences, backgrounds, and politics. Each of us might emphasize the importance of different parts of the Preamble, if not outright disagree with other Preamble statements as we formulate our own teaching goals. Those differences are what make this AIS 100 introductory text interesting. Our different approaches combine here to give a sense of the various disciplines and personalities that make up AIS at Palomar College. The various chapters also give a sense of other classes that we teach in AIS in the fields of art, anthropology, history, language, and sociology. The bulk of the classes are taught by Steve Crouthamel, Deborah Dozier, Linda Locklear, and Patti Dixon, who will chair AIS by the time this book is revised. Their bios and class descriptions are available from the main American Indian Studies/American Studies web site at http://www.palomar. edu/americanindianstudies/. Henrietta Moore, Alexandra Harris, and I are all contributors to this text and adjunct faculty at Palomar College as well. Students can reach us through the AIS office at (760) 744-1150, 2425. A minority of chapters are provided by outside authors David Wilkins and Mark Q. Sutton because they complement the content of our text with their excellent research.

The text roughly follows a chronological and disciplinary order. Crouthamel's archaeological survey of ancient American civilizations precedes the subsequent historical European invasions that Sutton covers. Sutton's ethnography on Arctic Natives contrasts with the agricultural southern cultures of ancient civilizations. Wilkins documents the eminence of Native American sovereignty from both a legal and historical point of view while Deborah Dozier's chapter takes a more humanistic approach to history through multiple lenses of art. Alex Harris' art history analysis makes parallel findings to Dozier's essay, although through the more modern media of photography. Contemporary Indian identities and lands make their way into the text thanks to Wilkins. Modern Native American prose and poetry by Henrietta Moore balance Wilkins' statistical and legal approach to American Indian identities of today. My own research on contemporary spirituality also relies on poetry and oral traditions. Finally, world systems and law structure my essay on Indians in a Latin American and international political context, ending this first edition of *An Introduction to American Indian Studies: Sovereignty, Culture, and Representation.*

1

America's Earliest Cultures and Civilizations

Steven J. Crouthamel

ANCIENT BEGINNINGS: ORIGINS

The origins and settlement of the American Continent remains one of the most controversial issues among scientists and indigenous people. On one hand archaeologists debate about minimal physical evidence that is further hampered by difficulty in technical dating methods, such as, measuring quantities of radiocarbon isotope, C14, in organic material such as bone or charcoal. On the other hand Native American people's knowledge that is grounded in traditional religious myths clashes significantly with Western scientific theories in emphasis, logic, and detail.

Myths of any culture are primarily stories of origins presented in a complex symbolic or metaphorical logic that does not emphasize historical chronology or other objective information. The myths are stories with a symbolic guide on how to live.

Native Americans produced and passed down their own myths about their experiences in the American landscape respective to each group's experience. Therefore, the myths are complex and highly varied between the many cultures from North America to the tip of South America. Many of the themes of the myths share common patterns with cultures throughout the world. For instance, peoples of the Northern Hemisphere, including many native North American peoples, share the common folkloric motif of an early hero/heroine that is viewed as "Earth Diver," that successfully dived for earth at the bottom of a perpetual sea to bring up the first earth/land that became this continent, "Turtle Island". As one traveled south from North America to Meso America the origin myth shifts to the folkloric motif viewed as "Emergence" with a hero/heroine emerging from an underworld (often a lake or body of water) to this middle world, which is soft and must be made hard. Similar folkloric motifs were found in Southern Europe, North Africa, and the Levant. Many try to read these stories as historical fact, but that was never intended since they were metaphors of the transcendent nature of things all humans experienced. Recent scholarship points out that some of these common metaphorical patterns may be based on universal human realities, such as, our emergence from our mother's womb, and universal environmental experiences, such as, flooding due to changes in climate during the recent Ice Ages (Pleistocene Epoch). Also, some Native American myths refer to complex origins and journeys of their ancient ancestors that do agree with archaeological, linguistic, and genetic information.

Western science, especially archaeology, relies on physical evidence about indigenous America. This physical evidence and in many cases the lack of physical evidence points to the relatively recent arrival of modern humans (Homo sapien sapien) in the Americas between 40,000–10,000 years ago. The current theories about the origins of Native Americans from Eurasia focuses on migrations from Asia into Alaska/North America over a 1,200 mile wide land bridge (Beringia) created by lower sea levels during Ice Ages. More recent theories propose alternative coastal routes from Asia or Europe along the Pacific and Atlantic Coasts. Actually, such theories had been proposed earlier and have been revived due to the realization that continental glaciers (2,000 miles wide; 2–3,000' thick) must have posed a tremendous barrier at the time of a land bridge. The inundation of the North American continent with these huge continental glaciers that created Hudson's Bay and the Great Lakes must have also destroyed most earlier sites and archaeological evidence. Even further south of Canada and Northern U.S there were alpine glaciers moving from higher mountain regions into lower valleys. Ancient archaeological sites older than 10,000 years ago are scarce or non-existent in the Arctic and Sub-Arctic; the very route migrations would have taken.

Physical evidence of genetic similarity of Native populations to earlier European and Asian populations is clear, but there is enough variation to agree that these migrations were multiple and represented a number of different populations. The Yupik, Inuit, and Aleut peoples still are distinct and no one refutes their Asian origins of 9,000–2,000 years ago after land bridges and the most recent glaciation. Furthermore, Yupik, Inuit, and Aleut have the B variant of the ABO blood system; which indicates a fairly recent time of leaving Eurasia. The NaDene or Athabascan American Indian people of the Subarctic, Northwest Coast, California, and the Southwest are O (without A, B, AB) and migrated to America between 12,000–8,000 years ago. All the rest of the people, American Indians (Amerindians) are mostly O and are speculated to have migrated 40,000–12,000 years ago.

In some ways indigenous people's myths and Western scientific theory do not fundamentally disagree since the variation of people's origins in Eurasia, variant environments and climate, and different routes and settlement areas would certainly lend to a tremendous diversity in detail of mythic themes. Also, some groups settled in initial areas of the Americas and relocated, sometimes further south, or even moved north again. The effect of 10,000–30,000 years in the Americas further effected diversification in genetics, language, and cultural traits.

ANCIENT HUNTERS AND GATHERERS: PALEO-INDIAN

A number of archaeological sites are identified as representing cultural remains of human use or occupation before 12,000 years ago, but most of these sites have problems that bring into question their age or even legitimacy as a human site.

Early Paleo Indian Sites	Original Dates/years ago
Old Crow, Yukon, Canada	22,000–43,000
Meadowcroft, Pennsylvania, USA	18,000–19,000
Wilson Butte Cave, Idaho, USA	14,500–15,000
Taima-taima & Muaco, Venezuela	13,000–15,000
Pikimachay, Ayacucho, Peru	14,500–20,000
Pedra Furada, Brazil	17,000–32,000
Monte Verde, Chile	13,000–17,000

In spite of problems in terms of accuracy of dating techniques, mixed stratigraphy, and legitimacy of artifacts, some of these sites may show enough merit to place people in America around 40,000–18,000 years ago. One of the most convincing sites of early human occupation in America before 13,000 years ago is Monte Verde, Chile. This site produced artifacts that indicate a more general hunting and gathering lifestyle that does not emphasize large Pleistocene game, but rather plants. Not only is the lifestyle different, but the occupation of around 13,000 indicates an entrance into America from the North at least 20,000 years ago. However, by 12,000–11,000 years ago a big-game hunting tradition, called Clovis, was a definitive lifestyle with evidence in numerous sites throughout much of the Americas.

The Clovis tradition was characterized by sites that produced large fluted bifacial points that are found in situ with mammoth (Mammuthus sp) or mastodon (Mammut sp) kills. Even more unique is the fact that the Clovis tradition is widespread throughout the Americas and consistently dated 12,000–11,000 years ago. This evidence implies a relatively rapid spread of a technological style and shared lifestyle involving big game hunting large Pleistocene megafauna as an important activity.

Chart I: Paleo-Indian Traditions

CLOVIS	12,000–10,500 years ago
FOLSOM	10,500–8,500 years ago
PLANO	8,500–5,500 years ago

Most of these early projectile points were used as spear/dart points for a lever launching weapon referred to as an atlatl (Nahuatl word) or spear thrower. This weapon increased the penetration of the dart foreshafts into these large mammals of the Pleistocene.

This big-game hunting lifestyle continued through the end of the Pleistocene to about 8,500 years ago, but changed as various animals became extinct. The causes of extinctions were a combination of climatic changes to drier conditions and increased human hunting pressures. This was a global phenomenon and over 100 species became extinct at the end of the Pleistocene.

Detail of a Hunt Scene from Newspaper Rock Petroglyph Panel. Courtesy of Corbis Images/David Muench.

The Folsom tradition used a smaller fluted point to hunt game, such as an extinct bison (Bison antiquus), but was limited to the American Southwest and Plains between 10,500–8,500 years ago. The Plano tradition continued only in the American Plains until about 5,500 years ago and involved hunting smaller and more modern bison (Bison bison). These changes caused ancient Native Americans to seek smaller game and gather plants. More than 60 species of Pleistocene mega fauna became extinct in the Americas.

ANCIENT HUNTERS AND GATHERERS: ARCHAIC

The effect of the climatic and environmental changes at the end of the Pleistocene pressured human cultures to adapt by hunting smaller game and to focus on wild plant gathering. In some areas, especially around lakes, rivers, and seashores, people intensified specialized food resources like shellfish. These changes occurred about 10,000 years ago and are usually referred to as the Archaic tradition. The physical evidence for these changes included the appearance of smaller projectile points and a substantial increase in milling tools to process seeds, etc. The shift in lifestyle is unde-

MANO: Milling Stone. Courtesy of S. Crouthamel, Palomar College.

niable, but varies in both detail and chronology depending on what part of the Americas and how long game animals persisted. In many harsh and desolate areas, the Archaic tradition led to the greater need to manage plant species that ultimately led to various forms of agriculture.

FARMING AND AMERICAN CIVILIZATION: INTRODUCTION

During the Archaic a gradual technological shift occurred to manage plants to the point of cross hybridization of more favorable characteristics especially in the more arid regions of the Americas. In fact, the development of domestic plants in Archaic cultures after the last Ice Age (Pleistocene) was a worldwide phenomena occurring in desert mountain regions and only later spreading to lowlands, tropical, and temperate regions. Recent research has also demonstrated that the domesticated grains (corn/maize, wheat, barley, rice) that become important to urban developments and civilizations are not the first or earliest to be domesticated. For instance in America, people of the Southwest, Eastern Woodlands, and Andes developed many domesticated plants before maize spread from Meso America. Over time, corn/maize, beans, and squash (CBS) became the most important crops in Native America. Considerable misunderstanding arises from the word corn, which was derived from the old English referring to any hard grain or kernel and therefore, can be found in the King James version of the Bible! However, American corn or maize (Zea mays) is a very specific

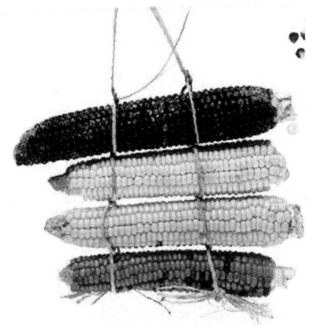

Corn. Courtesy of EMG Education Management Group.

grain/grass domesticated by Native Americans and is indigenous to America. Along with a variety of beans and squashes there are over 40 domestic plants developed by Native Americans. The impact for Native Americans was spectacular because these crops were the economic basis to civilization in America. Native Americans recognized the importance of CBS as embodied in the representation of CBS as deities: the three sisters.

Their kinship is reflected also in agronomy, since when the three plants are grown together they mutually benefit each other. Nutritionally the food products from CBS complement each other with nutrients the others do not have.

As production of CBS and other domestic plants increased in the Archaic, native peoples become more sedentary, which resulted in increased fertility and in turn increased populations. Ultimately, this generated larger villages, ceremonial centers, urbanization, and greater sociopolitical stratification. These urban civilizations developed in America, but with some unique expressions and in relative isolation from the other agricultural civilizations of the world.

FARMING AND AMERICAN CIVILIZATION: MESO-AMERICA

It is in Meso-America where the horticulture/agriculture first emerged based upon the American cultigens corn (maize), beans, and squash (CBS). However, many other domestics like the gourd and avocado are found in archeological sites at earlier levels than corn/maize.

Chart II: Meso-American Civilization

Time	Period	Cultures	Sites
AD 900–1519	Post Classic	Toltec, Aztec	Chichen Itza Tenochtitlan
300 BC–AD 900	Classic	Maya, Teotihuacano, Zapoteca	Tikal, Palenque Teotihacan Monte Alban
1500–300 BC	PreClassic/ Formative	Olmec	La Venta, San Lorenzo
9000–2000 BC	Archaic		Tehuacan Valley

Corn, beans, and squash (CBS) eventually became important enough to stimulate sedentary lifestyle, population growth, and urban empires that are the most dramatic and evident in Meso-America. These early cultural developments about 9,000–7,000 years ago point to Mexico as the "grandmother culture" of America. However, it was not until 1949 that Western scholars became aware of colossal basalt heads along the Vera Cruz and Tobasco Coast that were constructed by these early cultures. This culture is referred to as the Olmec (rubber people). The Olmec developed complex CBS agricultural systems and built ceremonial centers in these lowlands 3,000–4,000 years ago. The Olmec's most important development was writing and mathematics. Later, cultures of the classic period were centered in other areas, but exhibit similar cultural traits, such as, a common base 20 vegesimal mathematical and calendrical system; along with similar symbolic motifs, such as, were-jaguar.

Nino jaguar olmeca. Courtesy of Dumbarton Oaks Research Library and Collection,

Ruins of Temple I at Tikal. Courtesy of Corbis Images/ML Sinibaldi.

The Olmec influential sphere spread in Meso-America and many of the cultures it influenced, like the Maya, Zapotec, and Teotihuacano. Yet, it is not clear what happened to the Olmec people.

Cultures, like the Maya, who originated in the pre-classic in the lowlands (El Peten) of Mexico, Guatemala, Beliza, and Honduras, initially, were thought to be slash and burn (milpa) CBS farmers in small villages supporting elite priests living in temples on pyramids in great ceremonial centers. As archaeological research reexamined great centers like Tikal, Guatemala, with new research tools like satellite remote sensing, it became clear that these sites and their respective cultures were far more complex. Tikal consisted of larger urban development with more than 100,000 people that operated not only a religious center, but an elaborate trade center with markets, artisans, etc. In other words, there was a whole mid-range of people and activities.

In addition, there was a more elaborate agricultural production system (chinampas) that supported the people and generated a surplus for trade. Since these cultures were so complex, they also were more fragile in terms of social and environmental stress that resulted in changes that led to their ultimate collapse. As with many great cultural developments and civilizations, vulnerability from this stress can be exacerbated by peripheral cultures tired of paying tribute; eventually invading. Such invasion occurred in Meso-America by people from the north called Chichimecs ("Wild Ones"). The first of these groups of the Post-Classic are referred to as the Toltecs. They may have been responsible for the destruction of Teotihuacán (Valley of Mexico) around A.D. 600. Another group of Chichimecs that rose to power around A.D. 1100, are known as the Aztecs. According to their own legends the Aztecs came from the North, "Aztlan," and settled in the place where an eagle landed in a cactus with a serpent. This place was the area around Lake Texcoco, the center of what was to become one of five cities including Tenochtitlan (Mexico City). The Aztecs like many conquering cultures absorbed many of the earlier developments of religion, art, and science of the civilizations they invaded. It was this late cultural empire that by A.D. 1500 spread to Northern Mexico and to Costa Rica that the Spanish found as they invaded from the Caribbean. Subsequently, it took considerable time for Euro-Americans to understand that there were many earlier Meso-American civilizations like the Olmec and Maya.

Map of Meso-America. Courtesy of FAMSI, © Foundation for the Advancement of Meso-american Studies, Inc., www.famsi.org.

Many other peoples away from the Valley of Mexico had developed CBS civilizations in Meso-America. Some of these cultures are part of the various empires that are most powerful at any given time, but others can be rather independent. The Caribbean, for instance, can be viewed as having Meso-American and South American traits.

The Caribbean developed CBS-based farming cultures, but in rather isolated tropical island environments. There were millions of Native Americans on Caribbean islands like Cuba, Jamaica, and Hispaniola (Haiti and Dominican Republic). However, their population declined by 90% and was replaced with African slaves by A.D. 1580. Thus, European Americans seldom recognized that there were Native American civilizations in the Caribbean.

FARMING AND AMERICAN CIVILIZATIONS. SOUTH AMERICA

The South American continent is not as compact as Meso-America and has a huge tropical rain forest, the Orinoco and Amazon Basin, in the middle of the continent. There was as much diversity of environments that somewhat mirrors North America in reverse. However, the Amazon Basin was an environmental barrier to Native American people, colonial Euro-Americans and others, including archaeologists assessing these cultures in the 20th century. The spectacular cultures of the Andes tended to draw greater attention, so much so that maps of South American prehistory often only show the Andean area. South America's prehistoric cultures developed CBS agriculture in a variety of desert, mountain, and tropical environments. In the very southern parts of today's Chile and Argentina hunting and gathering continued as the subsistence base after the Pleistocene, similar to the North American Far West and Far North.

Chart III: Andean Civilizations

South America	Initial/Early Horizon 3,500 BC	Chavin	Chavin de Huantar
N. Andes			
S. Andes		Paracas	
C. Andes		Ancon	Garagay
N. Andes	Intermediate 300 BC	Moche	
		Chimu	Chan Chan
S. Andes		Tiahuanaco	Tiahuacano
		Nazca	
Brazilaian Highlands		Tupiguarani	
C. Andes	Late Horizon AD 1000	Chancay	
S. Andes		Ica	
N. Tropics Colombia		Chibchas (Tirona)	
Brazilian Highlands		Santarem	
Andes		Inca	Cuzco, Machu Picchu, Urubamba

The Andean civilizations were spectacular and unusual cultural developments. Similar to Meso-America they began from a mountain/desert horticulture but expanded to the coasts and even higher in the Andean mountains. Stone masons worked with immense granite rock and built fortresses with large stone blocks that are so tightly fitted that one cannot fit a razor blade between them. Yet, it was the relatively unknown crops, especially tubers like the potato that were grown at very high altitude that allowed for expansion, support of public works, and complex political systems. The potato is merely one tuber plant that was grown in thousands of varieties and literally freeze-dried for long-term preservation and storage.

Other seeds and nuts like the peanut or groundnut were also highly modified to adapt to high altitude farming. One of the earliest cultures to make an impact was the civilization called Chavin that was similar in time and culture to the Olmec. Common cultural elements included the were-jaguar motif and stone monuments.

Potatoes. Courtesy of
S. Crouthamel, Palomar
College

Later, a proliferation of kingdoms arose up and down the Andean cordillera producing spectacular ceramics and monumental architecture. These included groups like the Chimu and Mochica. The Moche have recently become even more known with recent finds of the unlooted tombs. Again, in similar patterns to Meso-America, later civilizations became more militaristic, with the last and most known group, being the great civilization of the Inca. Inca was actually a noble family name that rose to power and began to absorb surrounding kingdoms by A.D. 1200. Its sociopolitical system was thought to be socialistic and some European American scholars saw the Incan government as an example of pre-Marxist socialism in America. Such a comparison may not be very valuable and too manipulative of the Incan system. Work, resources, and state run economics were commonplace in America and even in other parts of the world. Recently, local way stations were discovered along the 8,000 mile road system of the Incan state. These way stations had food, including beer, clothing, and other accommodations for armies and/or officials that that traveled the royal roads on state business through the local areas.

We have good evidence now that other elaborate farming civilizations developed in Guyana, the Brazilian Highlands, and the Colombian-Venezuelan areas north of the Andes. In fact recent evidence suggests that the Amazon/Orinoco Basin was far more managed by Native Americans through a variety of techniques to include burning.

As one travels south in South America the climate and environments become colder and more barren similar to traveling north in North America. Here, too, hunting and gathering cultures developed in the pampas of Argentina or specialized fishing and shellfish gathering in Tierra del Fuego. These areas have similar counterparts in the Arctic/Sub Arctic and Plains of North America.

FARMING AND AMERICAN CIVILIZATION: NORTH AMERICA

North America is a large and highly diverse environment with some mountain and semiarid barriers in the west and large expanses of arctic and sub-arctic environments in the North. Like South America, North America's Native Americans developed CBS-based farming in the Eastern Woodlands, Plains, and Southwest. However, the CBS farming is quite different in each area and local or native plants augmented the subsistence considerably.

Corn, beans, and squash (CBS) agriculture originated in Meso-America, but how and when it spread to South America and North America is not clear. In both cases the Caribbean may have played a role in diffusion of cultural traits between all three areas. The blowgun and the hammock are technologies that spread from the Amazon basin through the Caribbean into the North American Southeast. Certain cultural traits may also have gone from Meso-America to South America via Panama; and from Meso-America to North America via the Gulf of Mexico or the Pacific Coast of Mexico. It must be remembered that Native Americans may have had less cultural separation than today's American states.

The Eastern Woodlands is as the name implies a temperate woodland area. Farming developed relatively slowly with indigenous plants and animal foods taking care of the people's needs for a long time. Some of the indigenous plants became early cultigens before CBS agriculture diffused into the Eastern Woodlands.

Chart IV: Woodland Civilizations

Eastern Woodland Traditions	Time Periods	Sites
Archaic Tradition	Early Archaic—9,000–6,000 B.C.	*Hardaway,* NC; St. Alban WV; *Icehouse Bottom,* TN
	Middle Archaic—6,000–4,000 B.C.	*Koster,* IL; *Windover,* FL; Neville, NH; Black Earth, IL
	Late Archaic–4,000–1,000 B.C.	Lamoka Lake, NY; Oconto, WI; Otter Creek, NY; *Indian Knoll,* KY; *Poverty Point,* LA
Woodland Tradition	Burial Mound I (Adena) 1,000–300 B.C.	*Koster,* IL; *Adena,* OH; *Moundville,* WV; Newark, OH; Augustine Mound, New Brunswick, CAN
	Burial Mound II (Hopewell) 300 B.C.–A.D. 700	*Mound City Group,* Scioto/Chillicothe, OH; *Quarry Crk/Trowbridge,* KS; Marksville, LA, Newark Site, Koster, IL
Mississippian Tradition	Temple Mound I A.D. 700–1200	*Weeden Island,* FL; Kolomoki, FL
	Temple Mound II A.D. 1200–≈1740	*Etowah,* GA; *Cahokia,* IL; *Town Creek,* NC; *Moundville,* AL; Spiro, OK; *Natchez,* MS

A similar pattern developed in Northern and Western Europe. In both cases nuts were an important food source with the hazel nut in Europe and the pecan in Eastern Woodland America. As CBS spread into the Eastern Woodlands the populations tended to move into the lowlands using slash and burn and later more intensive agricultural practices. This began in the Ohio River Valley with Adena and subsequent Hopewell cultures. These people also constructed effigy mounds and burial mounds, a trait not uncommon in other parts of the world. The effigy mounds were low 5' high x 15' wide earth mounds in uniform geometric or zoomorphic animal images. The great serpent mound in Ohio is an example. Burial mounds were more wide spread and were earthen cemeteries in which the subsequent generation's graves were capped with earth and new burials placed on top. Sometimes these reached 30' in height and covered 1–2 acres at the base. Many of these mounds were destroyed by colonists and many of the burial mounds were desecrated and looted.

About a thousand years ago an even more elaborate group of Native American cultures built huge earthen temple mounds in the Mississippi delta and the American bottoms near present day St. Louis, Missouri. The Woodland Culture in Ohio declined (A.D. 700–900) and new cultures that spread from the Mississippi delta were derived from earlier Archaic and Woodland influenced cultures that intensified agricultural techniques and built large ceremonial complexes with multiple temple

Overview of Serpent Mound and Foliage. Courtesy of Corbis Images/Richard A. Cooke.

mounds. These temple mounds were monuments for high ruling leaders to divine with their sky orientated deities. Burials were spread out in separate locations and varied depending on one's status. These cultures are generally referred to as Mississippian, but sometimes more dramatic labels have been used like Southern Cult, Buzzard Cult, or Death Cult. One of the difficulties with these early cultures is identifying the people and trying to connect various archaeological traditions to contemporary Native American people. This was further confused when early Europeans called all ancient Eastern Woodland cultures "Mound Builders" and did not attribute the culture to Native Americans at all. This was due to European American prejudice and a need to justify displacement and removal, especially around 1830. The controversy was referred to as the "Great Moundbuilder Debate" and was a dominate topic between 1790 and 1880. Eventually, as archaeology became more systematic it became clear that Native Americans were in fact the various "Mound Builder" cultures of the Eastern Woodlands.

Cahokia Mounds State Historic Site. Courtesy of Corbis Images/Michael S. Lewis.

Chart V: Southwest Civilizations

Southwest Traditions Desert Archaic Traditions	Time Periods	Contemporary Cultures
San Dieguito-Pinto (W) Cochise (S) Oshara (N) Chihuahua (SE)	all ≈ 6,500 B.C.–200 B.C.	
Anasazi (Ancient Pueblo)	Basketmaker II 100 B.C.–A.D. 400 Basketmaker III A.D. 400–700	Western and some Eastern Pueblo people: Hopi, Taos, San Juan, etc.
	Pueblo I A.D. 700–900 Pueblo II A.D. 900–1100 Pueblo III A.D. 1100–1300 Pueblo IV A.D. 1300–1700	
Mogollon (sub regions below) Sinagua Salado Mimbres	Mogollon 1 300 B.C.–A.D. 400 Mogollon 2 A.D. 400–600 Mogollon 3 A.D. 600–900 Mogollon 4 A.D. 900–1000 Mogollon 5 A.D. 1000–1400	Acoma, Laguna, Zia, Zuni, etc. Pueblo people
Hohokam	Pioneer 100 B.C.–A.D. 500 Colonial A.D. 500–900 Sedentary A.D. 900–1200 Classic A.D. 1200–1400	O'odham (Piman peoples)
Fremont	≈A.D. 400–1350	Pueblo/Numic people?
Patayan (Hakataya)	Patayan I < A.D. 400–1050 Patayan II A.D. 1050–1500 Patayan III A.D. 1500–	Colorado Plateau and River Yumans
Dene/Athabascans	? A.D. 900/1450–	Dene (Navajo and Apache people)

Cahokia was the largest temple mound site located near East St. Louis, Illinois, and was a large trade center in the American Bottoms with intensive CBS agriculture that flourished between A.D. 700–1400 and boasted a population of 20,000+. Their trade involved elaborate and far reaching networks bringing in obsidian from the Rocky Mountains, copper from the Great Lakes, and mica from the Carolinas; for local flint, salt, and lead.

In the Southwest CBS agriculture took on a variety of forms but generally develops into lowland irrigation systems or mesa/upland dry agriculture.

The Anasazi and Mogollon (ancient Pueblo peoples) peoples practiced dry agriculture techniques coupled with an intense religious strategy of rituals to control weather and fertility known as the Kachina cult. Often called "cliff dwellers," the Mogollon and Anasazi lived in a variety of arid environments in canyons and cliffs that were of a fairly high elevation (2,500–8,000'). As aridity increased after A.D. 1250 it was necessary for many of the people to move into the Rio Grande Basin (called Eastern Pueblo), where irrigation became communal and filled the need for water. Some groups, called Western Pueblo, continued their religious techniques and stayed on mesas and in canyon floors. Today, these groups are called Pueblo Indians of the North from the Spanish differentiation of more permanent looking stone masonry from thatched or jacal walled houses among what they referred to as "rancheria" people. At one point (about A.D. 1100–1300) these cultures had built integrated towns with multiple religious structures, called kivas, and multi-storied stone masonry structures reaching five stories. Pueblo Bonito was a spectacular version of such an integrated town. However, it is not clear if people actually lived there on a permanent basis.

Rather, Pueblo Bonito might have served as a trade and/or religious mecca in the Chaco Canyon area of present day New Mexico.

In the lowland area of the Gila and Salt River there was an irrigation-based CBS farming culture referred to as the Hohokam. They built ceremonial centers with small mounds and ball courts in the style of Classic and Post-Classic Meso-America. It is likely that trade from Meso-America to the Southwest was more developed than we once thought, especially via the great centers, in Mexico, like Casas Grandes or Tulum. Besides stone masonry these people made increasingly elaborate pottery, jewelry, and costumes.

Along the Colorado River another more moderate CBS irrigation culture developed called Patayan or Hakataya. These cultures used the natural flood plains of the Colorado River to irrigate farmland and augmented their food subsistence with mesquite beans and other wild plant foods. Today, Yuman cultures are descendents of the Patayan culture.

Unfortunately, European colonists and early archaeologists did not credit the living Southwest Native Americans with these various dry or irrigation farming civilizations and like the mound builder stereotypes of the East portrayed the ancient Southwest ruins as being built by Meso American civilizations. Thus, we get site names, such as, Montezuma's Castle or Aztec Ruins. Certainly, the influence was there, but Southwest civilizations are based on indigenous peoples. In fact, the Aztecs more likely came as rather modest hunters and gathers from the Southwest.

It is certain that one people came to the Southwest in recent times and these are the Navajo and Apache people or Dene peoples. They came from the Sub Arctic and adapted very well to desert conditions both in hunting and gathering; and some in farming subsistence strategies. However, their arrival in the Southwest was quite late in two or three waves between A.D. 1000–1400.

Corn, beans, and squash agriculture spread into the Plains from the Eastern Woodlands and into Southern California from the Southwest. However, most areas of the Far West and the Far North continued in the Archaic traditions with increased specialization of hunting and gathering strategies.

Ruins of Pueblo Bonito in Chaco Canyon. Courtesy of Corbis Images/Dewitt Jones.

CONCLUSION

As one can see American archaeology has always tended to emphasize the more materialistic ancient cultures of Native America. There may be other criteria of cultures and civilizations equal or more important that are beginning to be revealed. Regardless of the controversies with origins and technological innovations, Native Americans developed complex and diverse civilizations in relative isolation from the "Old World". These cultures represent true Americanisms and a tremendous time depth of experience in the American landscape. In recent years, Native American communities have taken greater control of their own histories and cultural resources.

2

European Invasion and Conquest

Mark Q. Sutton

The discovery of the New World by Columbus in 1492 was preceded by at least one Asian discovery of the New World some 14,000 years ago. Those intrepid people, all hunter-gatherers, explored and colonized the western hemisphere in a relatively short period of time. Europeans had themselves discovered the New World by about 1,000 years ago, and had visited and established colonies in North America hundreds of years before Columbus. However, for various reasons, these contacts were never substantial and the records of such visits were never widely known. Thus, most Europeans had no knowledge of the New World prior to 1492. After Columbus, though, Europeans quickly claimed, conquered, and colonized North America (see Jennings 1993; Allen 1997; and Wilson 1998 for discussions on the discovery and conquest of North America).

THE NORSE DISCOVERY

The earliest documented contact between Europeans and native peoples of the New World was that of the Vikings from Scandinavia, known as the Norse, about 1,000 years ago. Beginning in 982, the Norse established several colonies in Greenland, considered by many to be technically part of North America but not close enough to be regarded as the first discovery of North America. In 985, a lost Norse ship apparently observed some unknown land west of Greenland. Ten years later, Leif Thorvaldsson, son of Erik Thorvaldsson (or Leif, Erik's son, now commonly known as Leif Eriksson), sailed west to explore this newfound land (hence the name Newfoundland), and in 1004 a small colony was established. That colony lasted only a few years before the survivors moved back to Greenland. Remains of a small Norse settlement were discovered

Reprinted from *An Introduction to Native North America*, (2004), by permission of Allyn and Bacon.

by archaeologists at l'Anse aux Meadows, Newfoundland; they may be those of the colony founded in 1004 (see McGhee 1984; Fitzhugh 1985; Ingstad and Ingstad 2001).

Most Norse contacts in North America were likely with the Eskimo, but were probably never very intense nor sustained for very long; thus, there was no real opportunity for the transmission of disease. There is currently no evidence of any European diseases in North America prior to 1492, or for any major Norse influences on Eskimo culture. In the late fourteenth century, the Eskimo expanded east and south into Greenland, and by about 1400, the Norse had abandoned Greenland, perhaps due to a cooling climate. However, it may be that the Eskimo pushed the Norse out of Greenland; if so, it would be a unique case of Native Americans invading an area occupied by Europeans and supplanting them. It has been argued that the fighting abilities of the northeastern Indians and Eskimo so discouraged the Norse that the European invasion of the New World was delayed by 500 years (McGhee 1984).

COLUMBUS AND THE EARLY EXPLORATION OF NORTH AMERICA

On October 12, 1492, Columbus landed on a small island in the Caribbean, although no one is sure which one. He thought he was in the Indies of Southeast Asia, a region now called the East Indies; the eastern Caribbean islands were subsequently named

Columbus landing in the New World, from a 1728 etching.
Courtesy of Corbis Images/Stapleton Collection.

the West Indies. Thus, Columbus believed that the people he encountered were "Indians." In popular literature, Columbus is usually credited with the discovery of North America. However, when Columbus set out on his voyage, he thought he was going somewhere else; when he got there, he did not know where he was; and when he got back, he did not know where he had been (Brace and Montagu 1977:6).

The Spanish began their conquest of Central and South America while other Europeans rushed to exploit the resources of eastern North America. By 1497, the English were fishing for cod off Newfoundland and there is even a possibility that cod fishing by Basques predated Columbus (Quinn 1974). By the early sixteenth century large numbers of Europeans fished the waters off Newfoundland every summer. French Basque whalers were operating off the shores of eastern North America by 1536. The resulting very early contacts were relatively minor and their impact on the native peoples is unknown.

EUROPEAN COLONIES IN NORTH AMERICA

Initially, Europeans reacted to the discovery of the New World by attempting to conquer its people and loot its resources. Only some years later was any thought given to colonization. The Spanish began to explore the southern portion of North America in the early sixteenth century and in 1526 were the first to establish a colony in that region, located in what is now South Carolina.

Partly in response to this Spanish activity, the English founded colonies along the central Atlantic coast. The Roanoke colony was established in 1585, but it soon failed. A second attempt was made at Jamestown beginning in 1607; this colony struggled but survived, marking the beginning of a huge influx of English settlers into eastern North America. Another English colony was established at Popham Beach, Maine, in 1607 but failed the next year.

The French and Dutch also set up colonies in northeastern North America, first as fur-trading centers and later as colonies. The English eventually evicted the Dutch and took over their colonies and territories. The main Dutch colony, New Netherland, was subsequently renamed New York.

Most Europeans held the ethnocentric view that the Indians were either noble savages (idealized, simple children of nature) or primitive, bloodthirsty savages. It was also widely held that Indians had no God-given right to the land and that it was the "white man's burden" to bring civilization to them. Interestingly, most Indians also viewed the Europeans as bloodthirsty savages. In addition, Europeans and Indians often had different concepts about land ownership and use of resources, ideas that dominated many of their dealings (see Washburn 1988 for reviews of the relations between Indians and whites).

A number of European powers competed in the rush to claim portions of North America, including Spain, France, England, and to a lesser extent, Russia, Holland, and Portugal. Holland and Portugal quickly dropped out of the competition, but each of the other powers pursued particular policies and goals in the New World, resulting in different impacts to the native populations.

The Spanish Colonies

The first colonies in the New World were founded by Spain, in Central and South America, and later in what is now the southwestern United States and Florida. These Spanish colonies were government enterprises intended to establish an imperial presence, to control the native populations and economies, and to convert the Indians to Christianity. The procurement of land for settlers was not their goal, as relatively few Spaniards immigrated to the New World. The Spanish were primarily interested in appropriating native riches, particularly gold and silver, and enslaving the Indians to labor in exporting wealth to Spain. First, the natives had to be pacified, which was accomplished through ruthless and brutal campaigns of extermination, so that no doubt was left as to who was in charge (see Stannard 1992 for a gruesomely detailed account). To make matters even worse for the native populations, the spread of diseases introduced by the colonists reduced native numbers by as much as 95 percent in some regions during the first hundred years after the arrival of the Spanish (see Cook 1998).

Once the Indians were pacified, the Spanish introduced policies intended to control and enslave them. The Spanish established a new form of government to maintain political control of the various native cultures. This feudal system, called *encomienda*, entrusted large tracts of land to certain Spaniards; they could demand tribute and services from the resident natives, using military force if necessary. Eventually the Spanish themselves realized that the encomienda system, essentially a form of slavery, concentrated too much power in too few hands, so it was replaced by the *repartimiento* system, which divided the land into smaller units, the (still quite large) haciendas. These haciendas, owned by the elite, required the resident natives to work for the landowner. After the Mexican Revolution of 1910, many haciendas were broken up and the land redistributed to the peasants, either to individuals—who could not sell the land but could pass it on to their heirs—or to collective organizations such as villages.

French and Russian Business Interests

Unlike Spain, France and Russia were not much interested in converting Indians to European religions or in establishing direct control over their populations. The French and the Russians intended to conduct business with the Indians, primarily fur trading. Their policies toward the Indians were designed to ensure the success of the business ventures owned by their respective governments. They had the Indians do the difficult work of resource extraction, mostly of furs. Trading companies then purchased these goods at very low prices, sold them for their real value, and thus made gigantic profits. Neither the French nor the Russians made any concerted effort to colonize North America or to take large tracts of land from the Indians.

English Colonies

The English approached the New World quite differently. They wanted the land for themselves, rather than to exploit Indian labor or native resources. The first English colonies were established to provide living space for landless English citizens, a policy that resulted in large numbers of immigrants. Additionally, the English sent people to the colonies to ease the unemployment problem in England. They also exiled criminals to the colonies, a practice that continued during the colonization of Australia.

Once their colonies grew and became successful, the English began to reap economic benefits in trade and taxes. They considered the native peoples an obstacle, to be pushed out or killed to make way for more colonists. The Dutch had followed the same basic approach before England took over their territory. This pattern of genocide continued after the American Revolution, as the new United States undertook relations with the Indians.

Indian Slavery Among the Colonists

Many Indian groups had long taken other Indians captive, usually during warfare, for the purpose of acquiring hostages or slaves, or for adoption. Europeans eagerly joined in the market for slaves. Immediately upon their arrival in the New World, the Spanish began to export Indian slaves to Spain, but this practice did not last long because Indian population losses were so high. By the mid-sixteenth century, the Spanish, who required a large labor force to operate their new plantations, began to import African slaves to the New World to replace the rapidly disappearing Indians, thus ushering in the era of African slave trade to the New World. The English also joined in the trade of Indian slaves, encouraging an increase in native warfare in the Southeast in order to purchase Indian slaves from their Indian captors. A few Indian slaves were used in the South and some were sent to New England, but most were shipped to the West Indies as plantation labor.

In fact, all of the European colonial powers, but especially the Spanish and the English, used Indians as slaves. Even in the 1850s California, a nonslave territory, Indians declared as vagrants were arrested and essentially sold as slaves on the open market. The legal holding of slaves by Americans was not abolished until the 1860s.

GOVERNMENTAL POLICIES TOWARD NATIVE AMERICANS

Pre-Revolutionary Policies

By the middle of the eighteenth century, the Spanish had established themselves in southeastern, southwestern, and western North America. The French controlled Canada and the Mississippi drainage (later to be sold to the United States as part of the Louisiana Purchase). In eastern North America, the English colonies were expanding rapidly and aggressively, bringing the colonists into increasing conflict with the Indians and with the French, the longtime enemies of the British.

The British managed Indian affairs through several departments within their colonial government. In reality, however, the British never had much control over the colonists, who were living in many small and quasi-independent settlements that continually pushed against the Indians for land and resources. Between the early-seventeenth and mid-eighteenth centuries, the British and the local Indians fought many wars, most of them ending with the defeat of the Indians.

Conflicts also emerged between the European powers. The French in Canada allied themselves with the Indians against the British and their colonists to the south (the French wanted to keep the British away from the fur trade, and the English colonists wanted the land controlled by the French and Indians). The battles between them, collectively known as the French and Indian War, ended in 1763 with a British victory, leaving the British in control of Canada and all the land east of the Mississippi, except for Spanish Florida.

In 1763, following an uprising led by the Ottawa chief Pontiac, the British issued a decree limiting settlement west of the existing colonial boundaries. This line, called the Proclamation Line, was to be respected as the limit of English colonization until the government had signed agreements with the Indians. However, settlers ignored the line and streamed west. The 1763 decree implied an acknowledgment of Indian rights (Kelly 1990), as did certain attempts by the English to purchase land rather than to seize it. These somewhat enlightened government policies were largely ignored by the settlers, who wanted more and more land.

U.S. Indian Policies

Control of the lands south of Canada and west of the Mississippi passed to the new United States after 1783. Much has been written about the policies of the U.S. government toward American Indians, and an excellent overview is presented by Kelly (1990; also see Washburn 1973; Dippie 1982; Olsen and Wilson 1984; Prucha 1984; Deloria 1985; Weeks 1990; Hirschfelder and de Montaño 1993:8–35; Iverson 1998). During the late eighteenth century and throughout most of the nineteenth, for a variety of reasons, European Americans generally argued that it was necessary to either civilize or eliminate the Indians. However, the idea of "civilizing" the Indians seems to have served as a rhetorical smoke screen for the real purpose: eliminating the native peoples. Specific incidents reveal a discrepancy between the U.S. government's rhetoric and its actions. For example, even after the Cherokee had become "civilized"—having Americanized their way of life and established a modern state—they were ruthlessly uprooted from the Southeast and marched to Indian Territory in Oklahoma, an event known as the Trail of Tears.

Early in its history, the United States considered Indian tribes to be sovereign nations, though not *foreign* nations, and signed more than 400 treaties (by definition, agreements between independent political units) with various Indian peoples (see Prucha 1994 for a history of treaties between Indians and the federal government; also see Wilkins 1997 and http://www.councilfire.com/treaty/index.html for a list of full-text treaties). Many of these agreements were entered into in good faith by the respective governments, only to be broken by aggressive white settlers or, less often, by young Indian men continuing to raid after peace had been declared (see Prucha 1994:17–18; also see Deloria 1969). By the 1830s, Indian groups within the boundaries of the United States were considered to be *dependent* nations. This determination was based on an 1831 Supreme Court decision that denied a Cherokee request for an injunction against their removal; a year later, the government ignored a Supreme Court decision affirming Cherokee sovereignty (see Sherrow 1997). By 1871, most native groups without treaties had been defeated, so treaties were no longer sought. Thus, Indian political units evolved from sovereign to dependent status in relation to the U.S. government, occupying an ambiguous place in the political and cultural life of the United States—and this peculiar state of affairs still exists.

In 1775, the United States created several Indian Commissions, mostly in an effort to obtain Indian military assistance during the Revolutionary War. After the war, some Indians were punished for siding with the British, but there was generally a feeling within the government that the Indians should be treated fairly, perhaps because the U.S. military felt uncertain about its ability to quell potential conflicts (Kelly 1990:28). In 1790, the United States recognized the 1763 Proclamation Line and its provisions in an attempt to control both westward expansion and conflict with native peoples. However, it was virtually impossible to enforce this decision. When settlers continued to venture too far, the U.S. government felt obligated to protect them—it was preferable to fight Indians rather than its own citizens. This population pressure, and competition among European powers for control of the continent, doomed the effort (Horsman 1967).

In 1781, the Indian Department was created to manage native peoples. Its initial placement—within the War Department—provides some clue as to its mission. In 1824, the name of the agency was changed to the Bureau of Indian Affairs (BIA). The BIA became an independent agency in 1834 and was transferred to the newly created Department of the Interior in 1849. Initially, the mission of the BIA was to maintain good relations with sovereign Indian groups, in order to obtain land and promote trade. As the United States grew, however, its goal became the removal of the Indians from all lands east of the Mississippi River, then to their assimilation into American society. More recently, its mission evolved into supporting Indian groups.

The BIA is still the principal federal agency responsible for the welfare of native peoples in the United States and today has four primary responsibilities: (1) education; (2) providing other governmental services to native groups (e.g., law enforcement and health services); (3) management of the 56.2 million acres held in trust for various Indian nations; and (4) fostering Indian self-determination. Not until 1970 was an Indian appointed as the director of the BIA. A history and description of the BIA is provided by Jackson and Galli (1977; also see Porter 1988 and http://www.doi.gov/bia.html). In spite of the very checkered history of U.S. Indian policies, the federal government has spent many tens of billions of dollars to help its aboriginal inhabitants, a record no other nation can match.

Manifest Destiny

As European settlers continued to push westward, an idea evolved to justify the displacement of native peoples and the confiscation of their lands. Known as *manifest destiny*, it gave the European Americans a seemingly noble duty: to tame the wild lands of the west and to bring "civilization" to its native inhabitants. The idea gained momentum with the acquisition of the Oregon Territory in 1846 and of California and the American Southwest in 1848. As the Pacific Ocean beckoned, many Americans viewed it as their responsibility, or their "manifest destiny," to conquer and settle the lands west of the Mississippi River.

In the new territories, the West Coast was colonized first, due partly to the California Gold Rush. Two new American population centers, the West Coast and the region east of the Mississippi, were formed, with "Indian Country"—the Plains, Rockies, and Great Basin—lying between them. Many agreements between the government and Indian groups were breached as transportation corridors for wagon trails and railroads between the Mississippi River and California/Oregon were established. These broken treaties created considerable hostility between white settlers and the Indians, setting the stage for the famous Indian Wars of the west (a good history of these conflicts is presented in two volumes by Utley [1967, 1973]; see Brown 1970 for an Indian perspective).

Removal and Reservations

Though the early official U.S. Indian policy might be characterized as one of moderation (still, actual events tell a somewhat different story), after the War of 1812, the policy changed to removal and segregation. Entire cultures were relocated west of the Mississippi River, away from white settlements. This policy was formalized with the Indian Removal Act of 1830. Most of the Indians in the southeastern United States were forced, some at bayonet point, to walk to the Indian Territory established around 1830 in what is now Oklahoma (the word *Oklahoma* is from a Choctaw word meaning "red man"). Thousands of Indians died in these treks. Oklahoma essentially became a large reservation for many disparate groups, most of them separated from their homelands and economic bases. Ironically, oil was later discovered in Oklahoma, much to the dismay of the whites. In 1904, the Indian occupants of the Indian Territory petitioned Congress to admit the territory to the Union as an "Indian State," but their petition was rejected. Oklahoma was admitted to the Union in 1907.

In 1865, it was formally proposed that all Indians be put on reservations to protect them from whites, since neither the government nor the Indians themselves could do so. Over the next few years, a number of reservations were created on the Plains, this time located in the homelands of the affected groups, and a number of large groups moved to these reservations. Other groups were moved to Indian Territory and placed on lands that had been taken away from the Cherokee and Creek as punishment for their support of the Confederacy.

The government attempted to provide for the groups within the various reservations, but many of the politically appointed Indian agents prevented much of the money and supplies from getting to the Indians. Due to this corruption and greed, starvation became a serious concern, so some groups left the reservations to find food. The government perceived these actions as "uprisings," which they often quelled through bloodshed. Other Indians revolted at the poor treatment through raiding and warfare. Finally recognizing the corruption of Indian agents, the government appointed religious organizations—presumed to have higher morals—to administer the reservations and Indian payments through the Board of Indian Commissioners. This also failed, and the plight of the Indians worsened.

The Military Solution

Throughout the history of contact between native peoples and Euroamericans, the Indians almost always fared poorly. Few treaties were honored by the whites. Most of these accords were vague, poorly worded, negotiated with the wrong people, and never ratified by Congress. Virtually all were broken, usually by the whites, who were dealing with expanding populations. The affected native groups often reacted violently, and numerous military confrontations ensued. Many native groups possessed substantial military power and were adept at small-scale warfare. Most groups preferred not to fight but were quite capable if provoked. Small-scale conflict between armed settlers and native groups was a constant feature of the frontier. Large-scale warfare between Indians and the U.S. Army (or with the British prior to 1783) was uncommon and pitched battles were rare. Man for man, the Indians were more than a match for any European or American military force; however, the Indians lacked a sufficient number of modern weapons and were not able to sustain an army in the field for years on end.

Indian military power waned through defeat and population loss. By 1871 no more treaties were negotiated with Indians, and conflict between Indians and whites became an internal affair. In 1867, the United States instituted a "Peace Policy," forming the Indian Peace Commission to try to stop the incessant warfare. To the United States, peace meant the defeat and submission of the Indians, and a central component of the Peace Policy was to impose peace on the native peoples by force if necessary. To accomplish this goal, Gen. William T. Sherman (of Civil War fame) was appointed General of the Army in 1869. Sherman decided that the best way to obtain peace was to exterminate the Indians, although many Americans were opposed to this policy. While the Indians were not exterminated, the ruthless pursuit, defeat, incarceration, and maltreatment of Indians crushed their resistance, thereby achieving "peace."

Assimilation

From the early nineteenth century, many believed that the Indians were on the verge of extinction and that the survivors should be assimilated. Beginning in the 1870s, government policy began to shift from segregating Indians on reservations to attempting to assimilate (i.e., "civilize") Indians into mainstream society. Thought to be a humane solution to the Indian "problem," it was to be accomplished through educating the Indians, converting them to Christianity, and transforming their economies to farming (many Indian economies were already based on farming, but this was ignored).

It was reasoned that if the Indians became civilized, they would no longer require all of the lands of the reservations. Whites generally considered the Indians to have too much land already and proposals were made to parcel out reservation lands to individuals; thus, the Indians could be property owners, like whites. The Dawes Act (or General Allotment Act) of 1887 allowed for the disposition of group-owned Indian reservation land—mostly within actual states, rather than territories such as Arizona and New Mexico. These allotments were made to individual Indians (including women) in 40- to 360-acre parcels, depending on the quality of the land. Some reservation land was exempted due to earlier treaties. Lands that the government considered to be surplus could then be sold to whites, with the money, in theory, being used to help the Indians. The Dawes Act also made citizens of those Indians who received an allotment and moved away from their reservations. (All Indians in the United States were finally granted citizenship and the right to vote in 1924.) Individual ownership of land meant that the owners had to pay property taxes, which most Indians could not afford. Thus, the government held the allotments in trust, tax-exempt and non-transferable, for twenty-five years. Much reservation land was never allotted and remained in tribal hands. Many of these provisions were later changed, resulting in a further loss of Indian lands to whites.

Efforts were also made to educate Indian children. After 1877, schools were established, some on reservations and others as boarding schools. Frequently, Indian children were forcibly removed from their families, taken to boarding schools, and "educated" either to "become" whites (see DeJong 1993) or to serve as domestic help for white families. They were often punished severely if they spoke their native languages or observed their customs. This practice continued until the 1960s, when boarding schools were dropped in favor of local public schools.

The Indian New Deal

As the United States gained a New Deal during the presidency of Franklin D. Roosevelt, so did the Indians. Roosevelt appointed a new director of the BIA, John Collier, who initiated sweeping reforms in the BIA and major changes in Indian policy (see Philp 1977), moving away from assimilation and toward cultural pluralism (partly based on a 1928 report that was highly critical of Indian policies). Many of these reforms were passed into law with the Indian Reorganization Act of 1934. With this act, the allotment system was ended and unsold reservation lands were returned to federally recognized tribes. In addition, efforts were made to purchase land to "close up" the allotments and restore the land base. Groups were then allowed to organize tribal governments to manage their own affairs, although to a limited extent. The act also provided for improved education and preferential employment of Indians in the BIA. Collier resigned in 1945 amid accusations of favoritism toward Indians. The Indian Claims Commission was formed in 1946 to resolve the various Indian complaints against the government (see Sutton 1985).

World War II provided an opportunity for many Indians to participate in American society, including work in war industries and in the military. Some 25,000 Indians joined the military and fought overseas. Indians have fought for the United States in every war in its history. Patriotism and the chance to earn battle honors were incentives to join. The movement of Indians to the cities was accelerated by those seeking jobs in war industries and by the return of war veterans, eventually setting the stage for more politically sophisticated Indian activism.

Beginning in the late 1940s, the U.S. government initiated the Termination Policy to end the recognition—including status and rights—of some native groups, to eliminate their reservations, and to move them into white society. After 1958, the government ceased its efforts to terminate tribal governments. In the 1960s and 1970s, the civil rights movement and the war on poverty provided some funding and programs to help many Indians.

The establishment of the National Council on Indian Opportunity and the passage of the American Indian Civil Rights Act, both in 1968, initiated better legal protection (see Pevar 1997 for an outline of Indian legal rights). In 1970, the BIA changed its basic policy from managing Indians to serving them. Beginning in the early 1970s, Indians began to campaign more actively for their rights and a revitalization of their cultures, led in part by the American Indian Movement (AIM). As a result of these efforts, Congress passed the Indian Self-Determination Act (1975, designed to allow tribal governments to administer federal funds provided to them, funds that were subsequently cut in the 1980s), the American Indian Religious Freedom Act (1978, designed to prevent interference in the practice of Native religions), the Indian Gaming Regulatory Act (1988, to allow gaming on Indians lands), and the Native American Graves Protection and Repatriation Act (NAGPRA) (1990, to require the return of skeletal remains and sacred objects). These newfound legal rights allowed a number of groups to sue some states for the loss of their lands, and many have won substantial monetary damages. As a part of self-determination, many groups have established their own school systems, including community colleges.

Today, the government administers some 275 Indian reservations (including reservations, pueblos, and rancherias; see Tiller 1996 for a profile of each) and holds some 56 million acres of land in trust. In 1994, the government issued an executive memorandum directing government agencies to cooperate on a government-to-government basis with federally recognized tribes.

Canadian Indian Policies

As of 2001, there were about 675,000 native people living in Canada. They are organized in some 610 recognized native groups, often called the First Nations, living on 2,240 reserves (equivalent to reservations in the United States). The reserves are held in trust by the Canadian government. Before Canada became an independent nation, its native peoples dealt with the British government. Native peoples in Canada probably endured the Euroamerican invasion better than those in the United States, as Canada had far fewer immigrants and much less development than the United States and the British were a little more sympathetic to their needs. Nonetheless, problems remained. Slavery was not outlawed in Canada until 1834, and Indians were the primary slaves.

In 1867, Canada gained independence (actually dominion status within the British Empire), thereby taking over the responsibility of regulating the native populations. The Office of Indian Affairs was established within the office of the Secretary of State. In 1873, the Office of Indian Affairs was placed in the new Department of the Interior and was renamed the Department of Indian Affairs in 1880. This department was later changed to the Ministry of Indian and Northern Affairs.

Between 1871 and 1921, the Canadian government signed eleven major treaties with native groups, who were moved to reserves where the government was to protect and support them. The Indian Act of 1876 was passed to manage the Indians, although it did not apply to Eskimo groups until after 1939. The act designated Indians as either Status Indians formally recognized with treaty rights, or Non-Status Indians who, for some reason, had lost or given up their status. Another group, the Métis, requested and gained recognition. The Métis are the "third aboriginal group," consisting of the descendants of European fur traders and their Indian (usually Cree) wives (see Slobodin 1981; also see Payment 2001). Over the centuries they had developed their own cultural identity, speaking French or English rather than an Indian language. In 1991, the Métis numbered some 240,000 people in Canada (Payment 2001:675). The Indian Act also denied Indians the right to practice their social and religious customs. To enforce the ban on religious activities, the government confiscated religious paraphernalia from a number of groups, particularly on the Northwest Coast (see Cole 1985). The Indian Act remains the Canadian measure most emblematic of Indian mistreatment.

In 1888, Canada passed a law similar to the U.S. Dawes Act of 1887. The intent of the law was to break up reserve lands through an allotment policy. The Indians had very little power to stop it, but the loss of Indian lands was not as severe as it was in the United States.

An alliance of groups on the Northwest Coast won a small land-claims case against the Canadian government in 1927, which prompted Canada to pass a law forbidding all collective native political action. However, in reevaluating its Indian policies in the 1940s, the Canadian government passed the Indian Act of 1951. In this act, natives were granted citizenship and local voting rights (although they could not vote in national elections until 1960), were allowed to practice their religions, and could pursue claims against the government. Also, Indian groups on reserves, usually called "bands," were expected to establish councils to make decisions that related to the bands. Nevertheless, many of these decisions were subject to approval by the Canadian government.

In 1966, the Department of Indian Affairs and Northern Development was created; in 1969 the Canadian government repealed the Indian Act of 1876 and moved to break up the reserves, in a move similar to the failed U.S. Termination Policy (see above). This caused the politically dormant Canadian native peoples to unite, protest, and make demands, forcing the government both to abandon its termination policy and to repeal the 1927 law against native political activity. The native groups went to court to have their treaty provisions honored and won some victories. In 1974, the government set up the Office of Native Claims. In the past few decades, a number of land claims have been settled with various native groups, resulting in the formation and enlargement of reserves, special rights to land use, and cash payments. Several treaties, known as Comprehensive Land Claim Settlements, have recently been signed with a number of groups (see summary in Bone 1992: Table 10.1; also see Crowe 1991). As a result of one of these agreements, a new Canadian province, called Nunavat, has been created in the eastern part of the current Northwest Territory. Most of the population of the new province is Eskimo, who govern it.

Indian Policies in Northern Mexico

The majority of Mexicans today have some Indian ancestry, but only about 20 percent of the population identify themselves as Indians, or *Indios*. Mexican Indians are less vocal and have less political power than their counterparts in the United States and Canada, partly because Indians in Mexico have even less opportunity for education, employment, and social mobility. Centuries-old customs and traditions have marginalized Mexico's native cultures. Indeed, even after Mexico gained its independence from Spain in 1821, the Mexican government continued the use of the old Spanish system of repartimiento (see above), and the mind-set reflected in this feudal system still exists today in many parts of Mexico.

In the 1850s, to promote market-oriented practices, the Mexican government passed "reform laws" that prohibited communal ownership of land, thus breaking up lands owned by tribes. Much of this land was obtained by non-Indians during that time. The Mexican government also passed laws to abolish the status "Indian" so that only "Mexicans" would be recognized. The laws further stated that anyone could colonize "unoccupied" lands—that is, Indian lands—if one promised to develop them.

A number of groups resisted these policies and led several revolts. The Yaqui have been particularly resistant to the expropriation of their lands by both the Spanish and Mexicans for the past 450 years. The Yaqui led an armed resistance well into the twentieth century, which has gained the Yaqui a good deal of respect in Mexican history. Nevertheless, the Mexican government responded by sending in the army to crush the Yaqui. Many fled the region, and numerous Yaqui now live in Arizona.

After the revolution in 1910, the Mexican government pursued two different and seemingly contradictory policies. The first emphasizes assimilation through government education and economic development programs. The second emphasizes preserving the cultural and artistic heritage of Mexico's Indians. As part of the second policy, the government created the Asuntos Indígenas and the Instituto Nacional Indigenista to help the Indians in their disputes with private firms and government agencies.

Conflict between the government and Indians continues. In southern Mexico, the recent rebellions of Zapotecs in Oaxaca (1980) and of Maya populations in Chiapas (1990) are examples of growing problems. In northern Mexico, non-Indians continue to flood the region, exploitation of the environment remains unregulated, and the Indians continue to lose their lands and culture.

THE CULTURAL AND BIOLOGICAL IMPACTS OF EUROPEAN INTRUSION

Our knowledge of the consequences of European intrusion on native cultures is growing. First, we now better understand exactly how many native people were affected. Previous estimates of the number of people living in North America in 1492 stood at about 500,000, but it is now thought that eight to twelve million, or as many as eighteen million, lived on this continent. Second, we have gained a broader knowledge of the complex nature of the native cultures that were destroyed or damaged—a catastrophic loss in traditional knowledge and cultural achievement. Together, these impacts on population, land, and culture are astonishing in magnitude. The topic of European impacts on native cultures has been explored at some length, particularly in the past twenty years or so (see Fitzhugh 1985; Ramenofsky 1987; Stannard 1992; Dobyns 1993; Larsen and Milner 1994; Settipane 1995; Baker and Kealhoffer 1996; Cook 1998; Mancall and Merrell 2000; Thornton 2000; Axtell 2001; Larsen et al. 2001).

The population decline suffered by native peoples throughout the New World as a result of European contact and expansion was enormous, perhaps as much as 95 percent in some areas (Stannard 1992:268). Thus, of a total New World population of perhaps approaching 100 million people (probably more than were in Europe at the same time), only some five million survived. In North America, a similar rate of population loss was suffered by the natives; of the approximately eight to twelve million people, only about 375,000 survived into the twentieth century (see Stannard 1992). This type of impact is not confined to the past; native peoples continue to face population declines in many countries, for a variety of reasons.

SIDELIGHT

European Disease in the New World

Diseases introduced into the New World from Europe had a devastating impact on native populations. Contact between native peoples and Europeans resulted in the transmission of European diseases to the natives, but few if any native diseases were transmitted to the Europeans; the exchange seems to have been overwhelmingly one way. Why would this be so?

Humans originally evolved in Africa in relatively small groups, and immunity was evolved over millions of years. Asian populations originally migrated to the New World from northeastern Asia, and these populations were small and separated from diseases developing in the rest of the world. As people first moved into theNew World, they carried few diseases. Thus, New World populations were relatively free from contagious and infectious disease.

Disease is the complex of reactions and symptoms exhibited by the host in reaction to being invaded by a parasite. Contagious diseases generally involve small parasites such as viruses and bacteria and are spread from organism to organism mostly through the air or direct contact; infectious diseases involve relatively large parasites, such as worms and flukes. The development of contagious diseases requires a relatively large host population so that the pathogen (virus, bacterium, etc.) can be transmitted, and most pathogens must be transmitted to a new host rapidly before the host (and therefore the pathogen) dies. These "crowd" diseases have developed only relatively recently, since large, settled groups of people are a fairly recent phenomenon. Agriculture, which in many parts of the world displaced the hunting–gathering way of life, is only about 10,000 years old in the Old World and about 8,000 years old in the New World. Thus, only in the past several thousand years, as populations grew and cities developed based on agriculture, that crowd diseases had a means to emerge.

The other important factor in the development and dispersal of disease is that many human diseases first evolved in animals and then "jumped" to humans. Over the past 10,000 years, farmers have domesticated a wide variety of animals, including pigs, sheep, cows, chickens, dogs, horses, and many others. Large numbers of these animals were kept in close proximity to their human owners, providing ample opportunity for the transmission of disease. Many of the major killer diseases originally arose from animals; the influenza that killed some twenty million people in 1918 may have originated in swine. A similar influenza may have been the first of the New World epidemics (Stannard 1992:68).

Several other factors were also important in the transmission of European diseases. The major population centers in North, Central, and South America were mostly isolated from one another, and travel between them was quite time consuming. Such factors would have prevented the transmission of indigenous disease between these centers. However, in the Old World the extensive trading networks and rapidity and ease of travel between Europe, Asia, and Africa allowed disease to spread quickly. In addition, diseases apparently have an easier time moving east–west rather than north–south, perhaps due to climate and vegetation zones; European diseases dominated North America, whereas African diseases dominated South America.

Finally, humans were not the only ones to suffer from Old World diseases. Animal diseases (e.g., tularemia) brought over with European livestock, pets, and vermin (e.g., rats) may have ravaged native animal populations. Such epidemics would have exacerbated the already grim situation for the native peoples. A good, uncomplicated summary of disease transmission between the Old and New Worlds is provided by Diamond (1992; also see Cockburn 1971 and McNeill 1976).

Most population losses were due to the many diseases inadvertently brought to the New World by the Europeans, including smallpox, measles, influenza, malaria, typhus, bubonic plague, whooping cough, tuberculosis, diphtheria, yellow fever, cholera, and typhoid fever. The population declines associated with these diseases were usually due to multiple factors, including direct disease mortality across the population, greatly increased infant mortality, and a decline in birth rates. In addition, some of the population loss was due to direct action by Europeans (murder, overworking of slaves, failure to provide promised goods, etc.). Malnutrition resulting from imposed economic systems, such as forcing hunter-gatherers to become agriculturalists, lowered immune responses, increased disease, and decreased fertility. The effect of psychological stress on the immune system from the loss of life and culture may have added yet another layer of impact. However, some now believe that several native diseases also hit hard in Mexico in the sixteenth century, killing millions of people (Acuna-Soto et al. 2000).

The huge population decline resulted in loss of culture and knowledge. As the people who knew the ceremonies, songs, stories, technology, and other traditional knowledge died, less and less of this information was passed along to the next generation. After populations had stabilized and began to rebound, much had already been lost. Territory was also lost, making it even more difficult to reconstitute and rebuild cultures.

All of these factors continue to impact native groups. Racism, discrimination, despair, and poor health care are still widespread. Alcoholism is the most serious health problem facing Indians today. In some tribes the rate of alcoholism is as high as 85 percent. (A guide to sources on the current health of Native American populations is provided in Gray 1996.)

THE SPANISH MISSION SYSTEM

One of the major aspirations of the Spanish in the New World was to convert the masses of "pagan" natives to Christianity. In the late sixteenth century, the Crown had granted exclusive rights to missionize specific regions to the Jesuit and Franciscan orders, and after 1767, the Jesuit territories were given to the Franciscans. While small-scale missionary efforts were undertaken by the French and English throughout North America, the Spanish established mission systems in four major centers of North America: California, the Southwest, the Southeast, and northern Mexico.

In California, missions were established in both Alta and Baja California (see Costello and Hornbeck 1989; Mathes 1989; Crosby 1994). A series of seventeen missions was built in Baja California by Jesuit missionaries, and twenty-one additional missions were established by the Franciscans in Alta California. In the Rio Grande Valley of the Southwest, another system of missions was founded (see Kubler 1940; Spicer 1962; Kessell 1979; Jackson 2000). An extensive mission system was established in La Florida in the southeastern United States (see Thomas 1990; Milanich 1994), where as many as 130 mission localities were founded, although not all were occupied at the same time. The most extensive system was established in northern Mexico (the southern portion of the Southwest), where hundreds of churches were built (Dunne 1948; Polzer 1976; Roca 1979; Polzer et al. 1991; Sheridan et al. 1991; Jackson 1994).

In general, popular beliefs regarding missions and missionaries in the New World are highly romanticized, mythical versions of what people wish they had been: wonderful places where the natives could escape their primitive lives to discover and embrace the superior ways of the Europeans (see Thomas 1991 for a perspective on how this myth developed). This version is still widely taught in schools and remains the "party line" for tourists at many of the surviving missions, some of which are now parks. In truth, many (although not all) missions were little more than concentration camps, where the natives were imprisoned, forced to abandon their culture, and enslaved as labor, although it is true that these judgments are based on today's standards (see Guest 1979, 1983). These practices resulted in severe impacts to the Indians. Entire cultures were wiped out, dying from overwork, disease, and loss of the ability to reproduce. Native peoples were viewed as children, who required stern treatment and discipline if they were to be elevated from their savage or barbarian roots.

Organization of the Missions

Some missionary efforts were made at the actual village or town of a native group, while others were set up in different locations in order to separate the native individuals from their social, economic, and political communities and to concentrate them under Spanish control. This latter style, called *reducción* (or *congregación*), was established by the Spanish in California, the Southwest, and along the Southeast coast.

The missions were religious centers with priests, but military garrisons, or *presidios,* were built nearby to enforce the dictates of the priests. The state used the Church to help establish civil control over regions, while the Church used the state to protect its conversion efforts. The military was also sometimes used to gather new converts and to hunt down those who had escaped.

Missions typically consisted of a church building, housing for the priests, soldiers' quarters (if there was not a separate presidio), workshops, storage structures, animal pens, fields, irrigation works, and where necessary, dormitory-like buildings for the native converts. Buildings were often constructed from adobe (sun-dried mud) bricks, manufactured on site by native labor. Smaller missions, called *asistencias,* were sometimes established away from the major missions, and were often occupied by only a few people.

The Impact of the Missions

The Spanish were determined to subjugate and convert the native populations by pressuring them to settle at the missions so that they could be more easily controlled and their labor used. To do this, it was necessary to break down the traditional political, social, and economic systems of the Indians and remake them in the Spanish mold.

Central to the transformation of native culture was the forced adoption of new belief systems, although it was technically illegal for the Spanish to force someone to convert. Traditional religions were prohibited and replaced by Christianity. Attendance at daily mass was mandatory in some regions. People were baptized, often without even knowing what the ceremony meant. Marriages often had to be approved and performed by the Church. People were also forced to adopt European dress—including clothing of hot, lice-infested wool—foods, customs, and professions such as mason and carpenter.

Native people were usually compelled to learn Spanish, and native languages were often outlawed. In taking control of the native political system, the Spanish often replaced traditional leaders with others who were more cooperative. New laws and rules were instituted to control the movement of people. As they became entrenched, the Spanish then began to dismantle social institutions. Traditional kinship systems were broken up by reorganizing families and forcing children to attend boarding schools.

Economic systems were also changed, sometimes radically. Some groups were forced to adopt European-style agriculture in order to support the Spanish, who produced little. This often meant taking very productive native economies and converting them to less productive systems prone to drought and famine. The often unproductive agriculture required that food be rationed, with much less food given to the Indians than to the Spanish. Famine was a new phenomenon to the Indians and many learned what hunger was for the first time. Occasionally, a few Indians would be permitted to leave the missions to hunt and gather traditional foods. When the Spanish missionaries allowed these occasional excursions, they would hold family members hostage to ensure that the hunter-gatherers would return.

Finally, native people were often forced to live in dirty, overcrowded, unsanitary conditions, quite unlike their native villages. These conditions proved ideal for the spread of contagious disease, and the death toll among the natives, especially children, was staggering. In fact, some missions actually had to be abandoned when all the Indians within the region had died and there was no one left to work. The overcrowded conditions also fostered increased violence.

Native Resistance

Those resisting the Spanish were harshly punished. Many were beaten, some were imprisoned, and others were purposely starved. In some places, the death rate was so high from disease and overwork that the Indians desperately tried to escape. If they had a place to go, they simply ran away. Entire groups retreated into remote regions where the Spanish could not follow.

Other groups revolted violently. Indians at virtually all the missions planned revolts, but most were discovered in advance and thwarted. Large-scale rebellions did take place in La Florida in 1597 and in the Southwest in 1680, but these were so ruthlessly repressed by the Spanish that the Indians did not dare resist further. In California, the Indians at some of the missions revolted in 1824. This uprising was somewhat successful since the mission system was already on the verge of collapse by that time. Indians at several missions on the Colorado River revolted in 1781, eliminated the Spanish from the region, and successfully resisted reconquest until the 1860s.

THE FUR TRADE

The fur trade was a major economic endeavor undertaken by all of the European powers in North America, particularly by the French, British, and Russians, most intensively in northern North America between 1600 and 1850. Those native groups involved in the fur trade were, in essence, business partners with the European traders. The Indians were largely left on their own to provide furs and little effort was made to directly control them politically or to occupy their lands. Nevertheless, they were directly impacted by European diseases and suffered accordingly.

The French and Dutch initially dominated the early fur trade in northwestern North America, with the Dutch being pushed out by the English at a fairly early date. By the late seventeenth century, the French also controlled the fur trade in the interior of eastern North America, while the British dominated the fur trade in what is now much of eastern Canada and the northeastern United States. The British established the Hudson's Bay Company in 1670. The Hudson's Bay Company became very powerful, expanding across much of North America, and is still in business today, although on a much smaller scale. The French abandoned North America after 1803, leaving virtually all of the trade in central and eastern North America to the British and the Americans. The Russians moved into northwestern North America beginning about 1740 and dominated the fur trade in that region until they were pushed out by the British in the early nineteenth century.

Since its beginning, the fur trade played a dominant role in the economies of native peoples in the Arctic and Subarctic. The trade in furs declined in the 1950s, when the demand for furs decreased, primarily due to pressure from animal-rights groups. Nevertheless, there are still about 100,000 trappers in northern North America, about half of them native people (Bone 1992:213).

The fur trade profoundly altered the native cultures of northern North America, mirroring many impacts of Western cultures on indigenous groups around the world. These include changes in political and social structures, economic systems, settlement practices, territoriality, and technology.

To compete in the fur trade, European trading companies vied for partnerships with the various native groups, to form trading blocks against other companies. Competition was keen and frequently violent. Native groups sometimes found themselves at war with former allies and friends. Alliances dissolved and reformed, only to dissolve again as conditions changed. Native leadership fell to those who could manipulate the traders. Some groups were forced to completely restructure their political systems in order to deal with the trading companies.

Traditional economies were substantially affected. Prior to the fur trade, native economies were centered on obtaining resources necessary for the group. Then the economic focus changed from subsistence to trapping. Food and other goods were obtained from trade for furs, rather than directly by the people. After having survived for 15,000 years on their own, native peoples rapidly became dependent on the trading posts for their survival.

Prior to the fur trade, most groups did not own or defend territory. Afterward, specific territories became much more important since traplines had to be set out and

---

SIDELIGHT

Native Tobacco: Then and Now

Tobacco is a very popular substance that affects the lives of most people on our planet today. Tobacco is sniffed, chewed, and smoked in cigarettes, cigars, and pipes. Those who do not use tobacco are still subject to its effects through secondhand smoke or by having their taxes pay the medical bills for those who do use it. Since its first use, probably hundreds of millions of people worldwide have died of tobacco-related diseases, mostly cancer, and the death toll and associated costs continue to rise.

Tobacco (genus Nicotiana) is indigenous to the New World and includes about a dozen species distributed across the hemisphere. These species vary in their nicotine content; a strong tobacco can produce an immediate and almost hallucinogenic response. Native tobacco was used by Indians all across temperate North America, primarily for ceremonial purposes but sometimes for recreation (see Pego et al. 1999). It was smoked in pipes, sometimes chewed (as on the Northwest Coast), and sometimes snorted. Tobacco was cultivated by some native groups, while other groups managed wild tobacco plants, harvesting the leaves on an as-needed basis. Most groups mixed tobacco with either dogwood or sumac to lessen the effect of the nicotine.

Columbus observed natives in the Caribbean smoking "cigars"; in fact, the word tobacco comes from a Spanish translation of a native term meaning "cigar." Europeans rapidly adopted and began cultivating tobacco. By the mid–sixteenth century, snuff was being used, and then smoking tobacco in pipes became popular. Tobacco was first thought to be a medicinal aid. By the time people realized it was not, it had already become very popular and accepted in European society.

The primary native tobacco in eastern North America was N. rustica, but it was too harsh for the English, so a relatively mild species (N. tabacum) was imported from the Caribbean. This species was brought to the Jamestown colony in Virginia by John Rolfe, the husband of Pocahontas (see VIP profile in Chapter 11), who began tobacco farming in the colony. Tobacco farming spread all along the Atlantic coast from the Carolinas to Maryland, and soon the crop became an enormously important export. Farming of N. tabacum later spread across the world. Today, China is the largest grower and consumer of tobacco.

---

monitored. If the traps were raided, the fur would be lost. Thus, traplines and territories were vigorously defended.

Most groups involved in the fur trade had previously moved around the landscape in relatively small groups on a seasonal basis, following game, collecting plants, and/or fishing. But as they became dependent on traded goods, people tended to move closer to the trading posts, creating larger and more permanent villages adjacent to the trading posts. This new living arrangement brought relatively large groups of people into more or less permanent contact with each other. As food came from the traders, the value and prestige of hunters decreased and violence increased. Disputes over territory and/or women escalated, domestic violence became a problem, drinking and associated violence increased, and death rates began to soar. In addition, a number of health problems ensued from nucleation around the trading posts, including those related to poor sanitation, increased disease, poor nutrition from European foods, dental problems due to refined sugars, and alcoholism. People had lived for thousands of years in small, separate groups; they did not do well in large, permanent ones.

Traditional technology was finely tuned to a hunting lifestyle in the north. Then, in the late nineteenth century, the addition of rapid-firing guns and metal traps radically changed native technology and the people became reliant on European tools. This resulted in a loss of native knowledge, skills, and technology. Much later, additional technological changes, such as the use of guns and snowmobiles, increased the efficiency of killing, resulting in the reduction of certain fur species to the point where they could not be hunted profitably. Competing companies sometimes implemented a "scorched stream" policy that resulted in the complete extirpation of certain species from some areas so that other companies could not trap there.

Despite these great pressures, some of the northern North American groups have managed to maintain much of their traditional culture. They survive today partly by trapping, partly by government assistance, and partly by hunting. However, the loss of knowledge and skills over the past few hundred years has made it difficult for native people to return to traditional subsistence hunting, which is now regulated by the government to preserve species. Additional information on the fur trade can be found in Ray (1974), Wishart (1979a), Krech (1981, 1984), and Mackie (1997).

NATIVE PEOPLES OF THE ARCTIC

The Arctic encompasses all of the northern polar regions of the world, including parts of North America, Asia, and Europe. For the purposes of this book, however, only the North American portion of the Arctic is considered. The natural and cultural Arctic do not precisely match and there is some overlap between some Subarctic groups living in the Arctic environment and vice versa. In this book, the boundaries defined by the Arctic and Subarctic volumes of the *Handbook of North American Indians* (Vols. 5 and 6) are followed. The inhabitants of the Arctic are often collectively referred to by the general term *Eskimo*. Most people have heard of the Eskimo, and even have a basic idea of their adaptation to the Arctic environment; however, the popular understanding masks the substantial diversity and complexity of Eskimo culture (see Fienup-Riordan 1990:1–34). Nevertheless, for the sake of convenience, the term *Eskimo* is used throughout this chapter, with the exception of the case studies.

The term *Eskimo* was first used by Europeans in the late sixteenth century to refer to a specific group in the eastern Arctic, and was subsequently extended to include many other groups. The name was also used by Algonquian Indians in a derogatory sense to mean "eaters of raw flesh" (see Oswalt 1999:5–6). Interestingly, a small portion of the Siberian Arctic is also inhabited by Eskimo (see Fitzhugh and Crowell 1988), who are closely related to the people of the North American Arctic. The Eskimo are biologically distinct from the Indians living to the south. They are relatively recent entrants into North America and retain a number of biological traits traceable to northern Asia, including short and stocky bodies (for conservation of heat in cold climates) and epicanthic eye folds (extension of the skin of the upper eyelid over the edge of the eye) (see Szathmary 1984).

Following the *Handbook of North American Indians*, the native peoples of the Arctic are divided into two groups, the Aleut and the Eskimo. In a very general sense,

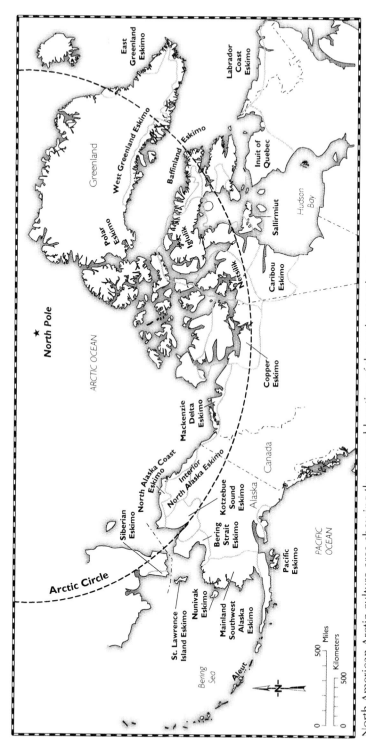

North American Arctic culture area showing the general location of the various native groups. Adapted from *Handbook of North American Indians, Vol. 5, Arctic,* D. Damas, ed., p. ix; copyright © 1984 by the Smithsonian Institution. Reprinted by permission of the publisher.

the Aleut are people of the open ocean and the Eskimo are people of the ice. The Aleut inhabit the Aleutian island chain extending westward from the Alaska Peninsula, while the various Eskimo groups occupy the rest of the North American Arctic. In Alaska, many Eskimo call themselves Yuit, while the Eskimo in Canada and Greenland prefer to call themselves Inuit, both terms meaning roughly "human being."

All North American Arctic groups speak languages of the Eskimo-Aleut language family; so do the Eskimo in extreme northeastern Siberia (see Woodbury 1984; Krauss 1988). The Eskimo-Aleut language is split into two major divisions: Aleut and Eskimo. The Aleut branch consists of one language, Aleut, spoken by people in the far southwestern Arctic, a region that is geographically in the Subarctic but is usually included in the cultural Arctic. The Eskimo branch is divided into three subbranches: Sirenikski, Yup'ik, and Inuit. Sirenikski is a single language spoken by Eskimo groups in far eastern Siberia. Yup'ik languages are spoken by Eskimo groups in southern and central Alaska and a small part of far southeastern Siberia, while the Inuit languages extend from northern Alaska eastward across Canada to Greenland. A very general classification of the North American Arctic people by language, culture, and geography is offered in Table 1.

GEOGRAPHY AND ENVIRONMENT

The North American Arctic covers about two million square miles (see Chester and Oetzel 1998 for a good overview of the geography of the Arctic). The Arctic is characterized by a cold climate, large bodies of water, icy terrain, and general paucity of vegetation. The land is bounded by the Arctic Ocean to the north, the Bering Strait between Alaska and Asia, and the Bering Sea to the south. The Arctic Ocean has many other named seas, bays, straits, and inlets, as well as many islands, the largest being Greenland. The ocean water is very cold, but fish and sea mammals are abundant.

Four major geographic regions are defined for the Arctic. The Canadian Shield, which consists mostly of exposed granite bedrock with few hills or mountains, encompasses much of the eastern Arctic to Greenland, and much of it is covered with ice. Several large mountain ranges, such as the Brooks Range in northern Alaska,

Table 1. Linguistic divisions of the Eskimo-Aleut language family and cultural divisions of the North American Eskimo

Language Family	Language Subfamily	General Culture	General Location
Aleut	Aleut	Aleut	Aleutian Islands
Eskimo	Sirenikski	Siberian Eskimo	Far eastern Siberia
	Yup'ik	Western Eskimo	Southwestern and central Alaska, far southeastern Siberia
	Inuit	Northern Eskimo	Northern Alaska and Canada
		Greenland Eskimo	Greenland

Source: Summarized from Woodbury 1984 and Krauss 1988.

dominate the western Arctic. The Arctic coastal plain stretches from northwestern Alaska east to western Canada. The Aleutian Islands, a series of island chains, run west from southwestern Alaska.

The Arctic receives low levels of solar radiation, about 40 percent less than at the equator, and much of what is received is reflected by snow and ice; thus, the climate is cold year-round. The region receives relatively little precipitation, and even less evaporation, so much of the Arctic can technically be considered a desert. The short but productive summers bring fairly warm weather, and coastal areas are ice-free by early July, although the polar ice pack remains year-round. By September, it begins to cool again and the snow and ice return. Strong winds can blow anytime and can be very dangerous in the winter, so shelter from these winds is essential. One of the major environmental distinctions made by the people who live in the coastal areas of the Arctic is the presence or absence of sea ice in the winter.

The Arctic Circle is the line that divides the nonpolar region of the earth, which has daily cycles of light and dark, from the northern polar region, where there are long periods of unbroken daylight, twilight, or darkness. Above the Arctic Circle, daylight is constant from about April through August, and it is mostly dark between about November and February. These cycles vary somewhat based on ones distance from the North Pole.

The Arctic has low biological activity and a small biomass. Vegetation communities are often divided into Polar Desert (or High Arctic) and tundra (or Low Arctic) (Bone 1992:19). The Polar Desert is permanently frozen and supports a few funguses and plants, mostly lichens. The tundra lies south of the Polar Desert and north of the Subarctic coniferous forest. The subsoil is permanently frozen (called permafrost), but the topsoil thaws during the short summer, creating vast wetlands and bogs (a favorite place for migrating waterfowl) and offering a limited growing season. The tundra supports a low-growing vegetation, such as dwarf willow, alder, and birch trees, as well as low shrubs, some grasses, lichens, mosses, and many flowering plants. The boundary between the Arctic and the Subarctic is often defined as the coniferous forest treeline. The treeline is not a discrete place, but rather a zone wherein the numbers of trees decrease until there are none (see Bone 1992:19). Because there is relatively little vegetation, it follows that the use of plant resources by the Eskimo was quite limited.

A number of land animals live in the Arctic. The most prevalent is the caribou, fairly large reindeerlike animals (up to 400 pounds) that migrate in large herds across vast tracts of the Arctic and Subarctic and graze on the short Arctic vegetation. In various parts of the Arctic are other animals, such as musk ox (except in the far southeastern Arctic), grizzly bears, polar bears, black bears, wolves, wolverines, lynx, many fur-bearing species (e.g., foxes, weasels, and mink), hares and rabbits, and many rodents. Marine mammals in the Arctic waters include nineteen species of whales, eight of seals, two of walrus, two of dolphin, and one of porpoise. Seals were probably considered the most important marine mammal by the Eskimo. Additionally, over a hundred species of birds nest in the Arctic during the summer. Some of these birds, such as ptarmigan, ducks, and geese, were hunted, and their eggs were also eaten. Many fish, including salmon, char, trout, pike, smelt, herring, whitefish, halibut, and cod, were caught and consumed.

A BASIC PREHISTORY OF THE ARCTIC

The Arctic has a remarkably complex prehistory. Summaries of what is known of the ancient Arctic are found in Dumond (1984, 1987), Maxwell (1985), McGhee (1996), and Fagan (2000). The information below is abstracted from those sources.

The Paleoindian Period (to ca. 10,000 B.P.)

A large portion of the western Arctic was not covered by ice during the last Ice Age. When Paleoindians crossed Beringia (see discussion in Chapter 1), they entered western Alaska, moving into the North American Arctic. A number of early sites known in the New World suggest an entry by at least 14,000 years ago, and there is some reason to believe that there may have been an even earlier migration into the New World. The technological and economic adaptations of these early people are poorly known. By at least 12,000 years ago, once the ice had melted to some extent, people in the Arctic began to move south to occupy the rest of the New World.

The Archaic Period (ca. 10,000 B.P. to Contact)

The people who remained in the Arctic after others had migrated into the rest of the New World essentially developed a generalized early Archaic, or "Paleo-Arctic," economy. It is possible that these people were the ancestors of the Na-Dene (speakers of Athapaskan languages). By about 7,000 B.P., perhaps even earlier, Na-Dene had begun to move into the Northwest Coast and western Subarctic, possibly from western Alaska. The Aleut occupied the Aleutian Islands by that time, though perhaps earlier.

By at least 4,000 years ago, some of the early Eskimo people moved east and inhabited the previously unoccupied northern portion of the Arctic, where they developed separate cultures from those remaining in the western Arctic. Beginning about 1,000 years ago, western Eskimo people began to move east, replacing those who had colonized those regions 3,000 years earlier, reaching Greenland by about 700 years ago. Thus, all of the people of the North American Arctic east of Alaska moved into that area in fairly recent times and share a common language.

The Contact Period

Sometime after about 1,000 years ago, the Eskimo of the eastern Arctic were first contacted by the Norse moving west from Iceland. Norse contacts were probably brief and never very intense. Thus, there was no real opportunity for the transmission of disease; at least there is no evidence of any Old World diseases prior to 1492, or for any major Norse influences on Eskimo culture. By the late fourteenth century, the Eskimo were expanding east and south into Greenland. By about 1500, the Norse had abandoned Greenland, perhaps due to a cooling climate. It is also possible that the Eskimo pushed the Norse out of Greenland; if so, it is a rare instance of Native Americans invading an area and replacing Europeans.

A Russian naval expedition landed in Alaska in 1732. In 1741, a second one, led by Vitus Bering, was dispatched to the region to claim it for Russia. The Russians contacted the Aleut, some of whom were forced to hunt sea otters for the Russians, an activity that rapidly depleted local sea otter populations. The trade in sea otter pelts expanded rapidly, and the Russian-American Company was established in 1799. The Russians fought—often in violation of imperial law—with the Aleut and Eskimo between 1760 and 1780, and with the Tlingit on the northern Northwest Coast between 1802 and 1804, before finally gaining control of the area. Alaska was purchased by the United States in 1867, and the Russians left the region at that time, although their cultural influences, particularly religion, persist to this day (see Black 1988 for a history of the Russians in Alaska).

After 1840, American whalers became very active in the northern Arctic, where whaling activities reached their peak in about 1900. This intensive hunting depleted whale populations to the point that the Eskimo were struggling to locate them. In addition, the whaling ships commonly stopped at coastal native villages, where the sailors spread venereal diseases. The Americans also distributed rum, which was ultimately detrimental to the Eskimo, as many became dependent on it. The introduction of rifles had a profound effect on the Eskimo as well, both by increasing their reliance on whites for ammunition and by depleting game populations.

For the most part, the governments of both the United States and Canada ignored the native people of the Arctic. There was some effort to build schools, but little other help was provided, and very little was done to control the effects that development in the region (e.g., mining, lumber, fishing, whaling) had on the native groups. The Aleut and Eskimo had to deal with major changes in virtually all aspects of their lives (see discussion of the fur trade in Chapter 2).

The Impact of European Contact

Although contacted in the seventeenth century in the east and in the eighteenth century in the west, most Arctic groups remained largely unaffected by Old World diseases. Most populations were small and dispersed over a vast landscape, impeding the transmission of disease. However, some groups were affected early due to intense contact with the Russians during the mid-to-late eighteenth century. In addition, by the late nineteenth century, many Eskimo were congregated around trading posts and other permanent settlements, ideal places for the spread of disease as well as other problems, such as increased violence. In Alaska, the smallpox epidemic of 1836–1838 was devastating, and epidemics of measles and whooping cough occurred repeatedly. The influenza epidemic of 1918 decimated native populations. The result was huge population losses, upwards of 90 percent in some places.

A BRIEF HISTORY OF ETHNOGRAPHIC RESEARCH

Contact with, and descriptions of, Arctic peoples began in the eastern Arctic in the sixteenth century and then in the western Arctic in the eighteenth century. However, as of the late nineteenth century, portions of the central Arctic and northern Greenland were still unknown to westerners. Thus, although the existence of the Eskimo has been known for the past 450 years, some groups remained uncontacted until fairly recently. The records of early explorers, ship captains, missionaries, and trading companies are exceedingly useful for descriptions of Aleut and Eskimo cultures.

Serious anthropological work on Arctic cultures began only in the mid-nineteenth century (see Burch 1979; Collins 1984; Hughes 1984). Among the most notable researchers were Hinrich Rink, Franz Boas, E. W. Nelson, and Knud Rasmussen, who himself was part Eskimo. Rasmussen worked with the Greenland Eskimo in the early twentieth century and his work displays "a depth of understanding, sensitivity, and insight that is unequaled in Arctic literature" (Collins 1984:10). In the central Arctic, the work of Diamond Jenness and Kaj Birket-Smith in the early twentieth century is particularly valuable.

Prior to World War II, most anthropological interest in Arctic peoples had focused on their technological adaptations to the Arctic environment. After 1945, when native life began to change rapidly with the encroachment of Western culture and anthropological research interests became much more sophisticated, many other questions were examined, such as those concerned with psychology, ecology, and acculturation. Today, considerable ethnographic work continues to be conducted in the Arctic (e.g., Condon et al. 1996; Burch 1998) and there is still much to learn.

There is a vast literature on Arctic peoples. Perhaps the best overall summaries of Eskimo culture were prepared by Weyer (1932) and Birket-Smith (1936). The Arctic volume (Vol. 5) of the *Handbook of North American Indians,* which was published in 1984 (Damas 1984a), was written mostly in the late 1970s and early 1980s and contains chapters on a wide variety of subjects and groups. More recent treatments of Arctic culture include Fitzhugh and Crowell (1988), Fienup-Riordan (1990); Crowe (1991), Morrison and Germain (1995), Condon et al. (1996), Burch (1998), and Freeman (2000). The summary of Arctic cultures presented below was taken from these sources and discusses groups as they were in approximately the middle of the nineteenth century.

A BROAD PORTRAIT OF ARCTIC GROUPS

The Arctic is a demanding, high-stress environment, and survival requires a very extensive knowledge and understanding of that environment. Arctic peoples have survived by living with the cold, rather than by struggling against it. Eskimo values include self-reliance, cooperation, modesty, sharing with others, and self-control.

There are four basic cultural divisions and adaptations in the Arctic: (1) Aleut; (2) Western Eskimo; (3) Northern Eskimo; and (4) Greenland Eskimo. The Aleut, speaking the Aleut language, lived on the relatively warm Aleutian Islands in fairly large, permanent communities. They subsisted almost entirely on fish and sea mammals.

The Yup'ik, or Western Eskimo, speaking Yup'ik languages, lived in western Alaska in a sort of Subarctic coastal/forest environment (the Yup'ik remain in their homeland and retain much of their traditional culture today; see Fienup-Riordan 1990). In the winter, the Western Eskimo lived in villages with substantial semisubterranean houses. In the summer, the families moved about the landscape, living in skin tents. Firewood was abundant and food was usually cooked. The major food resource was salmon, which was dried and stored. Hunting was important, and a variety of animals, including caribou, moose, bears, squirrels, and waterfowl, were exploited. Men hunted and women gathered plants (willow leaves were a favorite) and performed the main household and maintenance chores.

An Inuit family in Greenland, ca. 1950. Courtesy of Corbis Images/Hulton Deutsch Collection.

The Northern Eskimo, speaking western Inuit languages, occupied the northern coast of the Arctic from northwestern Alaska to eastern Canada. These were the Eskimo stereotypically familiar to most people. In northwestern Alaska, the Eskimo lived in permanent villages, but in most other areas, small, highly mobile bands were the rule. People lived in houses of snow or sod in the winter and skin tents in the summer. Dogs and dogsleds were critical for survival. Sea mammal hunting was the major economic focus, seals being the most important game animal, followed by whales and walrus. Other animals were also essential, including the musk ox and fish, and a few groups depended heavily on caribou.

The Greenland Eskimo, speaking the eastern Inuit dialect, inhabited the coasts of Greenland. They lived in large, permanent coastal villages with substantial structures and fairly large populations. Whales and other sea mammals were the major game animals; fish and land mammals were less important.

Dogs were essential to Eskimo life all over the Arctic, performing many tasks. Dogs pulled sleds packed with family belongings. People did not usually ride on the sleds, but walked alongside, often carrying other materials that did not fit on the sleds. In addition, dogs carried loads on their backs, helped in seal hunting by locating breathing holes, assisted in hunting bears by harassing them while the hunter attempted to kill them, and guarded camps from strangers and bears. Dogs could also be eaten in times of famine. Since food was scarce, most Eskimo kept a relatively small number of dogs. They were fed scraps of meat and human feces mixed with oil (it is common around the world to feed human feces to dogs). Grown dogs could usually withstand the cold and stayed outside, but puppies had to be brought inside during particularly harsh weather.

Political Organization

In general, Arctic groups were organized at the band level and had no tribal organizations until fairly recently, when such organizations were imposed on them by the Canadian and U.S. governments. Bands were usually identified by general geographic location by adding the suffix -*miut* (meaning "people of") to the location name. Thus, the name Kuskowagamiut translates to "people of the Kuskokwim River."

Many groups practiced a seasonal round, moving about the landscape throughout the year to exploit different resources. The band would stay together for only part of the year, splitting into smaller units of a few households (or even a single household) for the rest of the year, with the band reassembling the following season. Some other groups were larger and more complex, staying together throughout much of the year, sometimes in permanent villages, although small groups ventured out to perform specific tasks.

Most disputes took place between men, and they usually concerned women. Killing someone over a dispute was usually not acceptable (but probably not rare) as it could lead to retaliation and the initiation of a feud; if a married man was involved, it could deprive a family of its provider as well. However, if someone's behavior endangered the group, swift action would be taken, even if killing the offender was necessary. Most disagreements were resolved through contests, including punching, wrestling, and singing. In a song contest, each individual involved in a dispute would make up a song insulting the other's parentage, hunting abilities, looks, etc. After both had sung their songs, the assembled community would decide whose song was better and therefore who had won the contest. If the dispute was over a woman, she was under no obligation to leave with the winner, but at least the man's need to defend his honor had been fulfilled.

Wife-sharing was not an uncommon custom. The purpose of the practice was to establish and/or cement partnerships between men, or simply to satisfy a desire for sexual variety. Both the husband and wife had to agree to the arrangement, although the wife seems to have had a bit less power in the decision. Such exchange was not considered adultery. It might even create a "kinship" relationship between the two families, who could then ask each other for help in the future.

Most Arctic groups participated in some kind of warfare, usually motivated by revenge. Much of this warfare was supernatural in form and was conducted by shamans. Actual combat was relatively rare. Nevertheless, most males were skilled in warfare and were well armed with bows and arrows, spears, and knives. Many groups used body armor made of wood, bone, and skin. Combat would usually consist of surprise attacks on the enemy by small groups of men, whose goal was to kill everyone in the targeted camp. In the east-central Arctic, the Eskimo were frequently at war with some of the Subarctic groups to the south.

Social Organization

For most Eskimo groups, the primary social unit was the nuclear family, which was also the main economic unit. However, the extended family was not uncommon and formed the main social unit in some groups. The lineage was also important to a few

Arctic groups. Most Eskimo employed a bilateral kinship system, similar to that used in most of the United States. The advantage of a bilateral system is that one has twice as many close relatives than in a system where one is related only through the mother or the father (matrilineal or patrilineal).

Most marriages were arranged, often very early in an individual's life. However, some of the arrangements did not work out and some people married whomever they wanted. Females married at about the time they reached puberty, or even before; males tended to marry later, in their late teens. Polygyny was allowed, and in rare cases women could have multiple husbands. Divorce was a simple matter, though rare after the birth of the first child, and women could leave whenever they wished. Divorcees, widows, and widowers remarried as soon as possible, as marriage was necessary in order to constitute an effective labor unit; no one could function as an unmarried person for long in the demanding Arctic environment.

Due to the practice of wife-sharing, a child could be biologically fathered by someone other than the husband of the mother. However, as it was believed that conception could not take place during a wife exchange, the husband was always considered the father and was thus responsible for the child. When a child was born, the husband and one or two midwives would assist, and a shaman might be called if there were serious problems. Afterwards, the mother rested for a few days. If a child was due while the group was traveling, the mother and one or two others might stop to deliver the baby, catching up with the group later.

As in all cultures, children were valued, loved, and cared for. However, infant mortality was very high, and a major cause of infant death was pneumonia. At times, newborns could not be supported without endangering the entire group. In such cases, infanticide might be practiced, but it was always a traumatic decision made by the husband; women were the life-givers and men were the dealers of death. Infanticide of females was more frequent than that of males. Because hunting was very dangerous, resulting in a high adult male mortality rate and thus a constant shortage of males, males were more highly valued and more likely to be kept as infants. If any baby was born during times of famine, it would be killed to preserve the life of the mother. Children were not named until a decision was made whether to keep them, and since one was not believed to be an actual person until one was named, infanticide was not considered murder.

Names were very important, as the name determined the demeanor of the individual as well as the nature of his or her soul. Names were generally passed along through either side of the family; for example, a child might be given the name of a deceased grandparent. Since many Eskimo believed in reincarnation, the child could actually be his or her own grandparent.

An infant was carried by its mother on her back within her parka, and as infants rarely wore clothing, there was skin-on-skin contact with the mother. Without being removed, the infant could be maneuvered to the front of the parka to nurse. Thus, a very close relationship between the mother and child resulted. Strong ties also existed between children and grandparents. Up to the age of five or six, children were allowed to do mostly as they pleased; they ate and slept when they wished, played with other children and puppies, frolicked in the snow, and entertained themselves with various toys, including dolls, models (of boats, sleds, and other things), and wooden tops spun with a sealskin cord. Beginning at an early age, girls were required to start help-ing their mother with child care, but boys had a bit more freedom. Sex was not hid-den or discouraged, and children slept in a common bed with the parents, even while parents were engaging in sexual activities. Most Eskimo people did not keep track of their precise ages, but did know who was older and younger.

In most instances people defecated somewhere outside, but if it was very cold a con-tainer was used indoors, to be emptied later. Feces were sometimes saved, mixed with oil, and fed to the dogs. Bathing was not frequent in most areas, but when it did occur, cold water was used. Mothers cleaned their small children with spit instead of water.

Males formed partnerships, or cooperative friendships, with a number of other men. These partnerships varied in intensity, from joking relationships to serious asso-ciations for hunting pursuits. These relationships, often cemented with an exchange of wives, were important economically and socially, and a man's partners could be counted on in bad times.

When they were not working, many groups passed the long winter months with constant socializing, including singing, dancing, romancing, acrobatics, and playing games such as tug-of-war, cat's cradle, cup and pin, hoop and pole, tag, and guess who. Many Eskimo enjoyed the blanket toss, where a group holding a walrus skin (later a blanket) tossed a person into the air. In addition to the entertainment involved, tossing a person twenty feet into the air would enable him or her to see game at a greater distance. In portions of the eastern Arctic, houses were often con-nected by tunnels so that people could pass back and forth without being exposed to the cold weather. A "proper" winter village would have a community dance house where everyone could gather to socialize.

If the elderly became a burden, they might commit suicide for the good of the family. They might have a party to say goodbye or simply walk out into the landscape without telling anyone; at other times, they would be killed (at their request) by oth-ers. Everyone recognized that this act was a great and loving sacrifice to assist the group in bad times. Euthanasia was occasionally practiced when an individual was unable to keep up, thereby endangering the group. The dead were rarely buried below ground, as it was extremely difficult to dig graves in the frozen ground. Cremation was also uncommon, as it required a great deal of precious fuel. Instead, the dead were usually placed in rock cairn graves or on platforms, or sometimes just left in the snow, often with their clothing and personal possessions.

Economics

Arctic peoples were organized socially and politically to maximize the individual and communal procurement, distribution, and consumption of food. Eskimo men were the hunters and procured most of the food. However, women played critical eco-nomic roles as well; they gathered plants for food or manufacturing material, took care of the children, butchered the animals and distributed the meat, prepared the meals, educated the female children, tanned the skins, made the clothing (which required great skill), and did other tasks (see Guemple 1995). No family could survive without a good hunter and a skilled woman.

Both group and individual hunting were important and food was always shared. Most food came from animals, and this meat was prepared in various ways, such as drying, smoking, boiling, frying, and barbecuing. Few food taboos were practiced. The Eskimo generally ate almost every part of an animal that was possible to eat, including muscle tissue, organs, marrow, fat, and the contents of intestines. One exception was the livers of polar bears, which were not eaten because they made people ill (they contain so much vitamin A that they are actually toxic). The fat (blubber) of sea mammals was an important food, and large quantities were consumed. Interestingly, the Eskimo have a very high metabolism, and in spite of their high fat consumption they have lower average cholesterol today than westerners.

Different species of animals were taken by different groups, depending on the region. In general, a number of sea mammals were hunted, including seals, walrus, and whales. Seals were the most popular and would be captured whenever possible. Groups of hunters would sneak up on seals or walrus lying on the shore or on the ice and harpoon them. Animals in the water would be harpooned from kayaks. In open water, a good kayaker could glide up to an animal unobserved and harpoon it from behind. A float, made from an inflated sealskin, would be attached to the harpoon head to ensure the animal could not escape. Sometimes a team of kayakers might drive a number of animals into an area where other hunters could dispatch them. Walrus are large (about 2,000 pounds), aggressive, and very dangerous to hunt from boats, so hunters would wait until they came on shore to hunt them.

In the winter, when the sea was frozen over, a hunter would locate seals' breathing holes in the ice, often with the help of dogs. A hunter would wait patiently, for hours or even days, until a seal came to the hole to breathe, then harpoon it. When the seal tried to escape, the hunter would hold on to the harpoon line until the seal tired and drowned, or the hunter would dig out the hole enough to drag the seal out and then kill it. The hunter would sometimes need the help of his family and/or dogs to pull the seal out of the water. The wounds of the seal, as well as other sea mammals, were closed by the hunter so that the valuable blood (eaten as food) would not be lost during transport to camp.

Many Eskimo groups also hunted whales. Small species such as beluga and narwhal (the latter found only in the eastern Arctic) were hunted at sea using large, open boats called *umiaks*. Whales were harpooned and a number of sealskin floats were then attached. The hunters would follow the whale until it was exhausted and then kill it. Larger whale species were not hunted; rather, their carcasses were scavenged when they washed up on shore. Umiak owners were rich men, often the heads of households, and were the leaders of whale hunts; upon a successful hunt, they would divide the meat among the crew and then distribute what was left to the rest of the people.

Some groups of Eskimo hunted caribou, which do not occur in large numbers in the Arctic (they live mainly in the south, in the Subarctic). The animals were hunted communally, driven into places where they could be shot with arrows. To assist in driving the caribou, piles of rocks would sometimes be built to resemble humans. Caribou skins were essential to the manufacture of clothing and shelter.

Polar bears inhabited the far northern Arctic and were exceedingly dangerous to hunt. Nevertheless, they were hunted for both skins and meat. Polar bears would sometimes raid Eskimo houses for stored food, increasing the threat of food shortage. Other animals hunted by the Eskimo included musk ox, hares and rabbits, squirrels, and birds, including waterfowl. Fish, both freshwater and ocean species, were also critical resources for some groups. Fish could be obtained during most of the year and were captured from the shore or from kayaks, using weirs, harpoons, nets, and jigging with hooks and lines. The Eskimo did not have the technology to take most ocean fish living in deep water.

Hunters were required to be respectful and thankful to the animals they killed, as the souls of the animals would eventually be reborn and, if they were unhappy about their treatment, would not allow themselves to be killed for food again. Sea mammals and ocean fish were classified as animals of the sea, while caribou, bear, freshwater fish, hares and rabbits, and so on, were considered animals of the land. The two categories could not be mixed in either cooking or storage. Plants never formed a large part of any Eskimo diet, although some groups used more than others.

Hunger was not uncommon and famine was always a threat. Shortages of food occurred on a regular basis, some very short-term and others longer. Short-term shortages were solved by sharing food among successful and unsuccessful hunters and their families, with partners, and with other people in general. Long-term shortages were resolved by storing food for later use. In very cold regions, stockpiles of food would be placed on platforms outside of houses and in stone-covered caches in the landscape. This food would remain frozen and thus preserved for years. In warmer areas, food was dried in the sun and then stored. In times of actual famine, about once per generation, people would eat spare clothing (the skins could be eaten), dogs, and even the dead.

Hunting was a very dangerous activity; bears and walruses killed many hunters, and others died in accidents, such as falling through thin ice or tipping over in their boats. If a person fell into the water, there was little chance of survival; if one was able to get out of the water, there was no way to get dry and stay warm and the individual would freeze very quickly, although it might be possible to roll around in dry snow to absorb enough water to survive. Adult male mortality was so high that there was almost always a shortage of men, despite the practice of female infanticide (see above).

Material Culture and Technology

Eskimo technology was dominated by the use of skins. All clothing was made from skins and fur. Skins of caribou and/or bear were used for bedding and blankets, for containers, as wrapping material for transport, for tents, and for many other items. Skins were also used to cover the frames of boats, and sealskin floats were utilized in sea mammal hunting. Other important materials in Eskimo technology were bone, antler, stone, and wood, and most items were beautifully decorated.

The Eskimo built various types of houses, depending on location, conditions, and length of stay. Strong and warm houses were needed, particularly in the winter. The most well known of these structures is what the Eskimo call a snow house but is referred to by westerners as an *igloo*. In actuality, the Eskimo refer to any dwelling as an igloo, the snow house being just one type. Snow houses were used by the Northern Eskimo in the winter as temporary housing or as quarters for the entire season. Else-

An Eskimo family building a snow house (note the kayaks in the background). From an 1870 engraving. Courtesy of Corbis Images/The Bettman Archive.

where, snow houses were not generally used. Some snow houses were quite large and so sturdy that adults could safely stand on their roofs. Many groups constructed large, permanent, semisubterranean dome houses (for use as family dwellings and as men's houses) made from driftwood and whalebones, then covered with sod and insulated with moss. Houses were constructed with a "sunken living room" and benches on which to sit and sleep. This type of construction kept the coldest air collected at the bottom of the house, making the rest of it warmer. The size of the house was related to how much oil could be spared from the food supply for use in lamps to warm the house; the less available the oil, the smaller the house. In the summer, when the men were hunting or fishing, skin tents, brush shelters, or rock shelters were used.

Two major types of boats were used by the Eskimo, the umiak and the kayak. The umiak is a large, open, walrus-skin boat that could carry a fairly large number of people and material possessions. Umiaks are often called "women's boats" because the women usually rowed them. However, when umiaks were used in whale hunting, they carried an all-male crew.

Kayaks were made in a variety of forms, depending on their intended use. Generally they were small, covered boats, with one or two hatches, used by men in hunting and fishing. Most kayaks were built around a flexible wooden frame, tailor-made to fit the owner. Women would then fashion a sealskin covering for the frame, sewn on so well that it was watertight. The kayak was propelled and controlled by a double-bladed paddle. In use, the kayak became a part of the man, "worn" like a piece of clothing, and was often considered to be a "living being." Boys were trained from infancy to handle a kayak and to withstand wet and cold. Contemporary sport kayaks have borrowed Eskimo technology almost exactly, and today the act of righting a cap-sized kayak is called the "Eskimo roll."

Sleds were used by many groups and were built of bone and/or wood. The sled runners were made from bone or antler and were covered with a layer of ice to decrease friction on the snow. Frozen fish were sometimes used as sled runners.

The Eskimo's main weapon was the harpoon, which was used to kill most sea mammals. Harpoons were used by hunters in kayaks, but since the hunter was sitting and could not get much weight behind the throw, an atlatl was used to propel the harpoon. Spears were also used. Bows and arrows were not commonly used for hunting from boats, although Eskimo bow technology was sophisticated. The Eskimo employed several distinctive cutting tools. The crescent-shaped woman's knife, the *ulu*, was made from slate or chipped stone (and later from steel), and was used to cut skins for clothing, to butcher animals, and for just about every chore where cutting was required. Men made long-bladed knives from walrus tusk for many of their tasks, such as cutting snow blocks for a snow house.

Bowl-shaped lamps made from stone were essential for light and heat. Moss wicks were placed in the bowl and seal oil was used for fuel. Stone was also used to manufacture drills and other tools. Snow visors, necessary to survive the constant exposure to snow and ice glare, were made of wood, ivory, or antler. The Copper Eskimo in the central Canadian Arctic are known for their cold-hammered native copper tools and ornaments (see Damas 1984; Morrison and Germain 1995; and Condon et al. 1996 for further discussion of the Copper Eskimo). Some other groups also used copper in the same manner.

Probably the most important aspect of Eskimo material culture and technology was their clothing, all made from animal skins. Adequate clothing was vital to daily life, in order to keep warm and dry. Everyone dressed in three major items of clothing: a hooded parka and pants made from caribou hide, and the extremely important *mukluks*, watertight boots made from sealskin. Women wore long pants and short boots; men wore short pants and tall boots. Everyone also wore mittens. Most Eskimo wore several layers of clothing, depending on the weather and temperature. For the inner layer of clothing, the hair side of hides and skins was placed against the body; for the outer layer, the hair side faced away from the body. Most clothing was removed at night and used as pillows, bedding, and/or blankets. Boots would usually stiffen during the night from the cold, and one of the important tasks of an Eskimo wife was to chew her husband's boots first thing in the morning until they were softened enough for him to put them on. When possible, new clothing was made every year.

Most clothing was decorated to some extent. Women went to considerable effort to decorate their clothing, often with patterns of different-colored furs. A woman might have a large wardrobe, with fancy clothing for special occasions. A mother's parka was made large enough so that an infant could be carried on her back inside the parka and maneuvered around her body to nurse.

After puberty, many women would tattoo their faces, arms, and breasts; men rarely had tattoos. Tattooing was accomplished using a bone needle and a mixture of oil and soot. Both sexes wore their hair long, and women often had braids. Men frequently plucked their facial hair; otherwise, ice might form on it and cause frostbite.

Religion

The religious beliefs of Arctic groups were quite complex and primarily concerned with maintaining a relationship with the animals to ensure their continued cooperation in being hunted (see Fienup-Riordan 1988, 1990; Lowenstein 1993). All manner of beings, including humans, animals, and other entities, had souls (sometimes many souls), which determined the nature of the existence of the being the soul inhabited. Many Eskimo believed that humans had three souls; an immortal soul that left the body at death to journey to an afterlife (or to be reincarnated), a soul of breath and warmth that died with the body, and a soul associated with the person's name. Many Eskimo also believed in reincarnation, that the immortal soul would be reborn into a later generation. This included the souls of animals—who, if angry, would not allow themselves to be killed for food. Humans and animals thus shared two major characteristics: they had souls and awareness. These two attributes allowed humans and animals to interact to the benefit of both.

Good and bad spirits inhabited the world and could manifest themselves in any form, including human form. Bad spirits attempted to do harm, but people could be protected by charms or amulets, and also by shamans. A major goal of religious activity was to control evil spirits.

Shamans were the primary religious practitioners, as they had some access to, and control of, the supernatural. They could also cure illnesses or curse others with disease or bad luck. Shamans conducted warfare by putting spells on the enemy. Death was not considered a natural occurrence; when someone died (other than through infanticide or euthanasia), it was reasoned to be the result of the spell of an enemy shaman, and retaliation would follow. Shamans acquired their power through a number of means, generally by seeking a spirit-helper, either during some trial or quest. In other cases, new shamans were initiated by established shamans, who taught the trade to the novice. Both men and women could be shamans but most were men.

Arctic Peoples Today

Until fairly recently, many Eskimo lived in a largely traditional manner, but after World War II, radical change came to the Arctic. Many military bases were opened and employed Eskimo workers. Western material culture became more prevalent, and many Eskimo moved to small towns around bases and regional centers, where they now live in Western-style houses that do not stay as warm as traditional housing.

Traditional subsistence activities, such as whaling (see Freeman et al. 1998), hunting, and fishing, are still very important in the economy and social identity of many Eskimo. Dogsleds are still used, along with snowmobiles ("metal dogsleds"), and many communities are connected by air service. In 1991, there were some 36,000 Eskimo (Reddy 1995: Table 925) and about 2,400 Aleut (Reddy 1995: Table 113). Most Eskimo are now Christian.

In the U.S. portion of the Arctic, all groups have signed the 1971 Alaska Native Claims Settlement Act (ANCSA). At that time, the ANCSA settled land claims by giving native groups title to forty-four million acres, a payment of $962 million and a royalty of $500 million on mineral rights. Thirteen native corporations were established to administer the settlement monies and lands. Native people with at least one-quarter native blood became "shareholders." Many worried that the ANCSA would have a result similar to the Dawes Act and termination policies of the 1950s; however, housing, health care, and education have improved for many people in the Arctic (see Burch 1984).

The Canadian government remains in negotiations to settle other native claims (see Crowe 1991). One agreement resulted in the creation of a new Canadian province, Nunavat, from the eastern part of the Northwest Territory in 1999 (see Rigby et al. 2000). Nunavat is governed by the Eskimo who live there. Many Canadian Eskimo reject the idea of claims settlements, arguing that the land is not for sale.

Greenland won province status from Denmark in 1979 and now governs itself, and the majority of the members of the Greenland legislative assembly are Eskimo. Due to a warming trend in the past 200 years, the seal population in western Greenland has declined considerably and many Eskimo rely on fishing to a much greater degree than in the past. Greenland Eskimo still hunt narwhals from kayaks, but it is illegal for others to do so.

The Eskimo face a number of serious problems today. Alcoholism, with its associated violence and economic impacts, is a huge problem among the Eskimo. There are few jobs in the Arctic, and being dependent on public assistance (welfare) is not an Eskimo value. Teenage pregnancy is also a problem. *Gussak* (white man's food from stores) is very expensive, as much as 400 percent more costly than in other regions, and many people do not like it. The sugar and refined foods have greatly increased dental problems and have even contributed to malnutrition.

Nevertheless, the future looks promising. The Eskimo themselves are working to reinvigorate their culture, and they have regained some measure of control over their territories. Native languages are being taught in schools, and the use of native technologies (clothing, weapons for hunting, dogsleds, etc.) and skills is being encouraged. Some Eskimo families have even returned to a traditional lifestyle, hunting animals and fishing, living in igloos, and traveling by dogsled (which are actually more reliable than snowmobiles).

LEARN MORE ABOUT CONTEMPORARY ARCTIC PEOPLES

The discussion above is only a very brief description of Arctic people today. What else can you discover? Go to the library, and look on the Internet (you can begin with http:/www.ainc-inac.gc.ca./ or http://arcticcircle.uconn.edu/) to learn more about how Arctic groups are managing. Topics you can explore include the following:

1. Chose a particular group or two, and investigate how land claims settlement has affected them economically, politically, and in other ways.

2. Which groups have concluded treaties with either the United States or Canada? Which are in the process? What is the status of the new Canadian province of Nunavut?

3. What traditional practices have been retained by a particular Arctic group? What are the roles of traditional religion, economics, and politics in this Arctic group today?

4. How is having traditional knowledge integral into one's identity as an Inuit?

5. How are Arctic people coping with Western culture? What are the problems faced by Arctic people today?

3

Indian Peoples Are Nations, Not Minorities

David E. Wilkins

We claim that the "constitution, and the laws of the United States which shall be made in pursuance thereof . . . shall be the supreme law of the land." But we also claim to recognize the sovereignty of Native American nations, the original occupants of this land. These claims—one to jurisdictional monopoly, the other to jurisdictional multiplicity—are irreconcilable. Two hundred years have produced no resolution of the contradiction except at the expense of the tribes and the loss to non-Indians of the Indians' gift of their difference.

Milner Ball, 1987 [1]

A quick perusal of recent national newspaper headlines searched under the category "Indian politics" uncovered a number of articles with alarming headlines such as "Backlash Growing as Indians Make a Stand for Sovereignty," [2] "The New Indian Wars: A Growing National Movement Is Gunning for Tribal Treaties, Reservations, and Rights," [3] "Tribal Nations Fight Challenges to Their Sovereignty," [4] and "Senate Measures Would Deal Blow to Indian Rights." [5] But what is the "backlash" about? What prompted and who are the protagonists in the "New Indian Wars"? What are Indian "rights" and "tribal sovereignty" anyway?

The situation of the 561 indigenous polities in North America is and has always been distinctive in comparison to the status and place of African Americans, Asian Americans, Latino Americans, women, and other racial or ethnic groups in the country. This is so for a number of important reasons, some obvious, some little known. First, tribal peoples are the *original—the indigenous—inhabitants* of North America and they are *nations* in the most fundamental sense of the word. That is, they are separate peoples inhabiting specific territories that they wield some governmental control or jurisdiction over. While speculation abounds in scientific circles about how

Reprinted from *American Indian Politics and the American Political System*, by David E. Wilkins, (2002), by permission of Rowman & Littlefield Publishers, Inc.

long Native peoples have inhabited the Americas and whether or not they originated here or arrived from distant lands,[6] it is safe to say that they remain the original inhabitants of the Americas.

Second, the preexistence of over six hundred independent tribal nations, bands, pueblos, etc., well in advance of the formation of the United States, each having a number of integral attributes, including a bounded land base, an appropriate economic system, a governmental system, and sociocultural distinctiveness,[7] necessitated the practice of aboriginal sovereigns negotiating political compacts, treaties, and alliances with European nations and later the United States. The fact of *treaty making,* which no other resident American group (states are also precluded from negotiating treaties) participated in, and the products of that process—the actual treaties, agreements, and negotiated settlements—confirmed a nation-to-nation relationship between the negotiating tribal and nontribal parties. See the chart on the next page for a graphical depiction of the structural relationship between American Indian nations and the United States, individual states, and local governments. A large number, over five hundred, of these important contractual arrangements form the baseline parameters of the political relationship between tribes and the United States and are still legally valid, though their enforceability has always been problematic.[8] A majority of these treaties involved land cessions by tribes and reservations of lands not ceded or sold to the federal government.

As tribes are treaty-recognized sovereigns, tribal rights are not based on or subject to U.S. constitutional law and are therefore not protected by the Constitution. This is because as preexisting sovereigns tribes do not derive their inherent governmental powers from the federal or state government. Thus, tribal nations have an **extraconstitutional** relationship to the United States that no other group has. However, according to article 6 of the U.S. Constitution, "all treaties made, or which shall be made, under the authority of the United States, shall be the supreme law of the land; and the judges in every State shall be bound thereby, any thing in the Constitution or laws of any State to the contrary notwithstanding." Hence, while tribal sovereignty is not beholden to or rooted in American constitutional law, a tribe's treaty rights are, at least in constitutional theory, the supreme law of the land and should be subject to full protection under the Constitution's rubric.

A third feature differentiating indigenous peoples from other racial/ethnic groups is the *trust doctrine.* While the federal government and tribes have rarely been in agreement on what the trust principle entails,[9] President Clinton, in an executive order on May 14, 1998, put forth a clear description of what the trust relationship entails from the federal government's perspective: "The United States has a unique legal relationship with Indian tribal governments as set forth in the Constitution of the United States, treaties, statutes, executive orders, and court decisions. Since the formation of the Union, the United States has recognized Indian tribes as domestic dependent nations under its protection."[10] In this statement the president sought to assure Indians that the United States recognized that tribes have a sovereign status which the federal government, as a separate though connected sovereign, is bound to respect under its own law. The hundreds of treaties and agreements that were negotiated in which the tribes were guaranteed all the rights and resources (e.g., rights to water and lands; to hunt, fish, and gather; to exercise criminal and civil jurisdiction;

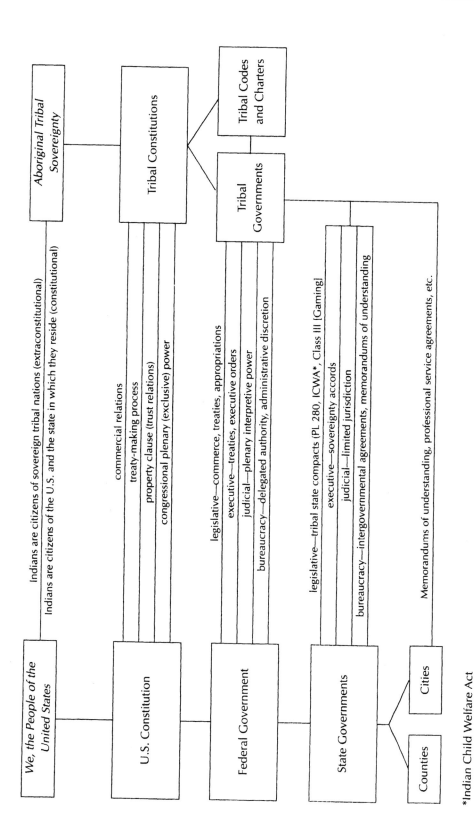

The figure contains the following labels:

Aboriginal Tribal Sovereignty

Tribal Constitutions

Tribal Codes and Charters

Tribal Governments

We, the People of the United States

Indians are citizens of sovereign tribal nations (extraconstitutional)
Indians are citizens of the U.S. and the state in which they reside (constitutional)

U.S. Constitution

commercial relations
treaty-making process
property clause (trust relations)
congressional plenary (exclusive) power

Federal Government

legislative—commerce, treaties, appropriations
executive—treaties, executive orders
judicial—plenary interpretive power
bureaucracy—delegated authority, administrative discretion

State Governments

legislative—tribal state compacts (PL 280, ICWA*, Class III [Gaming]
executive—sovereignty accords
judicial—limited jurisdiction
bureaucracy—intergovernmental agreements, memorandums of understanding

Counties

Cities

Memorandums of understanding, professional service agreements, etc.

*Indian Child Welfare Act

Indigenous Nations and the American Political System.

to tax) they had not ceded to the federal government when they sold or exchanged the majority of their lands—most of North America—were contractual rights that were also protected by the trust doctrine, which is the federal government's legal and moral pledge to respect those reserved Indian rights.

More important was the president's use of the phrase "under its [the government's] protection." This is a declaration that the federal government has a protectorate obligation to support indigenous peoples legally, culturally, economically, and politically. It is best characterized by the phrase *trustee (United States)-beneficiary (Tribes)* relationship. As Vine Deloria Jr. (Standing Rock Sioux), the leading scholar of Indian law and politics, has stated:

> The trust responsibility of the federal government toward the Indian tribes is mandated by the fact that Indians are extra constitutional. No constitutional protections exist for Indians in either a tribal or an individual sense, and hence the need for special rules and regulations, special administrative discretionary authority, and special exemptions. This special body of law replaces the constitutional protections granted to other members of American society.[11]

Tribal nations tend to think of "trust" as entailing four interrelated components: that the federal government—or its agents—was pledged to protect tribal property and sovereignty and would not move for or against tribes without first securing tribal consent; that the United States would act with the utmost integrity in its legal and political commitments to Indian peoples as outlined in treaties or governmental policies (e.g., provide health care, educational support, housing assistance); that the United States would act in a moral manner regarding tribal rights, as the Judeo-Christian nation it historically professed to be in its dealing with tribes; and that the United States would continue to support any additional duties and responsibilities in its self-assumed role as the Indians' "protectors."

A fourth concept, congressional plenary power, is yet another distinctive feature of the tribal-federal relationship that separates tribal nations from all other racial/ethnic groups in the United States.[12] Basically put, "plenary" means complete in all aspects or meanings in federal Indian policy and law. First, it means exclusive. The federal Constitution, in the commerce clause (article 1, section 8, clause 3), vests in Congress the sole authority to "regulate Commerce with foreign Nations, and among the several States, *and with the Indian tribes.*" In other words, the founders of the American republic believed that the power to engage in treaty making with tribes should rest with the legislative branch of the federal government, not with the states, which, under the Articles of Confederation, had retained the right to deal with tribes in their proximity.

Second, and related to the first definition, plenary also means *preemptive.* That is, Congress may enact legislation which effectively precludes—preempts—state governments from acting in Indian-related matters. Finally, and most controversially, since this definition lacks a constitutional basis, plenary means unlimited or absolute. This judicially constructed definition (*United States v. Kagama,* 1886) means that the Congress has vested in itself, without a constitutional mooring, virtually boundless governmental authority and jurisdiction over tribal nations, their lands, and their *resources.* As recently as 1978 the Supreme Court, in *United States v. Wheeler,*[13] held that "Congress has plenary authority to legislate for the Indian tribes in all matters, including their form of government."

Federal plenary power when defined as unlimited and absolute should give one reason to pause from a democratic theory perspective. The idea that a democracy has exercised and continues to assert that it has the power to wield absolute authority over tribal people—and without tribal consent—whose members are today citizens of the United States, is deeply disturbing, yet that reality persists for indigenous peoples and their citizens, notwithstanding their treaty and trust rights as citizens of sovereign governments and, since 1924, with citizenship status in the states and federal government as well.

Plenary power, like the trust doctrine, has proven to be a mixed blessing for Indian peoples. On the positive side, Congress, under its plenary power, has been able to pass legislation that accords Indians unique treatment that other groups and individuals are ineligible for—medical care, Indian preference hiring practices in the BIA, educational benefits, housing aid, tax exemptions, etc. Such legislative and policy action is possible, again, because of the extraconstitutional status of tribes, which places them outside the protections of the Constitution. Tribal members are entitled to these distinctive considerations, and Congress is empowered to exercise a great deal of authority in Indian affairs because it must be "immune from ordinary challenges which might otherwise hamper the wise administration of Indian affairs."[14]

On the negative side, plenary power has been interpreted by the Supreme Court to allow the federal government to pass laws and enact regulations which prohibit Indians in some situations from selling their own land to whomever they wish.[15] Congress may also confiscate Indian lands held under aboriginal title and is not required to pay just compensation under the Fifth Amendment to the Constitution.[16] Congress may punish Indians under federal law for certain crimes, even if this means the individuals will be punished more severely than non-Indians who commit the same crime under state law.[17] And Congress may literally terminate the legal existence of tribal nations.[18]

How are Congress and the Supreme Court able to justify such discriminatory action if the Constitution prohibits discrimination on the basis of race? It is because while tribal nations certainly constitute separate racial groups, more important is the fact that they constitute separate political groups, recognized in the treaty relationship, the trust doctrine, and the placement of tribes in the commerce clause. In other words, European nations and the United States did not enter into treaties with tribes because of their racial differences, but because they were separate sovereigns—oftentimes with impressive military and economic clout—that the United States wanted and needed to establish diplomatic ties with. Hence, the relationship the United States has is with tribes as political entities, as governments, and is at its heart a political, not racial, alliance. Congressional action, therefore, that is based on plenary power does not violate the equal protection and due process clauses of the Constitution that prohibit discrimination on the basis of race.[19]

What all the preceding concepts confirm is that tribal peoples, unlike any other groups in the United States, are *sovereign nations,* not minority groups. A sovereign nation is a distinct political entity which exercises a measure of jurisdictional power over a specific territory. It is not an absolute or fully independent power in a pure sense because no nation or tribe in the world today, regardless of its geographic girth, population base, or gross national product, is completely or fully sovereign. "Our industrial world of mass communication, soaring population and global transportation makes isolation of sovereign nations virtually impossible. Economic and political factors also encourage and necessitate governmental interdependency."[20]

In addition to the practical limitations of sovereignty, a nation's sovereignty is also restricted by self-limitation, according to Sam Deloria, "as when the United States Constitution puts limits on the expression of this country's sovereignty. In the case of the Indian tribes, the United States agrees to recognize our [Indian tribes'] political, cultural, and land rights. In recognizing these rights [in treaties and agreements] the United States has voluntarily limited its sovereignty."[21]

This statement, in part, addresses the fundamental issue raised in the quote which opened this chapter: that of jurisdictional monopoly vs. jurisdictional multiplicity. In other words, the United States is certainly a distinctive sovereign entity and the U.S. Constitution is recognized as the "supreme law of the land." But the historical record and the Constitution itself also evidence the reality that the United States and the constituent states have always recognized, if not always supported, the preexisting sovereigns—the tribal nations—who have lived in North America for millennia. Thus, one of the tasks of this book is to discuss the reality that indigenous nations constitute the third set of sovereigns—along with the federal and state governments—whose politics deserve focused attention.

The sovereignty of tribes, it is important to note, was not delegated to them by the federal or state governments—it is original and inherent power. **Tribal sovereignty** has to do, on one hand, with a tribe's right to retain a measure of independence from outside entities and the power of regulating one's internal affairs, including the ability to make and execute laws, to impose and collect taxes, and to make alliances with other governments. On the other hand, tribal sovereignty has a unique cultural and spiritual dimension which differentiates it from the sovereign power of a state or the federal government. I define it this way: *Tribal sovereignty is the intangible and dynamic cultural force inherent in a given indigenous community, empowering that body toward the sustaining and enhancement of political, economic, and cultural integrity. It undergirds the way tribal governments relate to their own citizens, to non-Indian residents, to local governments, to the state government, to the federal government, to the corporate world, and to the global community.*

Because of the doctrines discussed above, the sovereign interactions of the tribes, the states, and the United States entail an ongoing and awkward minuet whose choreography has too often been unilaterally prepared by the federal government, with little regard for the inherent rights of the tribes, the original minuet partners. As we begin the new millennium the distinctive cultural, political, geographical, and legal status of indigenous nations still does not fit within the U.S. Constitution's matrix, and is completely let alone by state constitutional documents, especially of western states, which were required by Congress to include clauses in their enabling acts and then in their constitutions forever disclaiming any jurisdiction over Indian tribes or their lands and promising never to tax Indian lands held in trust by the federal government. These clauses continue in effect, even though tribal citizens have been citizens of the United States since 1924.

Consequently, tribal nations find that their collective rights, lands, and even inherent sovereignty lack substantive protection from the very government, the federal government, which is charged by treaties, by the trust doctrine, and by constitutional acknowledgment in the commerce clause with protecting Indian tribes. The internal political affairs of tribal nations and the relationship between tribal nations and the United States is, thus, full of perplexity.

INDIANS AS CITIZENS/SUBJECTS OF THE UNITED STATES

One of the fundamental differences between indigenous peoples in their relationship with the federal government and that of other racial/ethnic minorities and the United States is that from the beginning the relationship was a political one, steeped in diplomacy and treaties. It was, in fact, a nation-to-nation relationship, with the United States viewing Indian tribes as small, largely "uncivilized" nations it would have to deal with as separate political entities.

This is evident in several provisions of some of the key documents of early U.S. political history.

The Declaration of Independence, July 4, 1776. Drafted mainly by Thomas Jefferson, this document proclaimed the right of the colonies to separate from Great Britain and outlined the rights of man and the rights to rebellion and self-government:

> He has excited domestic insurrections amongst us, and has endeavoured to bring on the Inhabitants of our Frontiers, the merciless Indian Savages, whose Known Rule of Warfare, is an undistinguished Destruction, of all Ages, Sexes and Conditions.

Treaty with the Delaware Tribe, September 17, 1778 (7 Stat. 13). This is considered the first Indian treaty written in formal diplomatic and legal language:

> Article 6: . . . And it is further agreed on between the contracting parties [the United States and the Delaware Nation] should it for the future be found conducive for the mutual interest of both parties to invite any other tribes who have been friends to the interest of the United States, to join the present confederation, and to form a state whereof the Delaware Nation shall be the head, and have a representation in Congress.

Articles of Confederation, March 1, 1781. The compact among the thirteen original states that established the first government of the United States:

> The United States in Congress assembled shall also have the sole and exclusive right and power of . . . regulating the trade and managing all affairs with the Indians, not members of any of the States, provided that the legislative right of any State within its own limits be not infringed or violated.

The Federalist Papers, No. 24, Alexander Hamilton, 1787–1788. Part of a series of eighty-five essays written by Alexander Hamilton, James Madison, and John Jay—all under the name *Publius*—published in New York newspapers to persuade New Yorkers to support the newly proposed Constitution:

> The Savage tribes on our Western frontier ought to be regarded as our natural enemies, their [Great Britain's] natural allies, because they have most to fear from us and most to hope from them.

The Northwest Ordinance, July 13, 1787 (Journals of the Continental Congress 321: 340–41). A congressional enactment under the Articles of Confederation for the government of the territory north of the Ohio River and west of New York to the Mississippi River. It is the most significant measure passed by the Confederated Congress, since it established the policy that territories were not to be kept in subjugation but were to be developed for admission to statehood on an equal footing with other states:

> Religion, morality, and knowledge, being necessary to good government and the happiness of mankind, schools and the means of education shall forever be encouraged. The utmost good faith shall always be observed toward the Indians; their lands and property shall never be taken from them without their consent; and, in their property, rights, and liberty, they never shall be invaded or disturbed, unless in just and lawful wars authorized by Congress; but laws founded in justice and humanity shall, from time to time, be made, for preventing wrongs being done them, and for preserving peace and friendship with them.

U.S, Constitution, 1789. The fundamental document that established the framework of government, assigned powers and duties of governmental agencies, and established the relationship of the people to the government:

> Article 1, section 2, clause 3: Representatives and direct Taxes shall be apportioned among the several States . . . according to their respective numbers, which shall be determined by adding to the whole Number of free Persons, including those bound to Service for a Term of years, and excluding Indians not taxed, three fifths of all other persons.

> Article 1, section 8, clause 3: The Congress shall have Power to regulate Commerce with foreign Nations, and among the several States, and with the Indian tribes.

Trade and Intercourse Act, July 22, 1790 (1 Stat. 137). This act required white traders to secure license before trading with Indians and generally restricted transactions between settlers and Indians:

> That no person shall be permitted to carry on trade or intercourse with the Indian tribes, without a license for that purpose under the hand and seal of the superintendent of the department.

Cherokee Nation v. Georgia (1831) (30 U.S. [5 Pet.] 1). The Cherokee had filed an original action in the U.S. Supreme Court challenging Georgia's extension of authority within Cherokee territory on the grounds that they were a "foreign nation" within the meaning of the Constitution. The Court denied it had jurisdiction to hear the case and went on to describe what it perceived the Cherokee status to be:

> They [tribes] may, more correctly, perhaps, be denominated domestic dependent nations.

Worcester v. Georgia (1832) (31 U.S. [6 Pet.] 515]. The Court, in holding that Georgia did not have the right to arrest white missionaries for having failed to obtain a state license, declared that federal law was supreme in relation to state law:

> The Indian nations had always been considered as distinct, independent political communities, retaining their original natural rights as the undisputed possessors of the soil from time immemorial.

Each of these documents acknowledges that Indians belonged to their own nations and were not citizens of the United States. Although the phrase "excluding Indians not taxed" was included in the Constitution as recognition that some individual Indians in the thirteen original states had merged with the general population, the Indian commerce clause, the practice of treaty making, and the geographic and cultural separateness of native nations from the United States evidenced the reality that Indian tribes were seen as necessary political and economic allies and not as peoples whose citizens were likely to abandon their tribal nation in order to become American citizens.

Even as the nation-to-nation relationship was being reconfirmed via steady treaty negotiations, the U.S. Congress was already acting in ways that indicated its eventual goal was to extend American citizenship to certain individuals and groups of Indians. In such cases, Indians who requested U.S. citizenship were usually required to abandon their tribal citizenship and relinquish tribal property. For example, in 1817, in one of the earliest Indian removal treaties signed with the Cherokee Nation, a provision was included in article 8 whereby individual Cherokee heads of family who opted to remain in the east rather than relocate to the new lands in the west were given the opportunity to become citizens of the United States and receive 640-acre tracts of land.[22]

Other tribes, like the Stockbridge and Munsee, the Ottawa, the Potowatomie, and the Wyandotte, also had opportunities for their members to become American citizens, but nearly always on the condition that the individual abandon or sever all tribal ties, adopt the habits and customs of Euro-Americans, become self-supporting, and learn to read and speak English. In some cases, however, special statutes naturalized particular tribes or individuals. In others, general statutes, like the Dawes General Allotment Act of 1887, conferred citizenship on Indians who accepted land allotments. And finally, there were some statutes which naturalized special classes of Indians: Indian women who married white men in 1888[23] and Indian men who fought in World War I and were honorably discharged.[24]

Along with these sporadic attempts to naturalize particular tribes or individual Indians, and notwithstanding Congress's enactment of a "Civilization Fund," an annual sum of ten thousand dollars established in 1819 aimed at introducing Indians to the "habits and arts of civilization,"[25] the question of whether or not Indians were American citizens remained deeply problematic throughout the nineteenth and well into the twentieth century. In fact, the preponderance of evidence shows that, despite the several treaties and laws enfranchising some tribes and classes of individual Indians, the relationship between tribes and the United States remained one best described as a nation-to-nation association.

For example, in the devastating Supreme Court case *Dred Scott v. Sandford* (1857), which held that African Americans could not be citizens and lacked certain rights that whites had to respect, Justice Roger Taney wrote that Indian tribes by contrast "were yet a free and independent people, associated together in nations or tribes, and governed by their own laws." "These Indian governments," said Taney, "were regarded and treated as foreign governments, as much so as if an ocean had separated the red man from the white."[26] Taney did indicate that individual Indians could be naturalized by Congress, but only if they left their tribal nation and adopted the habits and values of whites.

The next opportunity to examine Indian citizenship arose in the wake of interpreting the Fourteenth Amendment, ratified by the states in 1868. This amendment provided in the first clause that "all persons born or naturalized in the United States, and subject to the jurisdiction thereof, are citizens of the United States and of the State wherein they reside." A cursory reading of this amendment would lead one to believe that Indians, virtually all of whom were born in the United States, were now citizens of the United States.

However, the Senate Judiciary Committee, which had been asked to determine whether the Fourteenth Amendment had, in fact, enfranchised Indians, reported in 1870 that Indians who remained bound to their tribal nations were not and could not be subject to the Constitution's Fourteenth Amendment, including its citizenship clause:

> To maintain that the United States intended, by a change of its fundamental law, which was not ratified by these tribes, and to which they were neither requested nor permitted to assert, to annul treaties then existing between the United States as one party, and the Indian tribes as the other parties respectively, would be to charge upon the United States repudiation of national obligations, repudiation doubly infamous from the fact that the parties whose claims were thus annulled are too weak to enforce their rights, and were enjoying the voluntarily assumed guardianship and protection of this government.[27]

The committee did state that individual Indians who had "merged in the mass of our people" became subject to federal jurisdiction, but stopped short of declaring even detribalized Indians American citizens.

A year later three important developments occurred that addressed ongoing federal ambivalence about the political status of tribes. First, Congress, by way of a legislative **rider** attached to an Indian appropriation bill, declared that henceforth it would negotiate no more treaties with tribal nations, although it would remain legally bound by all preexisting ratified treaties. Second, and conversely, a federal district court in *McKay v. Campbell* (1871) ruled that a Chinook Indian was "born a member of an independent political community" and therefore "not born subject to the jurisdiction of the United States—not born in its allegiance." Finally, the Supreme Court in *Cherokee Tobacco* (1871) held that Indian treaty rights could be implicitly overridden by subsequent federal laws, a particularly egregious ruling because of the recent enactment of the treaty-termination law, which froze tribes in political limbo and left them completely vulnerable to the Congress. As a result of the *Cherokee Tobacco* precedent, any federal law enacted after March 3, 1871, could be interpreted as having overridden any prior treaty.

The status of tribes as separate yet domestic sovereigns, subject to increasing federal legislative power, yet lacking any constitutional protection and with increasingly little treaty protection, was summarized in 1872 in Commissioner of Indian Affairs Francis A. Walker's annual report to the secretary of the interior:

> In a word, in the two-hundred and seventy-five thousand Indians west of the Mississippi, the United States have all the elements of a large gypsy population, which will inevitably become a sore, a well-nigh intolerable, affliction to all that region, unless the Government shall provide for their instruction in the arts of life, which can only be done effectually under a pressure not to be resisted or evaded. The right of the Government to do this cannot be seriously questioned. *Expressly excluded by the Constitution from citizenship, the Government is only bound in its treatment of them by considerations of present policy and justice.* Even were the constitutional incapacity of these people not what it is, and were there nothing in the history of the dealings of the United States with them to form a precedent for their being placed under arbitrary control, still, the manifest necessity of self-protection would amply justify the Government in any and all measures required to prevent the miserable conclusion I have indicated.[28] [emphasis added]

This was the status of tribal nations and their citizens. But the status of detribalized Indian persons who had voluntarily left their nation was not addressed until the 1884 Supreme Court case *Elk v. Wilkins*. John Elk, an Indian whose tribal affiliation was never stated, had left his nation and moved to Omaha, Nebraska. Elk had registered to vote but his application was rejected by Wilkins, the city registrar, on the grounds that Elk was an Indian and therefore not an American citizen. The Supreme Court agreed with Wilkins's decision and denied Elk the right to vote. The Court held that Indians, like "the children of subjects of any foreign government," were not subject to the Fourteenth Amendment's provisions since they belonged to "alien nations, distinct political communities, with whom the United States might and habitually did deal as they thought fit, either through treaties . . . [or] legislation."[29]

In other words, Indians were not "subject to the jurisdiction of the United States," so could not be citizens by birth. In addition, the Court said that even if individual Indians met the same basic citizenship requirements expected of other noncitizens they still could not be enfranchised unless Congress made an affirmative declaration—naturalization—authorizing by an act such a change in their standing.

However, federal policymakers, increasingly intent on the forced assimilation of Indians, continued their efforts to extend the franchise to Indians. In 1875 Congress extended the benefits of the Homestead Act of 1862 to those adult Indians who had or were willing to abandon their "tribal relations" and take up life as a homesteader on the public domain. These individuals were entitled to their per capita share of tribal funds, lands, and other property, although their 160-acre homestead was to be held in trust by the government, not subject to sale or voluntary conveyance except by court decree for a six-year period.

As the Board of Indian Commissioners, a quasipolitical body that helped set federal Indian policy, declared in its seventh annual report, in 1876: "This legislation was a step in the right direction, since it aims to recognize the Indian's property rights as an individual man, instead of his tribal rights as simply a ward of the Government."[30] Nothing in this law, however, suggested that Indian homesteaders were to become American citizens. A similar measure was enacted in 1884, also known as the Indian Homestead Act. The next major Indian land law, the General Allotment Act, did finally address the issue of citizenship.

Congress enacted the General Allotment Act in 1887. In this act, Indians who received land allotments and those who voluntarily took up residence apart from their tribes were to be granted citizenship. But although the law seemed clear on this subject, it was complicated somewhat because the allotments of land were held in trust by the federal government for twenty-five years on the Indians' behalf. Some courts maintained that Indians gained American citizenship at the end of the twenty-five-year trust period; others held that citizenship was gained as soon as an allotment was received. Trust or not, for many in Congress there was a sense that "allotment of land in severalty, and citizenship [were] the indispensable conditions of Indian progress."[31] Nonallotted Indians remained citizens of their respective tribal nations.

Second, in 1890, Congress enacted the Indian Territory Naturalization Act, which provided that any member of the tribes in Indian Territory (present-day Oklahoma and Kansas) were entitled to American citizenship upon application to a federal court.[32] Unlike in the Allotment Act's provisions, however, Indian applicants did not lose their tribal citizenship or the right to share in tribal assets. This law, "perhaps more than any other piece of legislation passed by Congress, seemed to imply that Indians held dual citizenship or could do so by performing the naturalization ritual in a federal court."[33]

In 1905 the question of the citizenship status of Indian allottees was firmly before the Supreme Court. In *Matter of Heff,* the Court held that upon receiving an allotment, an Indian immediately became an American citizen, and therefore federal laws prohibiting liquor sales to Indians were declared unconstitutional. Although the Court's ruling in *Heff* appeared to fit the thrust of what federal policymakers had been pushing for some time, namely, the unbridled assimilation of Indians, the outcry from a number of congressmen, the BIA, and Christian reform groups was immediate and vehement. These groups and individuals feared that Indians would be overrun by liquor-hawking whites, intent on defrauding the Indians of their remaining lands and funds.

Congress reacted in paternalistic fashion by enacting the Burke Act in 1906, which withheld federal citizenship from allotted Indians until the end of the twenty-five-year trust period or until the allottees had received a fee patent to their lands from the secretary of the interior. The government was concerned that if the Indian allottees were completely free of federal guardianship they would be subsumed by the "usual cycle of dissipation, drunkenness, disease, disaster, and death."[34]

Finally, in 1916, in *United States v. Nice*,[35] the Supreme Court expressly overturned the *Heff* ruling and enshrined in law the ambivalent status that Indians still have: they are citizens of their own nation and subjects/citizens of the United States. Justice Van Devanter, problematically mixing the status of tribes as sovereigns with the status of individual Indians, held that "citizenship is not incompatible with tribal existence or continued guardianship, and so may be conferred without completely emancipating the Indians or placing them beyond the reach of congressional regulations adapted for their protection."[36]

Nice was decided three years before American Indian World War I veterans were given the opportunity of becoming citizens[37] and eight years before Congress enacted the general Indian citizenship law that mandatorily extended federal citizenship to all Indians who were not yet enfranchised.[38] The 1924 General Citizenship Act unilaterally declared all other noncitizen Indians as federal citizens, but the act retained a section which confirmed that such citizenship would not diminish the Indians' right to tribal or other property.

Equally important, a number of indigenous nations, including the Iroquois nations and members of the **Five Civilized Tribes** (Cherokee, Choctaw, Chickasaw, Seminole, and Creek—so named because of the remarkable social, educational, economic, and political progress made by the tribes before and after their forced removal from the Southeast to lands west of the Mississippi during the Indian removal era), refused to accept federal citizenship, arguing that their preexisting tribal nation status was sufficient for them. And since they had not requested American citizenship, they questioned how the United States could unilaterally extend its citizenship to their people, who constituted separate governmental bodies previously recognized in treaties. Evidence of this is seen in actions by a number of tribal nations who continue to seek recognition before the United Nations as distinctive peoples.[39] Some of these indigenous groups—Hopi and Iroquois—travel abroad on passports issued by their own governments.

This is one of the unique realities, that tribal members are citizens of three polities—their nation, the United States, and the state—that make the study of Indian peoples such a dynamic pursuit. For if an Indian's tribal citizenship is an active one and he/she resides on or near Indian Country, he/she has rights as an Indian that may be adversely affected by federal plenary power. At the same time, such Indians enjoy certain protections, services, and benefits because of their treaty or trust relationship with the federal government that are unavailable to other individuals or racial or ethnic groups in the nation.

THE POLITICS OF AMBIVALENCE: INDIAN QUANDARIES

There is nothing in the whole compass of our laws so anomalous, so hard to bring within any precise definition, or any logical and scientific arrangement of principles, as the relation in which the Indians stand toward this [the U.S.] government and those of the states.[40]

In the opinion of your committee, the Constitution and the treaties, acts of Congress, and judicial decisions above referred to, all speak the same language upon this subject, and all point to the conclusion that the Indians, in tribal condition, have never been subject to the jurisdiction of the United States in the sense in which the term jurisdiction is employed in the fourteenth amendment to the Constitution. . . . Whenever we have dealt with them, it has been in their collective capacity as a state, and not with their individual members, except when such members were separated from the tribe to which they belonged; and then we have asserted such jurisdiction as every nation exercises over the subjects of another independent sovereign nation entering its territory and violating its laws.[41]

As the two quotes poignantly show, federal officials have struggled in their efforts to arrive at a consistent understanding of what the status of tribes is vis-à-vis the United States and what to do about Indian nations. Tribal nations and their individual members, as a result, have often suffered because of conflicting federal policies, which have vacillated between respecting the internal sovereignty of tribes and seeking to destroy tribal sovereignty in order to assimilate individual Indians into the American body politic. As such, the subject matter we are addressing encompasses at least four complicated quandaries about which I hope to provide some clarity.

First, tribes, as governments, face the conflicting tasks of "providing social services for people whose educational, health, and economic level is far below that of the general population in the United States, and running profitable and competitive businesses."[42] In their efforts to balance these two very different forces, tribes encounter complications from within and without that states and the federal government do not confront. The difficulties which have arisen for some tribes who have been successful in the gaming market that came in the wake of the Indian Gaming Regulatory Act of 1988 entail intratribal, intertribal, intergovernmental, and tribal-corporate conflicts that are examples of what can transpire when a government is also the chief employer.

Second, tribes have a real desire to exercise political, economic, and cultural self-determination—to maintain a degree of exclusion from the American polity—but the federal government defines its trust responsibility in a paternalistic manner not only to protect but also to make decisions for tribes that fundamentally conflict with any genuine definition of tribal self-determination. This second quandary is complicated by the fact that most tribes insist that one of the primary obligations of the federal government under the trust doctrine is to protect and strengthen tribal sovereignty and the assorted rights and powers that accompany that doctrine.

Third, American Indians are citizens of their own tribal nations, which are recognized as extraconstitutional governments. In other words, the federal Constitution does not apply to Indian tribes.[43] But by the middle of the twentieth century individual Indians had gradually been given the status of citizens of the United States, and of the states they resided in. Notwithstanding this treble citizenship, as described earlier, Indians have learned time and again that the U.S. Constitution provides only partial protection of their basic tribal and American citizenship rights. For example, the First Amendment has been interpreted by the Supreme Court as not protecting the religious freedom rights of tribal members.[44] The Fifth and the Fourteenth Amendments' due process and equal protection clauses are not extended to tribal members who continue to reside within a reservation's boundaries.[45] This is so, in part, because the Supreme Court determined in a major case in 1916, *United States v. Nice,* that U.S. "citizenship is not incompatible with tribal existence or continued guardianship, and so may be conferred without completely emancipating the Indians or placing them beyond the reach of congressional regulations adopted for their protection." In other words, Indians are indeed American citizens, but this status does not restrict the plenary powers of Congress with respect to Indians.

Fourth, Indian tribal governments are nations inhabiting territorial units—reservations, pueblos, or dependent communities—in which the U.S. Constitution is largely inapplicable. The political status of tribes, because of their preexisting sovereignty and treaty-making power, has been held to be "higher than that of states."

However, over the last century, and due to the passage of a number of laws like the General Allotment Act of 1887, a large number of non-Indians moved within the boundaries of Indian reservations. What is the relationship between these non-Indians and the tribal governments whose lands they inhabit? What powers may tribal governments exercise over non-Indians who are not politically represented in tribal politics? How is the jurisdictional minuet between the tribal governments, the federal government, and the state/county/local government to be administered since, constitutionally speaking, states and their political subdivisions have little or no jurisdiction in Indian Country because of Congress's exclusive authority under the commerce and treaty clauses?

These internal and intergovernmental quandaries are complicated by the indeterminate manner in which the federal government has dealt with indigenous nations, sometimes respecting, sometimes disrespecting their sovereignty. A brief, though not exhaustive, discussion of several of these federal indeterminacies, each rooted in legal precedent and political principles, will make clear why tribal nations enjoy little stability in their internal or external affairs.

First, tribes are sometimes treated as "distinct, independent communities" capable of exercising a significant measure of sovereign power, as when negotiating treaties or administering justice,[46] but they are also described as **domestic dependent nations** limited to exercising a reduced degree of internal sovereignty subject to federal dominance.[47] Second, tribal sovereignty has been defined as an inherent and reserved power,[48] but tribes have also been informed that they may exercise only those governmental powers that have been specifically delegated to them by express congressional action.[49]

Third, the tribal-federal relationship has sometimes been described as that of a "trustee" (federal government) to a "beneficiary" (indigenous group),[50] but on the other hand, the same relationship has been characterized as that of a **guardian** to a **ward**.[51] These are very different legal relationships. A "trusteeship" is a relationship that limits the property rights of the trustee, who is the beneficiary's servant; a guardianship relationship is one that limits the personal rights of the ward.

Fourth, a number of court cases have held that general acts of Congress are inapplicable to tribal nations unless they are specifically mentioned in the legislation, because of the extraconstitutional status of the tribes;[52] however, other cases have insisted that tribes are normally subject to congressional laws unless they are specifically exempted from the legislation, which would indicate that tribes are viewed as constitutional entities.[53]

Fifth, the federal government has sometimes acknowledged that its political power in relation to tribes is limited and must be based on specifically enumerated constitutional clauses (e.g., commerce, property);[54] on the other hand, federal law elsewhere asserts that the federal government has virtually unlimited political power over tribes and their property, and that this power is merely implied by constitutional clauses.[55]

Finally, there is much evidence that state laws have no force within Indian Country because of tribal sovereignty and federal supremacy under the commerce clause, unless the contrary is shown by an express act of Congress or some special circumstance;[56] but there is contrary evidence that state laws are valid in Indian territory unless they are expressly or implicitly prohibited by Congress.[57] There are other key inconsistencies in the way the federal government perceives its relationship to tribes that hinder stability in political affairs.[58]

These examples, with their radically different orientations, vividly point out that a tremendous ambivalence on the part of the federal government remains as to the actual political standing of tribal nations vis-à-vis their own peoples, the states, and the federal government. So long as this ambivalence persists, there can be no permanent resolution to many of the problems indigenous nations confront internally and externally.

A major reason for this ambivalence is that the status of Indian tribes and individual Indians has three very different sources in law, policy, and popular attitudes.[59] One source is the *cultural distinctiveness* of tribal peoples. It was this cultural sovereignty that the federal government for the better part of its history sought to obliterate in its powerful push toward ethnocide—through Christian missionaries, boarding-school education, individualization of Indian lands, etc. Now, the federal government sporadically seeks to protect cultural distinctiveness through bilingual education programs, protection of sacred sites, and allowances for Indians to practice traditional religions, but still finds ways to allow commodification and commercialization of American Indian culture—e.g., the perpetuation of degrading sports mascots and Indian caricatures like the Atlanta Braves and their "tomahawk chop," the Cleveland Indians' disfigured logo of an Indian, the derogatory football team name Washington "Redskins," and countless products that exploit stereotypical images of Indians, including the Indian maiden on Land-O'-Lakes butter and margarine, the "rugged" Jeep Cherokee, and the noble savage images perpetuated in movies like *Dances with Wolves* and *Last of the Mohicans*.

A second source of Indian status is the property rights of tribes and individual Indians as landowners and possessors of other important rights, like hunting and fishing rights identified in treaties. Of course, the subject of the transfer of Indian land title to the federal government through treaties and other agreements is the single most important fact animating Indian-white relations. Tribes went from being the landlords of the entire continent to owning less than 4 percent of their original lands by the 1930s. Laws like the 1887 General Allotment Act and its amendments, and the allotting agreement that ensued, exacerbated the land loss and contributed to the state of poverty most Indians found themselves in during the harshest days of Indian land dispossession.

As Vine Deloria noted, "Indian poverty was deliberately planned and [was] as predictable as the seasons," because of the allotment process and the way it was administered by the BIA.[60]

Hunting and fishing rights, water rights, and Indian tax exemptions from state law are the other major property rights of Indians reserved in treaties and federal laws. The manner in which these rights are exercised by the tribes, challenged by the local, state, or federal entities, or jointly administered by the tribal government, the states, and the federal government has important implications for Indian status.

A number of federal programs and agencies have historically been justified because a majority of Indians still suffered grinding poverty, high unemployment, and a host of other adverse socioeconomic circumstances compared with the U.S. population as a whole. Indians continue to suffer these conditions because of the manner in which their property rights, because of Indians' lack of a constitutionally recognized status, have been occasionally protected (when the right has been individually established, like an individual allotment of land) and more often exploited, when the rights are held in common by the tribal nation.

Some tribes have set up profitable gaming operations, other businesses, and resource-based enterprises in the form of cattle ranches, oil and gas operations, the timber industry, coal mines, recreational resorts, and electronic assembly plants.[61] But these tribal business successes remain greatly outnumbered by tribes whose governments and members struggle with intense poverty, largely artificial economies, and a virtual colonial relationship with the federal government.[62]

The third source, the rights of tribal nations as distinct political entities exercising inherent sovereignty, affirmed in international law, treaty law, the U.S. Constitution, and a wealth of congressional measures, Supreme Court cases, and presidential policy pronouncements, is the one source that is "constitutionally necessary to enable the society to make a legal distinction between Indian tribes and other cultural groups or other groups of poor people."[63] It is this political status of tribal nations and their treaty- and trust-based relationship to the United States that is the "foundation for the entire structure of policies, programs, and laws. Yet it is the one source of Indian status which, as a practical matter, probably cannot stand alone."[64]

CONCLUSION

These three sources—cultural distinctiveness, property rights, and political sovereignty—are braided together in the public and federal and state governments' perceptions of Indians. The inability or unwillingness of the public and the governments to distinguish between the three perpetuates the legal and political confusion of tribal status described earlier. In other words, tribal cultural distinctiveness and property ownership generally find some support in "the simultaneous humanitarian impulse and sense of cultural superiority that are the peculiar heritage of Anglo-American society."[65]

But as tribes have learned, their legal and political status as sovereigns will be and has been terminated or seriously diminished when they have been perceived to have "lost" their cultural uniqueness in the eyes of Euro-America, or, as is happening now, when tribes are deemed to be to well-off financially—the false perception that all Indians are wealthy because of gaming revenues—and are therefore perceived to no longer need federal protection or support. Phillip S. Deloria (Standing Rock Sioux) sums up the status dilemmas by noting that:

> Indian governments are thus subjected to a different status than other governments. There are not constant reviews of the demographic status of all the little countries in Europe that are frequently compared in size and population with Indian tribes. No one asks whether Monaco and Liechtenstein are sufficiently culturally distinct from neighboring countries to justify their continued existence. Unlike that of Indian tribes, their political status is taken for granted.[66]

Clearly, this is complicated academic terrain. But by unbraiding and closely examining the four quandaries discussed, as well as the issue of treble citizenship for indigenous peoples, the national or sovereign status of indigenous polities, and the federal government's inconsistent understanding of its relationship to tribes, I hope to bring needed clarity to the status and internal and external powers of tribal nations as the First Nations in the Americas, nations who have entered into distinctive economic and political relations with other tribes, interest groups, the states, and the federal government.

REFERENCES

[1]Milner S. Ball, "Constitution, Court, Indian Tribes," *American Bar Foundation Research Journal* 1 (1987): 1–139.

[2]Timothy Egan, *New York Times,* 9 March 1998, A1.

[3]Margaret L. Knox, *Los Angeles Times,* 7 November 1993, 28 (Magazine).

[4]Brad Knickerbocker, *Christian Science Monitor,* 3 April 1998, 1.

[5]Timothy Egan, *New York Times,* 27 August 1997, A1.

[6]See Vine Deloria Jr., *Red Earth, White Lies* (Boulder, Colo.: Fulcrum, 1996) for a critical, indigenous analysis of the Bering Strait theory and tribal responses to such scientific speculation.

[7]Jeanette Wolfley and Susan Johnson, "Tribal Sovereignty," National Council of State Legislatures, http://www.ncsl.org/programs/esnr/tribsove.html, June 1996.

[8]See Vine Deloria, Jr. and Raymond J. DeMallie's recent two-volume study, *Documents of American Indian Diplomacy: Treaties, Agreements, and Conventions, 1775–1979* (Norman: University of Oklahoma Press, 1999) for an outstanding treatment of this diverse diplomatic record.

[9]See David E. Wilkins, "Convoluted Essence: Indian Rights and the Federal Trust Doctrine," *Native Americas* XIX, no. 1 (Spring 1997): 24–31 for an analysis of the conflicting federal definitions. And see David E. Wilkins, " 'With the Greatest Respect and Fidelity': A Cherokee Vision of the 'Trust Doctrine,' " *The Social Science Journal* 34, no. 4 (1997): 495–510 for a discussion of one tribe's views on what "trust" means to them.

[10]Executive Order 13084, "Consultation and Coordination with Indian Tribal Governments," in *Weekly Compilation of Presidential Documents,* vol. 34, no. 20 (18 May 1998), 869.

[11]Vine Deloria Jr., "The Distinctive Status of Indian Rights," in *The Plains Indians of the Twentieth Century,* ed. Peter Iverson (Norman: University of Oklahoma Press, 1985), 241.

[12]However, the United States has asserted that it wields "plenary power" over Puerto Rico, a commonwealth, as well. See Nell Jessup Newton, "Federal Power over Indians: Its Sources, Scope, and Limitations," *University of Pennsylvania Law Review* 132 (1984): 195–288; Laurence M. Hauptman, "Congress, Plenary Power, and the American Indian, 1870–1992," in *Exiled in the Land of the Free,* ed. Oren Lyons and John Mohawk (Santa Fe, N.Mex.: Clear Light, 1992), 318–36; and David E. Wilkins, "The U.S. Supreme Court's Explication of 'Federal Plenary Power': An Analysis of Case Law Affecting Tribal Sovereignty, 1886–1914," *American Indian Quarterly* 18, no. 3 (winter 1994): 349–68.

[13]435 U.S. 313, 319.

[14]Deloria, "Distinctive Status," 240.

[15]*Johnson v. McIntosh,* 21 U.S. (8 Wheat.) 543 (1823).

[16]*Tee-Hit-Ton v. United States,* 348 U.S. 273 (1955).

[17]*United States v. Antelope,* 430 U.S. 641 (1977).

[18]In the 1950s and 1960s Congress enacted several "termination" laws in which the government divested itself of its legal obligations and moral responsibilities to certain tribes and in effect denied the right of those tribes to legally exist in the eyes of the federal government.

[19]Ralph W. Johnson and E. Susan Crystal, "Indians and Equal Protection," *Washington Law Review* 54 (1979).

[20]Wolfley and Johnson, "Tribal Sovereignty," 3.

[21]Sam Deloria, "Introduction," in *Indian Tribal Sovereignty and Treaty Rights* (Albuquerque, N.Mex.: La Confluencia, 1978), s23.

[22]7 Stat., 156.

[23]25 Stat., 392.

[24]41 Stat., 350.

[25]3 Stat., 516.

[26]60 U.S. (19 How.) 393, 404–5 (1857).

[27]Senate Committee on the Judiciary, *Report to the Senate the Effect of the Fourteenth Amendment to the Constitution upon the Indian Tribes of the Country,* 41st Cong., 3d sess., 1870, S. Rept. 268, 11.

[28]House, Commissioner of Indian Affairs, *Annual Report* 42d Cong., 3d sess, 1872, H. Exec. Doc. 1, 400.

[29]112 U.S. 94, 99 (1884).

[30]*Seventh Annual Report of the Board of Indian Commissioners for the Year 1875* (Washington, D.C.: Government Printing Office, 1876), 13–14.

[31]Felix S. Cohen, *Handbook of Indian Law,* reprint ed. (Albuquerque: University of New Mexico Press, 1972), 154, quoting from Senator Orville H. Platte.

[32]26 Stat., 81, 99–100.

[33]Vine Deloria Jr. and Clifford M. Lytle, *American Indians, American Justice* (Austin: University of Texas Press, 1983), 220.

[34]U.S. Supreme Court. *Records and Briefs.* Transcript of Record. *The United States v. Fred Nice.* Brief for the United States by Solicitor General John W. Davis, November 1915, 22.

[35]241 U.S. 591 (1916).

[36]241 U.S. 591, 598 (1916).

[37]41 Stat., 350.

[38]43 Stat., 253.

[39]See, Franke Wilmer, *The Indigenous Voice in World Politics* (Newbury Park, Calf.: Sage, 1993), for an excellent treatment of the persistent efforts of indigenous peoples, both in the United States and in other nation-states, to gain full admittance before the United Nations as separately recognized sovereign entities.

[40]U.S. Attorney General Hugh Swinton Legare, as quoted in House, Commissioner of Indian Affairs *Annual Report,* 32d Cong., 1st sess. (1851), H. Exec. Doc. 2, 274.

[41]Senate, *Report on the Effect of the Fourteenth Amendment,* 10.

[42]Deloria, "Introduction," s24.

[43]*Talton v. Mayes,* 163 U.S. 376, 384 (1896).

[44]*Lyng v. Northwest Indian Cemetery Protective Association,* 485 U.S. 439 (1988) and *Employment Division, Dept. of Human Resources v. Smith,* 494 U.S. 872 (1990).

[45]See *Groundhog v. Keeler,* 442 F. 2d 674 (1971).

[46]*Worcester v. Georgia,* 31 U.S. (6 Pet.) 515 (1832).

[47]*Cherokee Nation v. Georgia,* 30 U.S. (5 Pet.) 1 (1831).

[48]See, e.g., *Ex Parte Crow Dog,* 109 U.S. 556 (1883) and *Merrion v. Jicarilla Apache Tribe,* 455 U.S. 130 (1982).

[49]*Oliphant v. Suquamish,* 435 U.S. 191 (1978).

[50]*Seminole v. United States,* 316 U.S. 286 (1942).

[51]*United States v. Kagama,* 118 U.S. 375, 383–84 (1886).

[52]*Elk v. Wilkins,* 112 U.S. 94, 100 (1884).

[53]*Cherokee Tobacco,* 78 (11 Wall.) 616 (1871).

[54]*Perrin v. United States,* 232 U.S. 478 (1914).

[55]*Lone Wolf v. Hitchcock,* 187 U.S. 553 (1903).

[56]*Worcester v. Georgia,* 31 U.S. (6 Pet.) 515 (1832).

[57]Cotton Petroleum Corporation v. New Mexico, *490 U.S. 163, 173 (1989).*

[58]For instance, the **doctrine of discovery** is sometimes seen as a preemptive legal principle that limited the rights of competing European states and the United States and merely provided the "discovering" state with the exclusive right to purchase such lands as the tribes were willing to sell; but sometimes discovery is treated as a principle that irrefutably vested legal ownership of America in the discovering states, thereby permanently diminishing the land rights of tribes to the status of an occupant—a tenant if you will—with a lesser beneficial title and no power to sell.

[59]Phillip S. Deloria, "The Era of Indian Self-Determination: An Overview," in *Indian Self-Rule,* ed. Ken Philp (Salt Lake City, Utah: Howe Brothers, 1986).

[60]Vine Deloria Jr., " 'Reserving to Themselves': Treaties and the Powers of Indian Tribes," *Arizona Law Review* 38 (fall 1996), 978.

[61]Robert H. White, *Tribal Assets: The Rebirth of Native America* (New York: Holt, 1991).

[62]David E. Wilkins, "Modernization, Colonialism, Dependency: How Appropriate Are These Models for Providing an Explanation of North American Indian 'Underdevelopment'?" *Ethnic and Racial Studies* 16, no. 3 (July 1993): 390–419.

[63]Deloria, "Indian Self-Determination," 193.

[64]Deloria, "Indian Self-Determination," 193.

[65]Deloria, "Indian Self-Determination," 193.

[66]Deloria, "Indian Self-Determination," 193.

4

American Indian Art Markets and Traditions

Deborah W. Dozier

The world art market, in all of its diverse forms, treats American Indian art differently than the works produced by artists of the Western world. Further, the world art market values, or rather devalues, American Indian works of art quite differently than the artworks of Europe. Although some may argue that this is changing, the dissimilarity is still globally apparent in museums, galleries, and sweatshops, as well as in the strip malls, courtrooms, and classrooms of America. The reasons for this are many, but all stem from the prevailing notions non-Indians have about Indian people. Our discussion of American Indian art then, begins with an effort to understand these stereotypes and the cultural conditions that fostered their formation. That story can be traced to events that occurred more than five centuries ago.

THE BIRTH OF A STEREOTYPE

Six hundred years ago, the pressure was on in Europe. The fresh water sources were so polluted that touching water was equivalent to infecting oneself; personal hygiene among the wealthy was replaced with perfumes—heavily scented sterile alcohols. People drank beers and ales rather than water because the brewing process sterilized the beverages. The deforested landscape, overpopulated and overburdened by man and domestic beast, could no longer produce enough to keep pace with the hunger of the poor.

Disease, crime, and poverty were the lot of the majority of Europeans, but those who were not victims of privation enjoyed a life of unparalleled luxury, even though many suffered from the physical effects of generations of marriages to close relatives as a way to maintain their wealth and position.

This was the way it was in the 1500s in Europe when the bored children of the filthy rich, as well as those disenfranchised from property and status in Europe, took to the oceans of the world to go exploring. The things these travelers saw were far more amazing than they ever anticipated, and this created a sort of cognitive dissonance between what they believed and the realities they perceived for themselves. Western ideas about American Indian people and art are rooted in this dissonance, which has resolved itself only slightly for most non-Indians.

What did these travelers believe? Simply, that they were the crowning jewel, the epitome, of creation. Proof of this would be offered in the 1530s by religious philosopher and lawyer, turned minister, John Calvin who saw wealth in the hands of the "elect" as manifest proof of God's favor, and authors like Francis Galton, who in the later 1800s, pointed to the ability of the wealthy of Europe to hang onto position and money as physical evidence not only of superiority but of genius.[1]

They believed that there was no more obvious or validating sign of God's favor than possessing the wherewithal to set out upon the seas on mercenary, pirating, pleasure, and educational voyages, where one could examine not only the cradle of their own civilization, but the faraway lands of "mysterious" peoples. Once visited, the peoples of these lands were judged, by the Christian-educated, European ruling class, as heathen and "savage," which literally meant what the word "wild" means today—indicating a people outside of the influence of the "civilizing" governmental and economic forces, languages, religions, and other systems of social control known to Europeans.

What did the travelers perceive? Arguably, the most elaborate, rich and finely wrought material culture[2] in the world. Every skill had practitioners who elevated their technical and esthetic ability to the highest possible level, producing unparalleled work in shell, feather, stone, metal, and hide as well as masterworks of watercraft, basketry, ceramic, textiles, sculpture, books, paintings, drawings, and architecture.

The quality and quantity of fine work was equal to or exceeded that of any other place in the world. Atahualpa, the Incan Emperor, had life-size, solid-gold models cast of all of the animals that inhabited the Incan lands as well as a full-length cloak made of small square plates of beaten gold interlocked with golden rings. The Aztecs, at the time of European contact, had developed a fabulously wealthy culture where the well heeled wore some of the most finely manufactured and embellished garments the world has ever seen. Mexican libraries held hundreds of thousands of volumes in the 1530s.

What did the travelers retrieve? Expeditions of discovery and pleasure became common, but more nefarious voyages were underway, too. Other branches of these royal or merchant families were involved in the exploitation of these "mysterious" populations and the extraction of their resources. Like their relatives on pleasure cruises, the Europhones marveled at the things they saw and brought many away with them—taking them home to show those who had stayed behind and who would never believe the verbal descriptions of what was encountered in these far off-lands. These other members of the family were busy looting and pillaging any and everything that they could put aboard their ships. Nothing, including people, was spared.

The books of America were all burned, but the gold and silver were melted and otherwise organized into units for transport to the treasuries of Europe. Some ships carrying the wealth of the Americas sank; tales of their unrecovered riches spawn television adventure shows and get-rich-quick stories. Others ships made the voyage across the Atlantic, laden with wealth Jack Weatherford says knocked the bottom out of both the African gold market and the Chinese silver market by flooding the economy of Europe with more wealth than they could ever have imagined. More than 12 million Indians died laboring to remove gold and silver from the Americas so the churches of Europe could become gilded and the children of the wealthy could sail the world on voyages of education and discovery.

What did the travelers conceive? Europhone contact gave birth to drastic change in the number and variety of goods produced that can be measured in three ways. First, whole new forms with new functions were created, as in the case of the North American Great Plains, where the reappearance and subsequent domestication of the horse prompted an explosion of new types of material culture objects, such as saddle blankets, saddle bags, and riding whips. Another locus of inventiveness was the intersection of Native skills and European traditions that produced walrus-tusk cribbage boards in the Arctic, quilled chair backs in the Northeast, and clay oil lamps in Southern California.

Second, the impact of contact can be measured in the appearance and disappearance of materials from the American artists' works. Glass beads were unknown in America before contact, but after contact they begin to appear worked into garments, bags, pipe stems and so forth. Account books, also called ledgers, were adopted by Plains artists to replace the plentiful hides once used to record history. Likewise, certain materials and forms may have disappeared altogether or were reduced in variety and number—the number of dyed porcupine quills worked into baskets, ear rings and moccasins has dropped dramatically since first contact.

Third, the impact is also reflected in a reduction in the production of art forms overall as the deaths of artists and their teachers mounted. The deaths were due to murder and massacre of Indian men, women, and children, but most deaths were caused by the transmission of many contagious illnesses[3] of Western origin that attacked the vulnerable immune systems of most Indian people.

Disease is a great equalizer in that it does not recognize position or wealth; it only knows immunity or lack of immunity. Of course immunity was an undiscovered concept in Europe and the deaths of huge numbers of Native Americans were interpreted by Europhones as the Christian God's affirmation of the superiority of the Europeans. Some Europhones died from these diseases, to be sure, but the percentage of Europhone deaths from viral and bacterial illnesses was negligible when compared to that of the Indian peoples where, in some cases, whole tribal groups were wiped out within three or four generations. Much knowledge was lost because people, the main repository for information, died and took the information with them.

But do not think that all was lost. Individuals were able to collectively rebuild their communities in ways that embodied the ancient traditions, as always, adapted to the changeable nature of reality and the needs of the remaining Native people.

COLLECTING CURIOSITIES

The wondrous things produced in the Americas amazed the Europhones, but on some level they understood that the objects meant very little, except as curiosities, when they were taken out of context. What they really wanted was to recreate the feeling of the worlds they had visited, even if they had to do it in miniature. Toward this end they built windowless rooms lined with shelves, called *vunderkammer* (literally "wonder cabinet"). Here they kept their "curiosities," the naturally occurring items or material culture objects that had caused them to experience the cognitive dissonance we call wonder. Thus was born, not only the ancestor of the modern "curio" cabinet but also of the modern museum; after several centuries of continued "collecting," these curiosities really began to pile up around the castles. Many needed special care to protect them from mold, insect infestation, and the like. The wealthy of Europe began to understand what it was going to cost them to keep their curiosities.

The European interest in curiosities as things to be appreciated instead of shunned was transferred to the Americas with the Europhone immigrants. They collected the skulls and objects that they unearthed from Indian graves. The idea that these items were taken from graves is a very important point because it indicates two things about the attitude of the Europeans regarding American Indian objects of all sorts.

Foremost, they believed, as do many modern Americans, in the validity of the concept expressed by the child's taunt, "finders keepers; losers weepers"—the notion that anything unguarded can be taken fairly by anyone who comes upon it. Second, it demonstrates the relative ease with which Europhones interacted with the bones of the dead. In one such case, a skull unearthed in the central Woodlands has been passed from generation to generation in the same family since at least the 1850s. Today, the skull sits in a library bookcase in the family home in central California, with little hope of repatriation.

As repositories of curiosities, public museums are only about 100 years old, and they resulted from the release of private goods to public institutions. Primarily they are based on the collections of individuals. The Phoebe Apperson Hearst Museum at the University of California at Berkeley, for example, began as the personal collection of the Hearst family and is now a public collection in the care of the University.

The new Smithsonian Museum of the American Indian in Washington, D.C., began when the privately owned holdings of the collection of the George Gustav Heye Museum were transferred to the publicly owned collections of the Smithsonian Institution in 1989. The Heye Museum had fallen on hard financial times, and the collection was in danger of total ruination, as water leaking through the roof became a serious threat. The point is that the collections became too expensive for individuals to maintain and rather than lose them to ruin, many were donated to institutions, cities, counties, states, and even to the federal government.

So, how did the objects in the Heye Museum and the Hearst Museum get collected in the first place? Most cornerstones of museum and private collections are objects procured directly from Indian people. Before 1900, the populations of American cities wanted interesting things to do, and the first museums opened their doors to rave reviews. Among these first museums was one in New York City privately owned by P. T. Barnum, which he eventually took on the road under the name of "circus." Newly created public museums, too, were eager to draw crowds through their turnstiles, and the museums' directors ordered their curatorial staffs to recreate, for the public, the feeling of being in an archaic Native American setting.

This spawned a collecting frenzy among individuals and institutions desiring to create "dioramas," specifically, three-dimensional reproductions, using mannequins, of an archaic Native American event, usually something mundane, exhibiting the material culture objects acquired from a particular group. They were full-scale displays that included hundreds of objects "bought" in Indian communities across America. It was important to collectors that the objects be original and filled with data, for it was the data encoded within the object that made it valuable.

Some apologists would point to the money paid to Indians for their things to justify the holdings of American Indian art. Until ten years ago, only a small number of Indian artists received fair value for their work; the count is now a small number plus a handful. Before ten years ago, the purchases of those objects that were bought "fairly" were most often coerced or extorted purchases, at prices substantially less than the real value of the object. The sellers were often near refugees but more often complete refugees on the verge of starvation and death from exposure in their own lands; the objects were essentially looted from the near dead. The buyers were pleased with their "bargain" prices.

Perhaps as important as what collectors wanted were the kinds of things they didn't want. They wanted objects that supported the stereotypes they sold to the public, so when the "authentic" Indian objects ran out in communities, the collectors went away. They left behind the objects that showed the ugly reality of Indian life at the turn of the twentieth century. They didn't want the cast-off objects of Western origin salvaged by Indian people and used to replace the objects collected away by the wealthy and powerful. The public didn't want to see the tin cans used to replace the plates and bowls shipped away nor did they want to see their own cast-off clothing that Indian people wore. The public, and therefore the institutions, were not interested in portraying the suffering of living Indian people, only in using objects to maintain stereotypes that the public found easy to believe.

THE INDIAN PRICE TAG

It is important to understand that many objects were gained by foul means of one sort or another. Many things in museum collections were acquired from burials, taken through "grave robbing." While we might personally look down on the activity of grave robbing, most Americans certainly are fascinated by the idea of finding buried "treasure," and a significant number have achieved fame, made fortunes, and built careers by "exploring" and/or "excavating" Indian burials. The rightful Indian owners were seldom given the right-of-first-refusal to move their ancestors out of the way of the juggernaut of progress nor were they compensated for the seizure and removal of these burial objects.

Like the grave pilferers, collectors who worked among the living paid little attention to legal or moral title, and they made virtually no effort to determine if the rightful owner of an object was the seller. Stewart Cullin and Constance Goddard DuBois, who collected for different museums at the turn of the century, each document Indian people begging them to return some object that should never have been sold; in each case the collector turned down the tearful Indian petitioners, saying, "A deal is a deal." Cullin went so far as to have the woman who begged for the return of a basket arrested, when she resorted to theft after he refused to sell the basket back to her.

Most dumbfounding is how "Ghost Dance"-related objects have entered collections. The Ghost Dance religion taught that God would return peace and prosperity to Indian America by causing a deluge to sweep away the Europhone populations after which the ancestors and great herds would be healed and resurrected. The winter of 1890 found the Sioux people under the leadership of Big Foot confined to their encampment on Wounded Knee Creek by the military power of the United States government. They were facing death from exposure and starvation, and most were too sick or weak or young or old to go and search for food. The few able-bodied braved the snow and cold and went to find food and fuel. The ones who remained behind prayed the Ghost Dance in hopes that the salvation promised by the Prophet of the religion would come before they were all dead.

Just before New Year's Day American troops opened fire on the sick and defenseless worshipers, and an estimated 300 unarmed people barely clinging to life were gunned down with experimental automatic weapons by the United States cavalry. Toddlers were chased into the brush and shot in the back. Among soldiers there is an old tradition that demands trophy taking; anything from severed heads to weapons taken from an enemy during a battle seems to be universally desirable. The American soldiers—more than twenty subsequently received Congressional Medals of Honor for the massacre—stripped the bodies of the Indian dead of anything that might be sold to collectors or institutions and made a little extra income. To this day, applying the words "Ghost Dance" to an Indian object sends its value soaring, specifically because of the connection with this slaughter of so many defenseless Indian people by the U.S. cavalry.

Included in the price paid by Indian people is one cost not much noticed or worried about outside of the Indian community. Institutions and private collectors celebrate the importance of their amassed holdings, yet they seldom mourn for the deleterious effects collecting has had on the Indian side of the equation. The heartbreaking loss of objects to collections has been felt in Indian communities since the first things were taken away. The price paid for the loss of these objects and the data they embody is the greatest, aside from the loss of human life, paid by Native communities.

There is a more subtle and insidious damage done by collecting so many objects from Indian America than by the conversion of utilitarian objects into simple curiosities or *objets d'artes*. Once the objects were collected, they were rendered mute, the volumes of data encoded in their physical bodies now lost to the new owners. The data was still there, but the ones with the key to understanding were now those with the least access to the objects.

Finally, many collectors have taken actions that removed any foreseeable possibility of return to their communities of origin. Thousands of the objects in the collection of the Smithsonian Institution, for example, have been dusted with arsenic, so that anyone who wants to see these things must wear gloves, gowns, shoe covers, and masks so they will not be poisoned. Hundreds of beautiful twined baskets from the Northwest Coast peoples were further ruined by being folded in half and flattened to save money on shipping by reducing the volume of the baskets. These objects are never again to be used as their creators intended.

IDENTITY DATA BANKS

All of the material culture objects people surround themselves with are encoded with data. The data reinforces identity one way or another. Some objects do not carry enough information or they carry the wrong information and are thus ignored or discarded; other objects we recognize as satisfyingly valid signs of who we are.

To understand how much data objects carry, it is useful to employ the concept of "identity value." Simply put, "identity value" is the amount of information an object carries that allows a person to know who he or she is. Typically, we surround ourselves with objects that reinforce our identities; people often want to keep family heirlooms because they have a high degree of identity value. The more strongly (positive or negative) we feel about an object, the greater its identity value. Artists infuse identity value into each piece they produce, whether they intend to or not; as each piece becomes suffused with value, it simultaneously begins to function as an "identity data bank."

This is apparent when one looks at a basket from California. More than 1700 plants that grow in California are suitable for making baskets; nonetheless, basketmakers limited the number of plants they employed to no more than a dozen. In fact, most used only three or four plants on a regular basis. So tightly bound were basketry materials and tribal identity that modern researchers, many of whom are Native Indian people searching for the scattered objects of their foremothers and the data they contain, use materials as a clue to establish the tribal origin of the basket.

A good basketmaker knew how to make baskets, not only in the style of her people, but also in the styles of others. This might occur because a woman would marry into a tribe where she was expected to change her tribal affiliation to that of her husband's. She would learn to make baskets in the style of her husband's people, even though she could already make baskets in the style of her people. She would be taught how to load the proper identity data into her baskets through the use of color, form, design, materials, and techniques.

When a basketmaker produced a basket for someone of a different tribe, as sometimes happened, the basketmaker would use the combination of color, form, design, materials, and techniques appropriate to the tribal affiliation of the intended recipient. Baskets produced for the non-Indian market had identity data appropriate to the collectors incorporated into them. For example, basketmakers borrowed designs from Spanish coins in the 1700s, depicted the individual cattle brands of ranching families in the late 1800s, and used hearts from American and European needlework patterns in the 1940s.

Basketmakers very clearly distinguished between their different markets and adhered to the design rules for that market. If a basketmaker's family used only two colors for their daily use baskets, and a basketmaker decided that she wanted to use three colors, her mental solvency would most likely be questioned. No one would be likely to praise her innovative color use; people would simply think she no longer knew who her people were and wonder about her future. This is really not so unusual. The same would be thought of a football player who rejected the uniform of his team and wore the colors of the opposing team. Thus every material culture object is an identity data bank and removal from the community of origin means that data is no longer available to the community.

History is replete with examples of a dominant culture forcing those of a less dominant culture to replace the material culture objects of their birth culture with those that reference the dominant culture.[4] Indian children, when they were sent off to government schools, were stripped of the things they brought from home; their physical appearance was altered by bobbing their hair and making them wear uniforms; they were punished if they spoke their mother tongue or played games from home. They were denied identity data that affirmed they were Indian and were surrounded instead with the stuff of America in the hopes that they would somehow become Americans through an imagined process called assimilation.

Most modern Americans' ancestors came here with the intention of shedding their identity and acquiring a new American one.[5] When they shed their languages, clothing, foods, and housing, religion and economics, that changed everything because with them went a mountain of identity data. Stepping in to fill the gap, of course, is the globalization strategy, ready to extend a new identity to the self-less. For this reason, even if the old folks hang onto the language and some favorite foods, the subsequent generations have no trouble becoming "Americanized."

Humans, however, have a strong desire to know who they are and to surround themselves with things that reinforce their identity, so most Americans can say of their heritage, "I'm German," or "I'm Nigerian," or "I'm Laotian" and point to some reminder. But how many third-generation Americans can speak easily in the language of their ancestors? The point is that most Americans have been assimilated. Most don't resent the assimilation; American Indian people, however, resent the humiliation of hegemony they have suffered. They were, after all, multiple sovereign nations who successfully managed the courses of their own destinies for eons before the appearance of the light-skinned Europhones.

It is easy to understand the frustration felt by Indian people who know that all of the things that hold their identity data have been scattered to the four winds, sold by collectors and traded by public and private collecting institutions to others in Europe, Asia, Australia, Africa, and South America. Many modern artists cite the far-flung locations of objects they need to see and examine as a barrier they must overcome to continue their traditions. Travel is expensive and this adds to the difficulty of visiting the works.

THE NATURE OF THE ART OF THE WESTERN WORLD

Now that we have a basic idea of how Native American material culture objects were lost to their communities of origin and placed into collections, we can begin to talk about their similarities to and differences from Western art and the effect Indian America has on modern world and national art markets.

According to Western art historians, art making was born 25,000 years ago when someone carved the oldest known sculptural figure, a female form called the Venus of Willendorf, named after the German town where she was found. Art making really took off, though, when some ancient person/people entered a deep cave in what is now called Lascaux, France, and drew a series of portraits of animals.

Collectors of European "art" then, believe that before the twentieth century, art was produced in the media of drawing, painting, sculpture, architecture, and print making, exclusively.[6] Of course, the wealthy of Europe had fine clothes and furniture and books and carriages, but those things were not considered art; neither was pottery nor metalwork. All of these were considered to be "crafts."

Western works of art are not utilitarian objects; they are not meant to serve dinner upon nor to fend off enemies. They are intended to be seen. This is easily verifiable by looking at any standard Western art-history text and looking at the art forms discussed there. The more modern, open-minded volumes include photography and computer-generated art under the rubric of new media. But, typically, the old standards are still based in the discussion of forms that have no utility beyond propaganda,[7] except, of course, in the case of architecture.

The distinction between "art" and "craft" is a very subtle but rigid and important one and depends less on the quality of work produced than on the gender and ethnicity of the artist, the materials the artist uses, and the intended end use of the object. The idea is that there are "rules" of a sort for determining if a thing is art or craft is historically Western and based in class and privilege. It implies a class of people so wealthy they can surround themselves with things that serve no purpose other than to be looked at.

Some might argue that occasionally the preciousness of the materials would elevate a "crafted" object to the status of a "work of art," as in the case of the egg-shaped cache boxes made from cast and beaten gold and both filled and encrusted with precious stones by Fabergé for the Russian royal family. It can be debated whether the Fabergé eggs are craft or actually miniature sculptures, but, in general, the term "art" is reserved for use with drawings, paintings, statues, or prints.

The Western distinction between art and craft then is not based in the internal processes of the artist. It is not based in the thoughtful reflective processes of the artist, nor in the ability of artists to express with their hands what their minds envision. This is ironic because it is the internal creative processes of Pablo Picasso and Paul Gauguin that are so much admired for having given life to paintings that reflect and represent these inner processes.

The distinction between art and craft in the Western world is market driven, that is, an object's status is determined by the identity it is given and the subsequent place it occupies in the world of objects offered for sale. Its worth is based on a classification system that assigns higher relative value to objects produced by men and particularly by light-skinned men of European ancestry. The moral character of the man certainly has nothing to do with the value of the art. Gauguin, for example, was a known syphilitic pedophile who single-handedly brought enormous misery and suffering to the children and families of the people of Tahiti. In Tahiti this is still remembered, but this is not taught in art schools, and most collectors do not consider his moral character related to the value of his paintings.

THE NATURE OF THE ART OF THE NATIVE AMERICAN INDIAN WORLD

There has always been a market for Native North American Indian crafted objects. Craft specialization[8] was a given in every community in the Americas. Before the arrival of the Europhones, the trade networks in America were vast and covered nearly every inch of the hemisphere. The objects created and traded had utilitarian value of one sort or another. None were made with display as the only purpose for their existence. Each had a functional utility; it is fair to say that nothing was made or fashioned without a purpose in mind.

Long before the Europeans came to the Americas, Indian women made baskets for sale and trade to the surrounding tribes. Never using the style of her own tribe, the basketmaker would copy the style of the tribe of the intended recipient. Thousands of baskets were made specifically to sell to collectors across America as wastebaskets or storage containers for hairpins to raise cash for Indian families; the basketmakers, knowing they would never see these baskets again, often coded them with data appropriate to their intended audience by adorning them with cattle brands and designs from magazines they thought would appeal to the Europhones.

The thing that was different in Indian America was that there was no concept of art as a separate activity or an object's sole value resting in its visual appeal. In the Western world, we have developed a culture that makes sharp divisions between art, business, church, and state. Whatever divisions existed within Indian America, the idea of acting in a non-prayerful way or making an object less than perfectly were never among those divisions. If a thing was worth doing, it was worth doing well and with good spirit.

Most American Indian world views presumed that the people were living in the now; many languages have no words for yesterday, tomorrow, one o'clock, later, and after a while. The people understood the importance of living in the now, in the moment. After all, the only place we can exist is the now; we are not living in the future or the past if we are mentally healthy.

One way modern Americans can imagine how this would work in daily life is to imagine that today is the only day of your life and what you do and produce today will be used to represent who you are to the rest of the world. What would people think of you? A few folks, put in this position, might laugh and be happy to be known as clowns; a few more couldn't care less how they are represented; but it is fair to say that most people have enough personal pride to hope that they would leave a good enough impression to be taken seriously. They would work carefully, thoughtfully, with respect and dignity, so that what they produce would be esteemed with the same high regard they reserve for themselves. It is difficult for most of us to imagine a world where everyone works with high regard for themselves and their task, as a rule.

One of the things an artist hopes to do is reach a particular creative "zone" while working. This zone is well known to athletes, where perception is altered and a certain clarity of thought is possible, or rather thought is no longer required, *per se*, to accomplish the activity, for the focus has turned inward. During this time, the creative energy of the artist flows smoothly, and the work proceeds with a certain ease that is captured in the finished product, especially if the artist has fully mastered the materials.

The high regard with which life is given to an object or, more precisely form is given to a thought, reinforces that this is not something to be undertaken lightly or carelessly, and this is perhaps why the range of items that get classified as art objects by collectors is, at first glance, truly curious. Western paintings and sculptures, to be sure, are considered art, but a whole universe of mundane Indian objects is also considered "art." A short list of such things includes backrests, back scratchers, bed linens, boats, bows and arrows, calendars, clothing, cooking pots, cradles, decoys, dolls, fishing gear, netting shuttles, shoes, storage containers, and tools of all sorts. A long list would probably include every single thing ever made by an Indian person, especially if the thing is from the archaic (pre-1492) or historic (1492–1890) period.

The Western art world's acceptance of such a wide range of media as art from Indian people is due in part to the historic museum collecting/diorama craze that sent anthropologists and traders flocking to the Indian communities of America, hungry for whatever they could find that was authentically Indian.

Economics is also a strong impetus for the categorization of a back scratcher as art. Since art always costs more than back scratchers or clubs for killing fish, one sure way to increase the value of a mundane object is to include it in a museum collection and place it on public display; publishing information about and photos of the object will further increase its value.

Another technique for adjusting the value of an object is to reassign its use to a more "glamorous" arena. For example, a club used to kill a salmon has much less sales cachet in America and Europe than a "war club" or "slave killer." American collectors are particularly known for their love of war-related objects. Thus a new art market was born that persists to this day.

THE SURVIVAL OF MODERN INDIAN ART

The challenges facing living and future Indian artists are enormous. Oren Lyons, an Onondaga Chief, once used the metaphor of going down a river with one foot in each of two canoes to describe Indian interaction with the Western world; he pointed to how tricky it is to keep one's balance and stay on one's feet while traveling in two canoes. This can be used as an appropriate metaphor for describing the multiple challenges facing Indian artists.

The first obstacle facing modern artists is to find a teacher to instruct them in the old techniques. Compare the number of classes offered at institutions of higher learning in American Indian art history and Euro-American/Western art history; some schools still do not offer anything but Western art history. Then, look at the programs where students learn how to make art, and you will see that while there are many programs that teach how to paint on canvas, paper, and board, there is virtually no one teaching feather work, wooden bow making, or rug weaving in any style.

Another set of problems facing Indian artists revolves around having an Indian identity. The art market demands that Indian art contain the stereotypical imagery that buyers expect. In other words, if an Indian artist wants to paint skyscrapers and computers or even abstract designs their work will seldom be sold under the label of Indian art. The standard for Indian art is that the imagery must contain signs of "Indianness," such as feathers, wolves or Indian princesses, recognizable to even the most uneducated collector. Works that do not contain these tokens of Indianness are usually not shown or relegated to the back of the gallery.

Even if an Indian artist can break through this barrier, others, like federal law await them. The Indian Arts and Crafts Act signed into law by President George H. W. Bush in November 1990 was designed to protect Indian artists from cheap imitations from Asia and Indonesia, and from unscrupulous non-Indians who posed as Indian artists.

Simply, the law says that any artist who sells art under the label of "Indian art" must be an enrolled Indian. Seems simple, doesn't it? It is, until you consider that the legal status of Indians is controlled by the federal government and is based on the listing of Indian peoples' names as set down by the government recorders.

If a family was present during this recording period, they were considered to be "enrolled Indians." If a family was not in town on the day that the list was made, even though they may not have a single non-Indian ancestor, they were not enrolled and lost their legal status as Indian. In other cases entire tribes were legally "terminated" and lost their Indian identity as far as the government was concerned.

The law does allow a loophole, but it is not a loophole that all can squeeze through. If an unenrolled Indian wants to show his or her work under the label of Indian art, he or she must find an elder willing to certify their Indianness.

Although the challenges are many and the struggles will continue, there is good reason for optimism when considering the future of American Indian art. The Indian population of America is again increasing. This is a critical thing because it means that there are more Indian people to advocate for solutions to these problems. It also holds the promise that Indian people will one day be sufficiently credentialed to teach American Indian art history and production techniques in our schools. They now have the potential to attend classes in museum studies and become curators of Indian collections. Finally, Indian people are making great strides toward the control of the publishing industry that produces the art books that make and break artists' careers.

This development points to the strength and resilience of Indian culture and stands as a testimony to the viability of Indian art as a genre of its own. As Indian people take greater control of their artistic future we can expect that the work will only become stronger and that left in Indian hands the future of Indian art looks very promising indeed.

END NOTES

[1]Galton's writing, by the way, gave momentum to the European "eugenics movement" of the turn-of-the-20th century that fostered and grew the idea that it was the God-given right of superior humans to eliminate inferior humans in the quest for the genetically perfect breed of man. His writings were adopted as part of the rationale for the genocide perpetrated by the Nazi governments of Europe.

[2]A people's material culture is everything they make or use.

[3]The diseases that did the most damage were measles, small pox, syphilis, and influenza.

[4]This process is called **hegemony** and is part of the colonizing process.

[5]The notable exceptions were the slaves, the African folks (and by extension, their descendents) who managed to survive the grueling journey to America and the other horrors of slavery long enough to have children.

[6]Some might include pictorial tapestry weaving, but since they were actually utilitarian, used to keep castle walls made of stone from sucking away the heat in the room, I tend to think of them as craft.

[7]Although propaganda is a somewhat loaded word, I use it to mean materials which are visually instructive or display history or hierarchy or demonstrate power systems within a culture.

[8]Craft specialization is the ability of a culture to raise their artist class to the level where the basic needs of the artist are met and the artist has functional control over access to his or her materials.

5

Photography and Indian Identity: Imagining a Cultural Space

Alexandra Harris

Photography as a visual medium emerged only indirectly from other artistic genres like painting and drawing. Since the advent of photography in the 1820s, photographs have served to augment our knowledge of the world through both art and documentation. Building upon centuries of studying light and its ability to be reflected and manipulated, those who ultimately invented photography in the 1830s were not motivated by the creation of a new artistic medium but instead looked to create an entirely different, "non-manual technique for making pictures."[1] Because this new technology was made by the reflection of light from an object and not by an artist's hand, many considered a photograph to be a representation of what is—*reality*. William Henry Fox Talbot, who invented the first calotype, or "dry plate," photographic process (meaning that unlike daguerreotypes or wet-plate negatives, the chemical emulsion coating calotypes was dry) experimented with his recent invention by taking photos of his summer home in 1835. He exclaimed, ". . . this building I believe to be the first that was ever yet known *to have drawn its own picture.*"[2] His observation is a clear indication that the originators of photography believed the person behind the camera to have complete objectivity, perhaps even being fully removed from the artistic process, and defined the medium by technology and chemicals.

From the outset, however, neither was the camera nor the operator objective. The first still images were created by Jacques Louis Mandé Daguerre, the inventor of the first successful, yet poisonous, photographic process. He found that by burning mercury fumes his image became fixed to the plate, yet he lived long enough to produce one of the most famous images in all of photography. His first photograph was a blurred image of a Paris street corner. The image displays a near empty street; the only figures are those of a shoeshine boy and his seated customer. In reality, however, because of the exceedingly long exposure time needed to imprint an image onto the metal plate through the lens of the camera, which was often two or more hours, the only people featured on the plate are those who remained stationary long enough for their reflections to be recorded. Immortalized by Daguerre's invention, these individuals may be the first people to have had their picture taken. In reality, though, the street contained hundreds of people bustling past. Yet, because the slow absorbing chemical emulsion did not record their impressions, they do not appear in the final "daguerreotype." Contrary to the initial concept of photographs as fact, it was evident early on that the technical process limited the ability to capture true "reality" despite continuing public faith in the image's representation.

As photography appeared in the United States within the following decade, the American public likewise believed in the medium's inherent honesty and began to use the camera to document not only mundane aspects of everyday life, but the sensational and exotic as well. This ultimately included the country's indigenous peoples. As historian Lee Clark Mitchell explains, the terms "photograph" and "American Indian" are difficult to categorize, as they are both abstract and complicated.[3] From the outset, definitions of these two concepts have been assumed—the photograph as "reality," and the "American Indian" being what the audience, mostly East Coast Anglo-Americans, wanted to imagine from this version of reality. Catering to the audience's faith in the medium and their hunger for the exotic, the photographers manipulated the assumed reality to create a false identity for native peoples that still remains the prominent stereotype today. This Anglo-invented identity has had serious ramifications for Native self-image and esteem, countered only by the emergence of images of Indians in cultural context. These images have almost exclusively been created by indigenous people for themselves.

First to arise as a subject of photographic sensation and excitement for the American public was the Civil War. In the 1860s, wet-plate photography (where the plate required exposure to light while still wet and immediate development) reduced the exposure time from hours to minutes. This made "documentary" images feasible, if not quite convenient. During this time, portraits of prominent military figures were printed as well as the first *cartes-de-visite,* postcards imprinted with portraits so that they could be sold as tourist items and sent across the country. Because of the cumbersome nature of the wet plates, battlefields were photographed after the fact and published in newspapers, revealing the graphic results of war.

After General Lee's surrender at Appomattox, war-trained photographers were suddenly out of a job. With a renewed governmental interest in the West, these men were not unemployed for long. Soon, these men were commissioned for federal survey expeditions. After a hiatus during the Civil War, the United States resumed efforts to navigate the western frontier in order to build railroads and expand the nation. As a result, four massive geographical surveys were launched between 1867 and 1879, two by the War Department and two under the Department of the Interior. Known by the names of the survey leaders, these included the King, Wheeler, Hayden, and Powell Surveys.[4] Photographers accompanied these surveys in order to document the peoples and landscapes they encountered in the West. In this fashion, many heretofore relatively unknown indigenous tribes were quite literally exposed to the camera.

William Henry Jackson, eventually one of the most prominent photographers of Native Americans and the West, first began his trade in the 1870s in the employment of the Geographical and Geological Surveys of the Territories taking pictures of unexplored landscapes.[5] In the process, he helped define the West as open, virgin territory. Eventually, the Army hired others like Timothy O'Sullivan and John K. Hillers, both of whom also became prominent photographers of Indians. Although their initial documentary images were landscapes, these photographers chose angles and exposures to bring out the inherent beauty of the land.

The men soon discovered that the more sensational and exotic the images, the more their audiences begged for them. The Civil War had whetted the Eastern public's appetite for shocking material, so images of the "savage" appeased their curiosity easily. Photographers traveled out into the field for different reasons; some sought "art" to sell to tourists, others sought documentary images for anthropologists, many of whom wished to prove the inferiority of the indigenous population. Unbeknownst to the Native peoples, their images were being used for everything from war reconnaissance to anthropological studies and commercial postcards. For the native peoples of North America, the ability to capture a moment of reality was both a boon and an impediment to their survival. While in some instances the images captured visions of suffering that promoted philanthropic missions to the reservations, most often the photographs were used for anthropological evidence or tourist sale.

From the first photograph taken of an American Indian in 1845, photography decontextualized native people, or removed them from their cultural context, and subsequently categorized them as the "other." Kahkewaquonaby, half Welsh and half Missassauga, was portrayed holding a hatchet and wearing British-influenced clothing in front of a studio background during a visit to Great Britain. At this time, many East Coast tribes had already been dispossessed of traditional lands and been forced to change their lifestyles as a result of outside influence. From this image, taken by Hill and Adamson, the viewer gains little knowledge of the subject's personality, culture, or sense of place in his community or environment.

Before the calotype, the ancestor to the modern roll film, photography required a subject to sit frozen for long periods of time without moving. To accomplish this, the photographer would set up a series of head and neck clamps to keep the sitter still. By the time Kahkewaquonaby stood for this image, William Henry Fox Talbot had already invented the calotype in 1841, which had reduced the exposure time from an hour or so down to a few minutes. Even though thousands of photos of Native Americans were taken in a similar fixed studio setting, the development of this new dryplate process simplified photography in the field and thus contextualized "action" shots were more accessible. Thus, traveling photographers were able to choose the environment and circumstance of the images.

Exoticism, developed through photography for the purpose of dehumanizing Native people and thereby validating injustices towards them, is the earliest theme present in the photographic work of the American West. Although this motif continued well into the twentieth century, the bulk of these images seem to have been taken between 1844 and 1890, when many Native Americans still had not been forced onto

"Rev. Peter Jones (Kahkewaquonaby)," by David Octavius Hill and Robert Adamson, salted paper print from paper negative, ca 1845, 7⅞ x 5¹³⁄₁₆ inches, courtesy of Amon Carter Museum, Fort Worth, Texas.

reservations. At this time, the "Indian Wars" still seemingly threatened the nation's security and photographs of aggressive, "wild" Indians encouraged public sentiments towards the reservation system or, even worse, eliminating indigenous cultures altogether. Nevertheless, contact with whites was leaving a distinct impression on Native people as well, who began to adopt, if they had not already, notions of white "civilization." As Christopher Lyman observes, "insofar as one was interested in cultures because they were *different* from one's own, it stood to reason that as a culture became more *like* one's own it also became a less interesting object of study."[6] Therefore, the photographers were immensely motivated to keep the image of the Indian static and stereotypically different from the white American norm.

Some photographers so desired to portray an archetypal "Indian" that they removed evidence of modern or Western culture from their prints. Often, if there were an element of Euro-American culture, perhaps of Christianity, perhaps a federal peace medal awarded to the subject, the photographer would eliminate such an influence from the image.

Although "racism" was not a popularly used social term until the twentieth century, scientific experiments exploring the physical and mental attributes of the world's cultures, what we now call "scientific racism," emerged about the same time as did the medium of photography. Thus, after the development of roll film and snapshot cameras in the 1880s, perfected by George Eastman of Kodak fame, anthropologists flooded into the farthest reaches of Indian lands for visual specimens that they could bring back with them to the East. Concerned that the native race was nearing extinction, anthropologists documented ceremonies, petroglyphs, and even created a method of photographing a subject to measure intelligence through "racially specific" features. Using the "anthropometric" technique, an anthropologist would shoot a subject at both full front and at profile against a neutral background, similar to a police "mug shot."[7] This second generation of photographers wielded their cameras like weapons, and their photographic ammunition further alienated Native people from existing alongside a dominating white society.

Generally during this time period, however, photos of the "exotic wildman" were sent back East for their entertainment value rather than for scientific purposes. The majority of names were lost, further dehumanizing Native sitters by removing their

"Little Soldier Ponca, front view," courtesy of the National Anthropological Archives, Smithsonian Institution.

"Little Soldier Ponca, profile," courtesy of the National Anthropological Archives, Smithsonian Institution.

identities and individuality. Many image-makers titled their pieces dramatically, such as, "Crying to the Spirits," and "An Apache Belle," rather than describing any of the humanistic qualities of the individual. *Stereographs,* which placed two virtually identical images next to each other on a card to be seen through a viewer, were fashionable in the 1850s, 60s, and beyond. This mechanism allowed the "savage" to be viewed seemingly in three dimensions through the stereoscope. Alongside these visuals, *cartes-de-visite* also gained popularity, climaxing in the 1860s but waning thereafter. These postcards featured similar images, yet also introduced pictures of half-naked women and men. What Chippewa writer Gerald Vizenor terms a "cultural striptease," these scantily clad Native men and women were ultimately displayed in both stereographs and *cartes-de-visites*. These were created not for scientific or documentary purposes but for the confirmation that these barely clothed creatures were far from the "civilization" and culture of Western society.[8] For both men and women of the time to whom naked skin was scandalous, these cards were shocking. Yet at the same time, they fulfilled mild pornographic desires without conscience; less-than-human people were acceptable to be exploited as such and further proved that white society was "morally and culturally superior."[9]

Other photographs supported this view of a subordinate race, where Indians ate, slept, and sat in the dirt with a complete lack of "appropriate" clothing or manners. In addition, Eastman-Kodak's invention of the Box Brownie camera in the 1880s, where no processing knowledge was necessary, sent a surge of amateur tourists invading Indian ceremonies. The influx of non-Indians snapping as many pictures as possible of ceremonies and individual Indians served as another resource for sensationalism. In this way, the "savage" was immortalized in white common public consciousness as dirty, violent, and immoral, thus validating aggression and the appropriation of their land.

From the 1890 massacre at Wounded Knee, South Dakota, until the present day, the belief that Indians were disappearing resulted in the development of a nostalgic attitude towards their images—a sort of Romantic Era of photographing Indians. In the process, this created the stereotype of both the noble victim and the defeated prisoner. Even the genocide demonstrated by massacres like Wounded Knee were recorded, evidenced by the grisly photographs of Chief Bigfoot and his band of Lakota days after the tragedy. This macabre documentation is not extensive, but is nonetheless powerful. Through the images created by photographers at this time, the public was able to wistfully regret the "end of the Indian" as if mourning an endangered species gone extinct.

After much of indigenous life and culture had been eradicated through these practices, turn-of-the-twentieth-century photographers attempted to remake Native Americans into the identity that white Americans believed they "should" have. The hero of this era was Edward Sheriff Curtis, who went to perhaps greater lengths than any other photographer to preserve his own personal "composite Indian," the "true" Indian.[10] As a member of the second generation of American photographers, he was amidst the first to fully realize the potential of photography to be manipulated. Born in Wisconsin in 1868, he was raised with the awareness of the genocide surrounding him and the "scientific" reasons behind Euro-American success at populating the continent as Native people died off.[11] Funded by banking giant John Pierpont Morgan and endorsed by Teddy Roosevelt, Curtis' aim beginning in 1898 was to produce

"Wounded Knee—gathering up the dead," courtesy of the National Anthropological Archives, Smithsonian Institution.

a twenty-volume set of photographs documenting Native people, called *The North American Indian.* As Curtis began his endeavor, the national "obsession with racial bigotry was *beginning* to give way." Curtis admitted that he felt guilt for the genocidal practices of his countrymen, describing the situation as "more than the crime of the century."[12] This sense of guilt quite apparently motivated his romantic style of imagery.

His images were no doubt beautiful, yet at times ethics were compromised for aesthetics. Curtis occasionally dressed his subjects up in stock Plains-Indian-style war bonnets and jewelry collected throughout his travels, regardless of tribal congruence. In many ways, he imposed the "exotic" stereotype onto many of the people he photographed. When Navajo dancers were uncomfortable performing their sacred ceremonies for him, Curtis attempted to manipulate the events so that the subjects would participate. Afraid of spiritual and community backlash, the dancers' hesitation forced Curtis to make their masks himself as they danced their ceremony backwards to secularize it.[13] After causing trouble in the communities and dressing up his subjects, Curtis used a stylus to remove all trace of Euro-American influence from many of his negatives. His photograph, *In a Piegan Lodge,* originally had a large clock situated between the two men, Yellow Kidney (left) and his father Little Plume. In the final photograph, however, he almost succeeds in blending the object into the tipi wall. Armed with his stylus, he scratched out clocks, wagons, and umbrellas while attempting to picture the "Indian" before the deleterious effects of European influence.[14] Curtis called his work "art-science," where "science" implied objectivity and "art" equated to his own impressions of those he photographed, seemingly an oxymoron.

"In a Piegan Lodge—Little Plume and his son Yellow Kidney," by Edward Sheriff Curtis, courtesy of the National Anthropological Archives, Smithsonian Institution.

"In a Piegan Lodge, retouched version," by Edward Sheriff Curtis, courtesy of the Smithsonian Institution.

At the same time, the images do reflect his romantic style of photographic composition. "It isn't that Curtis was a bad photographer," said photographer Richard Hill (Tuscarora) in 1994, "He was *too* good . . . He used his subjects to create still another version of the Noble Red Man myth, giving whites a way to love an image of the Indian while ignoring the Indians themselves."[15] Curtis' approach ultimately reflected a stereotypical attitude towards American Indians that his non-Indian viewing public has internalized for almost a century.

However, romanticism towards Native people has not only been adopted into mainstream American culture, but within American Indian communities themselves. "And if there's a photograph of an Indian in an Indian home that's not of a family member," Hill continues, "it'll be a Curtis; we Indian people ourselves have bought into the whole thing."[16] The photographs taken of Native people over the decades ultimately filter through modern media to the people themselves. Sometimes these images are obviously damaging, but others, like Curtis', although beautiful only add to the prevailing undercurrent of fabricated public information concerning Native people.

Perhaps the most prominent propaganda of this period beginning before the turn of the century surfaced from the Indian boarding schools. The first institution, built in Carlisle, Pennsylvania, was developed for Indians by assimilationist General Richard H. Pratt to, in his words, "immerse him in civilization and keep him there until well soaked."[17] When Carlisle Indian Industrial School opened its doors in 1879, John Choate became the official photographer.[18] His collection focused on the swift

Sarah Walker, Annie Dawson, and Carrie Anderson, 1880's "Three Girls as They Arrived at Hampton Institute," courtesy of the National Anthropological Archives, Smithsonian Institution.

Sarah Walker, Annie Dawson, and Carrie Anderson, 1880's "Three Girls Fourteen Months Later," courtesy of the National Anthropological Archives, Smithsonian Institution.

acculturation of Native children. To document this metamorphosis, Choate's photographs were basically "before-and-after" images, the foremost taken of the children on their first day fresh from the train. Next, he took pictures weeks later to fully document the transition from blankets and bare feet to military uniforms and cut hair. Cree Artist and Curator Gerald McMaster asserts that although these children represented the "colonial experiment," their faces betray their resistance.[19] Much language and culture was lost through Carlisle and similar institutions, yet strength and unity under the pressures of assimilation persisted.

HIGHLIGHT: CAPTURING THE SPIRIT OF THE CROW

The abundance of photographers was perhaps most evident on the Great Plains and in the Southwest, where Native societies displayed a colorful and diverse material culture that most attracted urban Anglo-Americans. On the Plains, photographers and anthropologists alike rushed to capture and cultivate the stereotypical image of the "ideal" Indian.

The end of the nineteenth century marked the low point in the Native American presence on the continent. Soon after the brutal massacre of Lakota at Wounded Knee in December of 1890, the federal government officially declared the "Indian Wars" to be over, thus condemning indigenous people to struggle for health and unity while corralled onto reservations. The buffalo had been hunted to near extinction from the Plains in order to subdue the local Indians with starvation, which along with malnutrition also resulted in an increase of disease.

It was in this environment that two photographers named Richard Throssel and Fred Miller formed their opinions about Native Americans that, in turn, influenced their approach to photography. While both men focused their cameras on the Crow culture of Montana, their approaches reflect differing attitudes towards their subjects. Miller chose to interact closely with the Crow community. In this way, he was readily accepted and not deemed intrusive when photographing ceremonies or burial scaffolds. On the other hand, Throssel had several different approaches towards his subjects. Initially, he moved outside the main community to set up a private studio, catering to white tourists. Eventually, he documented health problems and took up Crow causes in the political arena. As a result, much of his earlier photography reflects a social distance between himself and his subjects as he relegated himself to observer. Although these men both photographed the Crow, Throssel and Miller originally had widely varying approaches to their subjects.

Although Richard Throssel was Cree, as a landless Metís he was alienated by his Canadian government and migrated with his family throughout the northern United States and Canada, ultimately settling with the Crow for Montana's comparatively drier climate.[20] Attracted by the impressive Crow design and artistry, he acquired a job as a clerk at the Crow Agency. He taught himself photography, and took painting lessons from Joseph Sharp, a resident non-Indian artist. Of all the many visiting photographers and artists at the Crow reservation, however, none influenced him more than Edward S. Curtis, whose ability to manipulate Indian reality to create romantic beauty on film enthralled Throssel as well as it did the rest of the world. Throssel was in his early twenties at the time and still artistically impressionable. As a result, much of Throssel's early work was developed in a similar style—so similar that Curtis claimed a print or two as his own creation.[21] In his photograph, "Sunrise on Custer's Battlefield," Throssel emulates Curtis' manipulative technique by apparently applying potassium ferricyanide or a similar bleaching agent to the natural highlights on the gravestones, thereby increasing contrast and drama within the image. Also reflecting Curtis' influence, he uses his stylus to eliminate the American flag carried by the man on the far right in his image, "The Feathered Horsemen," changing it into the appearance of feathers. Many of Throssel's early photographs are based on the documentary anthropometric style of shooting both the profile and full front of the individual so

"Sunrise on Custer's Battlefield," by Richard Throssel, courtesy of the Richard Throssel Collection, American Heritage Center, University of Wyoming.

"The Feathered Horseman," by Richard Throssel, courtesy of the Richard Throssel Collection, American Heritage Center, University of Wyoming.

"Barney Old Coyote," by Richard Throssel, courtesy of the Richard Throssel Collection, American Heritage Center, University of Wyoming.

as to highlight what anthropologists believed to be the "racially specific" traits. Scientists based numerous studies of racial intelligence on photographs such as these. Like Curtis, Throssel often deviated from this method, as in his photo of Barney Old Coyote. Although this subject is displayed in profile format, the lighting is dramatic and thereby loses its scientific "usefulness." In this way, Throssel was able to later promote his genre "Western Classics" to a non-Indian audience as art rather than to the scientific community.

    This style of art merged with documentary photography dissipated over the years as Throssel adopted greater respect for the Crow community and took up many supportive political causes as a representative in the Montana State legislature. His later

"Unidentified Crow Couple, Sitting in a Tipi," by Richard Throssel, courtesy of the Richard Throssel Collection, American Heritage Center, University of Wyoming.

images even include seemingly intimate moments with families, a few of which laugh and smile into his lens. In his early years of private business, however, Throssel created photos reflecting romantic Crow ideals for a non-Indian audience, which perpetuated a fantastic yet false illustration of native peoples.

Not all of his photography portrayed posed images of the Crow people. Many of his sitters considered the tastes of Eastern non-Indians comical and were amused by "dressing up" to pose.[22] The "Western Classics," catering to these Eastern attitudes, actually comprised only four percent of his personal collection. The other thousand or so images displayed moments of Crow life, such as his photo of an unidentified Crow couple laughing in their tipi. This joyous moment of life was an aspect of Throssel's art that set him apart from Curtis. These images of social interaction convey a sense of familiarity and comfort that Curtis rarely, if ever, achieved. With the exception of a few examples, Throssel generally did not attempt to erase from his photos the traces of non-Indian influence, accepting their inevitability. As time passed and Throssel adopted an increasing concern for Crow well being, he was able to photograph ceremonies, illnesses, and even deathbeds.

Fred Miller, a non-Indian white man, used a different approach, albeit from similar beginnings. Also having emigrated to the Crow reservation from another state, Miller came not simply to photograph but to attempt cattle ranching as well. Having already established himself as a photographer in Iowa and Nebraska, he was not as heavily influenced by photographers visiting the Crow lands as Throssel was. Eventually, he failed at ranching and like Throssel took a job at the Agency as clerk. During this time, however, he became friendly with the local children, and even taught them football.[23] This earned him the nickname *Boxpotapesh,* or High Kicker. Through the children Miller became respected within the community, and soon after marrying a Shawnee woman, Emma Smith, was adopted into the tribe by the prominent Chief Medicine Crow.

Unlike Throssel, Miller quickly recognized the Crow's attachment to their sacred land and captured this on film throughout the decades of his social interaction with them. In this way, his photographs gave the Crow subjects a sense of place through context, seen most explicitly in his photographs of children, but also within his many images of the surrounding Montana landscape and the Crows' place within it. For example, although the photograph entitled "Aloysius Holds The Enemy" is taken from Miller's height down onto the little boy below, the photographer goes out of his way to include the distant horses, wagons, and tipis in the distance to contextualize the subject's worldview, deeply rooted in the landscape. Rare, if any, photographs were taken by him of a Crow in a studio setting, although a few included an impromptu draped background. He approached the people without imposing a formality upon them, but allowed the intrinsic value of the relationship between photographer and sitter emerge. At times, the "shared confidence" between Miller and his

"Aloysius Holds the Enemy (1895–1941)," by Fred E. Miller (1868–1936). Copyright © Collection Nancy F. O'Connor.

"Has No Foretop, a.k.a. Smart Iron (1872–1910), on a Travois," by Fred E. Miller (1868–1936). Copyright © Collection Nancy F. O'Connor.

subjects emerges significantly as joking between the two. For example, his photograph called "Has No Foretop a.k.a. Smart Iron (1872–1910) on a Travois" features a young man demonstrating how a travois would carry him wounded from battle. Here, Has No Foretop seems to be enjoying the interaction as he poses for Miller, laughing. Through Miller's methods, the personalities of each Crow individual are conveyed rather than each photo taken as a documentation of their existence.

Both Throssel's and Miller's methods were successful aesthetically. However, each man had a different set of goals. Throssel acted more as an observer and at first exploited his own separate Indian-ness as a Cree apart from the Crow people. This conscious separation to appeal to the non-Indian audience is reflected in the images he created of them. Although they were more than willing, and at times amused, to sit for his camera, the level of comfort seen in Miller's Crow subjects is not often as evident in Throssel's images. For a white man with only one eye and no depth perception, Miller demonstrated tremendous respect towards the Crow people and in return gained theirs though his second eye, the camera.

Overall, Throssel's attempt at a "visual census," having photographed about ten percent of the tribe, is a more than admirable endeavor. In Albright's 1997 collection of Throssel's images, interviews of the descendants of his subjects reflect an appreciation that they are able to see their relatives at such vibrant moments of their lives. At the same time, Miller impacted his native audience deeply as well, indicated by the positive community sentiment and support for Nancy Fields O'Connor's compilation of essays regarding the photographer, written in 1985. Both Throssel and Miller made an attempt to portray their Crow associates without denying the influences of white society. Yet, because of Miller's inherent reverence for the Crow worldview, which he included as context in his photographs, his images appear as a respectful and honest portrayal of the Crow as a people.

Ultimately, sensitivity is key to accomplishing a successful photographic project of not only Native people, but of anyone who is considered by the majority to be the "other." Included under this umbrella of sensitivity is the cultivation of a relationship between the photographer and his subject as well as a necessary respect for the individual or group worldview. Inherently, there is a threefold relationship in photography between the subject, the photographer, and the audience—that which is intended or not. For the viewer, the subject is "present" because of their extended existence through the image. Art historian Lucy Lippard calls this relationship the "cultural space" within the photograph.[24] If a relationship has developed between the photographer and the subject, this will translate over time to the viewer through expression, attitude, and pose (or lack thereof). Regardless of the audience, a sincere cultural space may provide a connection between the viewer and the subject, in this case Native Americans, and initiate understanding on an equal, human level.

Depending upon the type of "cultural space" in the photograph, a Native audience may be informed about the lifestyle of their ancestors. By showing an uncontrived personality within the image, indigenous people have access to the attitudes, experiences, and environmental context that their elders and relations experienced long ago. In this way, Fred Miller was much more successful than Richard Throssel. Throssel still relied on unnatural studio backgrounds, even though he rarely went so far as to remove the influences of Euro-American culture.

At the same time, this relationship would provide a non-Indian audience with enlightenment and knowledge of the exotic "other," and may highlight humanistic qualities rather than those seen as "uncivilized." Although portraying aspects of joy and comfort with the photographer may ultimately have been the goal of both Miller and Throssel, prominent stereotypes prevailed because the vast majority of images were still documentary, as was the style of Native photography at the time. For example, few images included daily work, lifestyle, or emotion, even though religious ceremonies were well represented. Unfortunately, as the country was largely Christian, these "pagan" images were a further affront to the sensibilities of East Coast Americans.

This issue of inherent cultural respect can be generalized to any photographer or artist creating images of an unfamiliar group of people. Edward Sheriff Curtis blew in and out of communities like a tornado, sometimes in the dead of night. His self-imposed alienation is clearly reflected in his art. Although his images may be aesthetically pleasing, they nonetheless embody to his Euro-American audience the concept of "exotic," "uncivilized" peoples who, like an endangered species, are swiftly vacating the planet. If he had formed any significant relationships, they are not seen within his photographs. Arguably one of Curtis' most famous photographs, "The Vanishing Race—Navaho" depicts a group of Navajo riding horseback into the distant hills, symbolic of the historic forced removal of the tribe to Fort Sumner, termed the "Long Walk" by those who endured the journey. Heavily shadowed, this image prophesizes

"Vanishing Race—Navaho," by Edward Sheriff Curtis, courtesy of the Smithsonian Institution.

the end of indigenous presence as the group leaves the sacred lands for incarceration. Photos like this by Curtis and his contemporaries denied the Indians a place in the future of the Americas, showing a downtrodden remnant of primal evolution. The exception here is Miller who, even though he was an acquaintance of Curtis, did not notably allow the other man's artistic successes to influence his work. Instead, Miller retained sensitivity toward the Crow and their worldview, thereby creating an artistic and accurate representation of the tribe's transition from nomadic to sedentary reservation life. His work was thus successful to both Indian and non-Indian audiences as a respectful portrayal; unfortunately, many non-Indian viewers of his time preferred to use his photographs to substantiate old stereotypes rather than to develop new ideas.

Furthermore, Miller is a relevant example for contemporary photographers in the field who are attempting to capture images of Native and non-Native people alike. The reciprocity and cultural respect that characterized Miller's approach is necessary to a sincere depiction of a group and at the same time allows access to the information by both audiences. Rather than alienating one or another group, Miller's approach is all-inclusive.

HIGHLIGHT: IMAGINING THE PUEBLO OF LAGUNA

Initial Pueblo mistrust over the intentions of photographers originated around 1870 when military outfits would include in their number a photographer to document their activity. Associating the photographers with the army, Native people became cautious.[25] As distrust evolved, any goodwill that had arisen between individual photographers and tribes deteriorated.

After the great Geological Surveys, many photographers returned to the most "exotic" Native American sites, including the Pueblo Southwest. During the height of tourism from the 1880s into the first two decades of the twentieth century, photographers looking to record and to sell images of "vanishing Indians" and sacred ceremonies overran the Pueblo tribes of New Mexico and Arizona. By the turn of the century, business was booming. Men such as Adam Clark Vroman, George Wharton James, Benjamin Wittick, Edward Curtis, and William Henry Jackson visited the Pueblo Southwest countless times throughout their careers as photographers. Noted photographic essayist and author Susan Sontag wrote in her 1977 book entitled, *On Photography,* "The predatory side of photography is at the heart of the alliance [between the "scandalous" and the "beautiful"], evident earlier in the United States than anywhere else, between photography and tourism. . . . The case of the American Indians is the most brutal." She describes the photographic influx into Indian lands as a "colonization through photography," as tourists photographed sacred objects, dances, and sites for which they held no respect, "if necessary paying the Indians to pose and getting them to revise their ceremonies to provide more photogenic material."[26]

One of these men, Adam Clark Vroman, left his bookstore in Pasadena, California to capture the imagery of the Southwest. Like many of the photographers, he made several trips through the Pueblos during the 1890s, rarely pausing long enough to cultivate relationships with any of his indigenous subjects. "Vroman's handsome photographs are unexpressive, uncondescending, unsentimental," attests Sontag, ". . . they are not moving, they are not idiomatic, they do not invite sympathy. Sander [a German photographer who attempted to catalogue different "archetypes" within the German people in 1911] didn't know he was photographing a disappearing world. Vroman did. He also knew that there was no saving the world that he was recording."[27] This judgment of Vroman seems harsh, yet epitomizes the distance between photographer and subject evident within the photographs of this era; Native people stare curiously, coolly, and at times defiantly, into the lens towards an unfamiliar photographer, ultimately distancing the viewer from the individuals within the image. This relationship generally served to reinforce stereotypes of Indian primitivism, as the pictures conveyed little warmth and evoked no sympathy.

Because of this era of tourist and commercial photography in the late nineteenth century, communities such as the Pueblo of Laguna, near Albuquerque, New Mexico, endured exploitation and cultural and social duress for many years because of photographers. Charles Francis Saunders wrote as he toured the Pueblos in 1912, "Whatever essential good, if any, may have accrued to Laguna from all this [white influence from intermarriage and tourists], it cannot be said that it has helped Laguna's manners . . . for in no other pueblo were we so thoroughly given the cold shoulder as here, and we visited it several times." In his curiosity, Saunders spoke to an artist he encountered outside Laguna village during his visit, who confirmed the reasons behind the lack of hospitality. He quotes the artist,

> Oh, yes, we've spoiled them both with ill-considered philanthropy and continually dumping impertinent tourists on them from the railroad here to pester them out of their lives . . . if I were king for a day, I'd have a tight stockade built about every pueblo and put St. Peter at the gate to keep out all school teachers and missionaries whatsoever, and every tourist who had not passed a previous examination in good manners.[28]

Like the other pueblos, Laguna endured unwelcome influences from tourists that shaped their identity to the outside world.

In the tumultuous atmosphere of the late nineteenth century—post-Civil War, post-Indian Wars—non-Indian photographers began to flood into the Pueblos. In those last decades of the century, the Pueblo of Laguna's accessibility and strong connections to American society marked it as a pleasant detour for documentary photographers, commercial photographers, and tourists alike. According to Laguna Indian photographer Lee Marmon, his grandfather Robert hosted many of the visiting photographers at his home. "They built a two-story house," explains Marmon, "and then the kids were all gone to school . . . and you know, money was hard to come by in those days."[29] Robert Marmon's boarding house, along with others like the Eckermanns who could afford to build larger housing, became immediate hosts to anyone passing though.

Meanwhile, the Atchison, Topeka, and Santa Fe Railroad (ATSF) spread tourist propaganda throughout the non-Indian nation at the turn of the century, increasing dramatically the invasion of visitors to the Pueblos. Allied with tourism industry mogul Fred Harvey, both the ATSF and Harvey's company created advertisements and books touting the sights and arts of "primitive" Southwestern tribes.

In 1876, Harvey founded his first eating establishment in Topeka, Kansas. He proceeded to set up lunchrooms and hotels all along the ATSF line that catered to the curiosity of Native American cultures. Although Harvey died in 1901, his son Ford continued the company under his father's name. In 1902, the Santa Fe Railroad commissioned ethnographers, artists, and photographers to illustrate Native culture for promotional use. In response, the Fred Harvey Company developed an Indian Department that would buy and sell Indian-made objects. In the process, Native people themselves would be on display, making crafts or selling their wares. The photographs he contracted to sell at these venues and those he used in his books would illustrate Harvey's version of the Southwest as beautiful and exotic, enticing tourists to stop on their way to California.

According to Leah Dilworth, as the railroad destroyed and distorted the traditional practices of the region's Native people, the Harvey Company attempted to preserve and commodify it. "Fred Harvey and the ATSF were nostalgic not for what was actually destroyed, but for an Indian that never existed; in the interest of selling tickets and hotel accommodations in the region, the two corporations constructed a version of Indian life that reflected and spoke to American middle-class desires and anxieties."[30] This Indian was "peaceful" and "pastoral," as the Native people selling pottery and jewelry at Harvey's Indian and Mexican Building at the Albuquerque train depot portrayed. In this context, Indians mainly existed for tourist purposes—as creators of or posing as souvenirs. This mentality survives through the present, as many Pueblo people living today will tell of camera-toting tourists entering their homes and churches uninvited.

During World War I, the tourism industry in the Southwest slowed. In response to the decline in railway passengers, Harvey and the Santa Fe developed Indian Detours in 1926, which would shuttle people from train stations to the sights by car. The Detours could last one, two, or three days and would return the visitors to the train station. These tours were far more invasive than the depot attractions; the "Harveycars" delivered tourists to Pueblos to witness dances and to photograph them. Ultimately the Indian Detours halted with the onset of the Depression, not long after they had begun.

The foundation of the Harvey Company's business was in advertising. "In Harvey's Southwest," observes Dilworth, "an ancient oral culture was being replaced by a modern culture that was not so much literate as visual . . . photography was the medium that best captured the vanishing Indian." Harvey's photographic postcards were retouched and colored using a Phostint process to make the images look more "real" and natural. The Company manipulated the content of the images to create a more "primitive" and "authentic" portrayal of Indian people.[31]

Prominent Southwest photographer Karl Moon contracted to sell his images in Harvey's establishment at El Tovar in the Grand Canyon. He acknowledged his own preference for removing "evidence of the white man" from his photographs. Moon, like other photographers, was afraid that any self-consciousness evident in the images would "give place to that freedom and ease that is so natural and pleasing a part of the Indian."[32] In this way, Harvey's photographers eliminated the cultural context from within the images, thus portraying Native people as "innocent" artifacts from a bygone era, freezing them in the past.

The serious amateur and commercial photographers flocked to the Pueblos before Harvey, however, and fed the flame of distinctively photograph-oriented tourism. Adam Clark Vroman spent much time photographing the country "from the Colorado-Utah-Nevada line to the Mexican border," and publicly stated that, "for the amateur photographer it is the long looked-for land of opportunities."[33] The tourist craze in the Pueblos caused the Native people to begin restricting where people could go and what they could document. The abuse of native privacy was overwhelming. One British photographer, George Wharton James, confessed his disrespect of Hopi requests, having taken a photograph inside a Mishongnovi village kiva.[34] Photographers invaded kivas, handled sacred objects, and ignored the restrictions established by the tribes regarding sacred dances. Pueblo people were angry not only that sacred practices were recorded, but that the images were commodified and sold as well.

The rare outside observer voiced his or her dissent concerning the commercialization of the dances, but on occasion protests emerged. Photographic historian Beaumont Newhall expressed his discontent at the turn of the twentieth century, remarking on the principles of intruding in Native life, claiming that tourists "changed the life of the Indian by paying him to pose and making him so self-conscious that he even changed his ceremonies."[35] Not wanting to alienate, but frustrated by the voyeurs, the Hopi relegated photographers to a small, protected section of the plaza during the 1902 Snake Dance. However, the initiative of the photographers to capture an image of the most exotic of ceremonies was not suppressed. British photographer George Wharton James reported in an article of the November 1902 issue of "Camera Craft" magazine,

> Hitherto every man had chosen his own field and moved to and fro wherever he liked—in front of his neighbor or someone else, kicking down another fellow's tripod and sticking his elbow in the next fellow's lens. Half a dozen or more Indian policemen kept us in line, so we had to go ahead and make the best of it.[36]

Due to the remarkable nature of the Snake Dance, the Hopi were infested with photographers. Finally, the Hopi restricted their dances from photographers in 1917 due to the disruptions.[37]

So fanatical was one photographer of the Hopi Snake Dance that it eventually led to his death. Benjamin Wittick photographed the dance almost every year from 1880 to 1903. As Wittick was an outsider and therefore restricted from the ceremonies preceding the Snake Dance, he became obsessed. He attempted to make friends with the snake priests, and was allowed to stand inside the kiva during a ceremony. Apparently, a priest warned Wittick that if he did not leave, he would succumb to swelling and other malevolent ailments. Yet, he remained. Finally, during one visit, a snake priest was quoted as threatening the photographer: "You have not been initiated. Death shall come to you from the fangs of our little brothers."[38] Following the prophecy, Wittick died from snakebite on the thumb in August of 1903 as he attempted to bring a rattlesnake to the dance as a gift. Although this dance in particular was popular with the clientele in the East, this mad obsession with images was replicated at all the Pueblos to varying degrees.

Kate Cory was also one of the many photographers on the Hopi Mesas, but instead of visiting during dances, she lived near the village of Oraibi from 1905 to 1912. In this way, Cory captured images of everyday living rather than only the "exotic" dances. She reputably was invited into the kivas, a strictly male religious role.[39] Why she was so respected remains a mystery, yet her documentation of everyday life and even internal political divisions reflects the intimacy she achieved within the Hopi community.

However, it does not explain the motivations behind her life with the Hopi. Originally, Cory's goal was to live in an environment that would be inspirational to her painting. Soon after her arrival, she was pulled into an unexpected role. Left without a teacher in 1907, Cory acted as substitute for the Oraibi village children. Contrary to her public image of generosity and respect, she at one point attempted to take advantage of her hosts through photographs and money for the sake of anthropology. In a letter to the Bureau of American Ethnology in 1907 she writes,

> I have lived alone in the village with them and have seen them under all possible circumstances. I have a painting of the men at work in the kiva. . . . It has seemed to me that a collection of photographs of the various types of faces here would be valuable to the Ethnologist . . . in my present position as teacher I have an exceptional opportunity to get pictures bath morning of the little girls nude and

I could probably secure the same of boys, if this would be of value. I can also secure everything they make or use, I know the whereabouts of their sacred stone which might be bought.[40]

Cory's work demonstrates the importance of cultural context within photographs of the Pueblo people. At the same time, she still catered to her "civilized" worldview in attempting to exploit the community in which she lived.

Even more rare than an ethical protestation of the photographic influence was a photographer or artist who actually cultivated friendships or lived with the Pueblo people. Although Cory balanced her everyday life in Oraibi with her Euro-American biases, she regardless was able to document events during the village's political division. Eventually, even Wittick's photographs of Laguna and Acoma Pueblos reflect a less stereotypical view of the tribes due to his repeated visits and relationships with the people. He even attended the wedding between the Laguna governor and Tzashima.[41]

"Tzashima," by Benjamin Wittick, courtesy of the National Anthropological Archives, Smithsonian Institution.

On a spiritual level, the Pueblo people are still suspicious today of tourists desiring to see their ceremonies. The reasons are complex, but are mostly due to centuries of forced Christianity and a cultural tradition of internal secrecy. Unsurprisingly, the Pueblo of Laguna has developed a significant degree of mistrust for harbingers of drastic change in response to the complex history of relations with disrespectful whites. In 1680 Popé, the San Juan Pueblo man who orchestrated the Pueblo Revolt, decreed, "that no Spaniard should ever witness their custom dances or religious ceremonies . . ."[42] In a way, regulation of the flow of intellectual property such as viewing and taking pictures of ceremonies is a concept older than the problem. The Pueblo of Laguna has endured much outside traffic over the centuries, many having labeled them as "progressive." The history they experienced, however, has only served to reinforce the need for caution. Ironically, Lagunas still regard photographs as treasured aspects of that same history, a tangible memory of departed ancestors and old traditions. Laguna writer Leslie Marmon Silko writes of the complex Pueblo relationship with photography,

> At first, white men and their cameras were not barred from the sacred katchina dances and kiva rites. But soon the Hopis and other Pueblo people learned from experience that most white photographers attending sacred dances were cheap voyeurs who had no reverence for the spiritual. . . . Pueblo people may not believe that the camera steals the soul of the subject, but certainly the Pueblo people are quite aware of the intimate nature of the photographic image. Because Pueblo people appreciate so deeply the power and significance of the photographic image, they refuse to allow strangers with cameras the outrages to privacy that had been forced upon Pueblo people in the past.[43]

When Juan de Oñate brought Roman Catholicism to the Pueblos in the 1590s, he outlawed the indigenous traditions, forbidding traditional ceremonial and religious practices. When Americans arrived toting a document claiming the "freedom of religion," the Pueblo traditions were not protected and were once again outlawed by the government. From 1883 to 1934, the United States government enforced a Religious Crimes Code against the Native people, which was not officially repealed until the American Indian Religious Freedom Act in 1978. During both of these periods, however, Pueblo people were anxious that their dances and ceremonies would be halted completely by the government. Photographers' visual evidence of the practices then and since, combined with a tradition of internal privacy, has caused considerable tension within the communities. According to a Laguna woman interviewed in 2001, the Pueblos now meet annually to review policies on tourism and photography.[44] In this way, the Pueblos may coordinate restrictions so that tourists encounter uniformity of regulations and do not compare between tribes.

At the same time, photographers were, and still are, making financial profit from the images. Many of the early photographers had studios elsewhere, sometimes at multiple locations. Between 1895 and 1902, Adam Clark Vroman left a bookstore and studio in Pasadena to seek his visions in the Southwest. Edward Sherriff Curtis left family and business in downtown Seattle to travel the nation. Anthropologists like Ales Hrdlička took anthropomorphic photographs of individuals in front and profile views, hoping that the images would indicate scientific information about the cultures. Yet these images were not simply used as art or anthropological pieces, but were transferred to *cartes-de-visite* and stereographs. The last one hundred and thirty years has brought much profit to photographers of Native people, and the Laguna people retain much of this resentment and mistrust. This suspicion is not for the medium itself, as they harbor no taboo of photographic "soul-stealing." Instead, Native people are suspicious of the man (or the rare woman) behind the camera.

Aside from the practical reasons for distrusting photographers, cultural mandates also add to the negative sentiments. According to tribal members, reflective surfaces are not permitted at Laguna sacred dances. This includes sunglasses, eyeglasses, and, ultimately, the photographer's lens. At the same time, this would also apply to being reproduced as a photographic image. Just as an audience member would not look a dancer in the eye, these traditions are followed as a sign of respect for those dancers.* Likewise, a member of the tribe is expected to know this, having learned over the years by example and out of respect for elders. Therefore, an intrusive photographer is not likely to have had either the experience or the foresight to follow these customs.

Modern conservative sentiments towards public photography at Laguna represent both a reaction against past abuses as well as traditional methods of concealing information. The Laguna people today maintain a highly resistant attitude towards "outsiders" intruding into the community for photographs. This resistance is not a direct result of "anti-white" sentiment. Rather, because Pueblo culture has always been regulated internally by religious leaders, exposure of sacred information conflicts with traditional management systems. According to linguistic anthropologist Dennis Tedlock, "A prayer is valuable and potent in inverse proportion to the number of people who know it."[45] His observations of certain Zuni prayers exemplify the methods by which community religious leaders regulate information. He continues,

> Some prayers are so valuable to their owners that they are 'said with the heart,' without any interpretable sound. This is the case, for example, with the prayers of dance leaders during the winter night performances of the Kachina Society. A prayer of this kind would be spoken aloud on only two occasions during the lifetime of a religious officeholder, the first when he learned it and the second when he trained his successor.[46]

Not only are outsiders to Zuni barred from hearing these prayers, but so is most of the tribe.

This internal regulation occurs today at Laguna Pueblo, as well. Until a child is initiated into the community, that child is not allowed to learn certain aspects about his or her culture and belief systems. "Secrecy belongs to all the Pueblo people," asserts a Laguna woman during an interview with the author in 2001. "Everyone

---

*I am being decidedly vague here, as I do not wish to emulate my scholarly predecessors by betraying the trust of those who have confided in me. Much is written in reference to these dances, including several works by Elsie Clews Parsons, so I do not feel it necessary to include information of a sacred nature.

knows that you don't tell outsiders. Of course, [anthropologist] Elsie Parsons found a few people who were willing to sell out—it just shows we're human."[47] Laguna secrecy is not entirely a result of tourism and past abuses, but relates directly to their origin story. "The religious leaders were in contact with the spirits to know where to go," she continues. "Nobody was left behind when we came out from the earth." In this way, all the Laguna people had an equal share in later prosperity when they finally reached their destination. As a result, Lagunas remember the trust given to the spirits and religious leaders to guide their people. Even today, that association through trust and respect does not extend to non-Lagunas. Another Laguna woman interviewed by the author recalls the relationship between her Laguna mother and her white father, "There were things that my mom never told my dad in all the years they were married." While the men, not women, are responsible for actively learning and participating in religious activities in the kiva, they are expected to return home to the Laguna women and share the information.

A paradox exists, as community members nevertheless regard images themselves as highly valued objects that captured the history of culture and family. Not only is

"Lee Marmon," by Alexandra Harris, courtesy of the photographer.

"Eagle Dancers," by Lee Marmon, courtesy of the photographer.

there an interest in viewing photographs taken by the historic photographers over a hundred years ago, but stories emerge of events that occurred and familiar people within the context of the images. "I'm sorry that a long time ago we didn't take that many pictures," admits another Laguna woman.[48] Those who viewed the photographs in the author's study of photography at Laguna have a distinct knowledge of kin and of tribal history that inspired recollections of traditions and personal stories.

From within the Laguna Pueblo community has emerged photographer Lee Marmon, grandson of Robert G. Marmon, a white immigrant and surveyor to Laguna who married into the tribe. For almost sixty years, he has conscientiously taken pictures of elders and of Laguna life to ensure the preservation of collective Laguna memories. From the time of his first image of a Route 66 truck accident in the late 1930s, Marmon has created a visual chronicle of his people of Laguna Pueblo through photography. Having been raised within the Laguna community, he approaches his art with different motivations than mainstream professional or commercial photographers.

Yet, like the Laguna people themselves, each of Marmon's images is complex and contains an intricate history that transcends conventional limits of visual art. Rather than removing the individual from their cultural context, Marmon includes features of each subject's daily life into his photographs. One of his most popular images, *White Man's Moccasins*, features Jeff Sousea, the caretaker of the Laguna church at the time the photograph was taken in 1954. Within the frame, Marmon's experience with

"White Man's Moccasins (Old Man Jeff)," by Lee Marmon, courtesy of the photographer.

Sousea is revealed; the caption's ironic twist is illustrative of how "Old Man Jeff" told tall tales to the tourists that day, as the cigar Marmon traded for a photo dangles from his fingers, even though he didn't smoke. From his traditional bandana to his modern high-top Keds, Sousea illustrates the complexity of the Laguna reality and, ultimately, the humor within.

At the same time, however, some Native people have criticized Marmon for selling these photographs of elders and of old dances for a profit that he does not share with the tribe. Yet the photographs that hang on the walls of many of these same houses exist as a result of Marmon's many years of documenting his community. Like many Native Americans today, a number of Lagunas consider each photographer as potentially exploitative, regardless of the beauty or honesty of his or her image. Consequently, Marmon's chosen art form is accepted, but often questioned. This societal reaction to a non-traditional art form combined with his familial mixture of white and Laguna ancestry has led to a mediation of the two cultures. At the same time, this ancestral and personal history has given Marmon the opportunity to place the people of Laguna in the public eye with context, individuality, and the strong tribal identity intact.

During the last one hundred fifty years, the people of Laguna have been inundated with tourists, commercial photographers, and white settlers who have imposed their American values upon the Pueblo. To maintain the traditional process of regulating information, as well as to eject abusive photographers from their land, Laguna chooses to restrict photography. Lee Marmon, on the other hand, is both an artist and Laguna; his work embodies both the complex aesthetics of professional portraiture as well as the cultural concerns of his community.

RECLAIMING NATIVE IDENTITY

Euro-American photography of Native Americans has consistently, yet not exclusively, reinforced a false Indian stereotype upon indigenous individuals as well as non-Indians, causing lasting damage to Native self-image. Author and cultural critic Paul Chaat Smith (Comanche) observes that regardless of these false images that have been created, Native people love the camera—taking pictures and having them taken. "So it should hardly be a surprise," he continues, "that everything about being Indian has been shaped by the camera."[49] Further, he insists that Native people only became "Indians," rather than distinct members of their tribes, after the struggle was over in 1890. Here, the stereotypical illusion of the "composite" Indian has been a success. From photographs, the independent nations learned how to be what the rest of society imagined. Through photographs and Buffalo Bill Cody's Wild West Show, Sitting Bull became our "first pop star" as Native people still "secretly wish we were more like the Indians in the movies."[50]

Thus, as we look upon these fantastic images today, we as viewers of all races assume certain truths just as the audiences did at the turn of the century. Lucy Lippard calls this tendency "partial recall," as total recall of information, identity, or otherwise from these images is impossible. As Euro-American people of the time took on the "responsibility" of representing other races, they fell in love with their inventions. Lippard writes,

> If anyone has the right to nostalgia, to romanticize the past, it is Indians. . . . Too many of these pictures, whatever truths they may hold, have been mendaciously manipulated. It is, therefore, white people who tend to look with greater longing at the past not quite depicted here . . . Buried in the pride of past conquest, less accessible than guilt and shame, is a distorted memory of primeval contentment.[51]

Born from a European obsession to "own," there emerged also the desire to "be."

Today, American society still feels the need to appropriate images of American Indians for their own use. As in the past, as Euro-Americans attempt to construct their own identity, they travel to the margins to usurp the identities of others. Anthropologist Deborah Root describes an encounter with a Canadian hippie in the 1960s, "Karma," who claimed "his spirit was Native" and that he was a "white-skinned Indian."[52] Although on the surface Karma and other hippies appeared to be "sympathetic," the claim was inherently racist. Because the hippies could not find power within their dreary suburbs, Root claims, they resorted to stealing the power of others. In this case, Native culture, romanticized through photography and film, was the perfect model for the hippie movement. On the one hand, Karma believed that Native culture would "save him from alienation and despair." According to the author, however, he is still the model colonist—an exhibitionist reminding the indigenous peoples who remains "master."[53] By adopting Indian imagery, the hippie movement and subsequent "New-Agers" trivialize the 500-year-old struggle, reclaiming dominance rather than sympathizing with the victimized.

In contrast, Native people are using many methods to counter both the stereotypes and the appropriation of these images to regain power over their own identity. Artistry has not been a foreign concept to Native Americans; rather, it has always served to document sacred ceremonies, timetables, and other significant events. From the earliest petroglyphs to the Lakota winter counts, Native people have been using visual imagery for millennia. Jolene Rickard, a Tuscarora and modern photographic artist, believes that Native communities have always had a relationship between "objects we create and the words that surround us." Whatever Indians create, for whatever reason, be it sacred, personal, or for the tourist trade, represents "spiritual, economic, and cultural survival."[54] Where non-Indians have seen a vanishing race, indigenous people see the failure of colonialism to exterminate them.

In actuality, American Indians have been making photographs for over a century. One of the first, Jennie Ross Cobb, took photographs of fellow students at the Cherokee Female Seminary from around 1896 to 1906. At the age of twelve her father gave her a box camera, initiating her life's journey in images. During her time at the Seminary, she took pictures of the social interactions of her fellow students. Breaking away from the photographic norm (of which she likely had not seen a great deal), Cobb caught images of everyday life. Jennie was probably the only Aniyunwiya (Cherokee) photographer and one of the youngest women using the medium at the time. As Diné/Creek/Seminole artist and photographer Hulleah Tsinhnahjinnie describes, Cobb "truly imaged Native women with love and a humanising eye."[55]

Overall, the many Native artists creating images today are concerned simply with honesty in representation. Fred Kootswatewa, a Hopi photographer, observes, "Hopi photographers bring an honesty and a lack of commercial intent that other photographers did not bring to Hopi. . . . We simply want people to see us as we see ourselves. We are photographers working with a cultural conscience."[56] Jolene Rickard also seems to agree, yet projects greater power on the Native photographer, claiming that, "Photographs by indigenous makers are the documentation of our sovereignty, both politically and spiritually."[57] It seems clear that native people are not attempting to emulate past photographic techniques or even to intentionally create new ones, but rather are interested in *true* representations of their culture, which rarely if ever can be obtained by a non-Indian or even one outside their own tribe.

"Graduating Class of 1902," by Jennie Ross Cobb, courtesy of the Oklahoma Historical Society.

Ultimately, the photographic debate is reduced to who has the right to represent a people. According to present day sentiment, it seems that a people should represent themselves. Susan Sontag observes that there is something "predatory" about taking a picture. "To photograph people is to violate them," she says, "by seeing them as they never see themselves . . . it turns people into objects that can be symbolically possessed."[58] As a result, it was not the notion of the soul being "stolen" by the camera that indigenous people were afraid of, but the man behind the mechanism who now "owned" a representation that had the potential to outlive them.

To counter this oppressive system of ownership, the Zuni are taking back photographs of themselves that have been in museums for decades. This repatriation of intellectual property is progressive; although there is presently no law to require museums and other organizations to return these images, the willingness of many like the Smithsonian Institution's National Anthropological Archives' donation of over 1000 photos is an impressive statement on the Zuni's reclamation of identity. These photographs are housed at the A:shiwi A:wan Museum and Heritage Center (AAMHC) founded in 1992. In addition, religious leaders document every image in the Zuni language, creating an opportunity for the tribe's further education.

Reflecting this activism, founding executive director of the museum Nigel Holman argues that referring to the camera as the "technology of domination" assumes an unrealistic passivity on the part of Native people He prefers "exchange," or "transaction."[59] In this situation, Native people take a more active role in the photographic process, even those images that have been manipulated and staged. This accounts for the range of responses from native people—those who are amused, laugh, and those who are angry. Instead of playing the victim, the powerful personalities of the sitters a hundred years ago still transcend time to reach us today, evidence that a fundamental connection, whether oppressive or not, was made between the photographer and the Native American individuals.

Whatever the approach, it is clear that photographic images have inflicted chaos on the spirits and self-image of Native Americans. Native photographers today reinvent themselves through their medium and their life experiences. Hulleah Tsinhnahjinnie gives this advice to the contemporary artists, thinking of the next time she will tell a story to her nieces and nephews:

> First create in their young minds, photographic albums where the men are strong and handsome and the women strong and breathtaking, lustrous warm dark skin, lightening sharp witty eyes, with smiles that could carry me for days. A photographic album of visual affirmation.[60]

WORKS CITED

Albright, Peggy. *Richard Throssel: Crow Indian Photographer*. 1st ed. Albuquerque: University of New Mexico Press, 1996.

Bush, Alfred L., and Lee Clark Mitchell. *The Photograph and the American Indian*. Princeton, N.J.: Princeton University Press, 1994.

Cory, Kate. Letter to the Bureau of American Ethnology, 24 December 1907.

Dilworth, Leah. *Imagining Indians in the Southwest: Persistent Visions of a Primitive Past*. Washington: Smithsonian Institution Press, 1996.

Dockstader, Frederick J. *Shadows on Glass: The Indian World of Ben Wittick*. Savage, Maryland: Rowman & Littlefield Publishers, Inc., 1990.

Fleming, Paula Richardson, and Judith Luskey. *The North American Indians in Early Photographs*. New York: Harper & Row, 1986.

Gaede, Marc, Marnie Gaede, and Barton Wright. *The Hopi Photographs: Kate Cory, 1905–1912*. 1st ed. La Canada: Chaco Press, 1986.

Gattuso, John. *A Circle of Nations: Voices and Visions of American Indians, The Earthsong Collection*. Hillsboro, Or.: Beyond Words Pub., 1993.

Greenough, Sarah. *On the Art of Fixing a Shadow: One Hundred and Fifty Years of Photography*. 1st ed. Chicago: National Gallery of Art; Art Institute of Chicago, 1989.

Gunn, John Malcolm. *Schat-Chen; History, Traditions and Narratives of the Queres Indians of Laguna and Acoma*. Albuquerque, N.M.: Albright & Anderson, 1917.

Harris, Alexandra. "A Picture to Remember Them By: Photography and Community at Laguna Pueblo." Master of Arts, University of California at Los Angeles, unpublished, 2001.

Hill, Rick. "High Speed Film Captures the Vanishing American, in Living Color." *American Indian Culture and Research Journal* 20, no. 3 (1996): 111–28.

Holman, Nigel. "Photography as Social and Economic Exchange: Understanding the Challenges Posed by Photography of Zuni Religious Ceremonies." *American Indian Culture and Research Journal* 20, no. 3 (1996): 93–110.

James, George Wharton. "The Snake Dance of the Hopis." *Camera Craft: A Photographic Monthly* VI, no. 1 (1902): 3–10.

Lippard, Lucy R., and Suzanne Benally. *Partial Recall.* 1st ed. New York: New Press: Distributed by W.W. Norton & Co. Inc., 1992.

Lomawaima, K. Tsianina. *They Called It Prairie Light: The Story of Chilocco Indian School.* Lincoln: University of Nebraska Press, 1994.

Lyman, Christopher M. *The Vanishing Race and Other Illusions: Photographs of Indians by Edward S. Curtis.* 1st ed. New York: Pantheon Books in association with the Smithsonian Institution, 1982.

Marmon, Lee. Interview by author, tape recording, 3 August 2000.

Masayesva, Victor, Erin Younger, and Northlight Gallery. *Hopi Photographers, Hopi Images, Sun Tracks; V. 8.* Tucson, Ariz.: Sun Tracks & University of Arizona Press, 1983.

McDowell, Steve. "Images across Boundaries." *El Palacio,* Winter 1994, 38–78.

McMaster, Gerald. "Colonial Alchemy: Reading the Boarding School Experience." In *Partial Recall,* edited by Lucy R. Lippard and Suzanne Benally, 76–87. New York: New Press: Distributed by W.W. Norton & Co. Inc., 1992.

Miller, Fred E., and Nancy Fields O'Connor. *Fred E. Miller, Photographer of the Crows.* 1st ed. Missoula, Mont.: University of Montana and Carnan Vidfilm, 1985.

Rickard, Jolene. "Sovereignty: A Line in the Sand." In *Strong Hearts: Native American Visions and Voices,* edited by Nancy Ackerman and Peggy Roalf, 51–54. New York, NY: Aperture, 1995.

Root, Deborah. "White Indians: Appropriation and the Politics of Display." In *Borrowed Power: Essays on Cultural Appropiation,* edited by Bruce H. Ziff and Pratima V. Rao, x, 337. New Brunswick, N.J.: Rutgers University Press, 1997.

Saunders, Charles Francis. *The Indians of the Terraced Houses.* New York: G.P. Putnam's Sons, 1912.

Smith, Paul Chaat. "Every Picture Tells a Story." In *Partial Recall,* edited by Lucy R. Lippard and Suzanne Benally, 199. New York: New Press: Distributed by W.W. Norton & Co. Inc., 1992.

Sontag, Susan. *On Photography.* 1st Anchor Books ed. New York: Anchor Books, 1990.

Tedlock, Dennis. *The Spoken Word and the Work of Interpretation, University of Pennsylvania Publications in Conduct and Communication.* Philadelphia: University of Pennsylvania Press, 1983.

Tsinhnahjinnie, Hulleah. "When Is a Photograph Worth a Thousand Words?" In *Native Nations: Journeys in American Photography,* edited by Jane Alison, 41–55. London: Barbican Art Gallery in association with Booth-Clibborn Eds., 1998.

Vizenor, Gerald. "Ishi Bares His Chest: Tribal Simulations and Survivance." In *Partial Recall,* edited by Lucy R. Lippard and Suzanne Benally, 64–71. New York: New Press: Distributed by W.W. Norton & Co. Inc., 1992.

Webb, William, Robert A. Weinstein, and Natural History Museum of Los Angeles County. *Dwellers at the Source; Southwestern Indian Photographs of A. C. Vroman, 1895–1904.* New York: Grossman Publishers, 1973.

END NOTES

[1] Sarah Greenough, *On the Art of Fixing a Shadow: One Hundred and Fifty Years of Photography*, 1st ed. (Chicago: National Gallery of Art; Art Institute of Chicago, 1989), 4.

[2] Ibid., 12.

[3] Alfred L. Bush and Lee Clark Mitchell, *The Photograph and the American Indian* (Princeton, N.J.: Princeton University Press, 1994), xiii.

[4] Paula Richardson Fleming and Judith Luskey, *The North American Indians in Early Photographs* (New York: Harper & Row, 1986), 104.

[5] Greenough, *On the Art of Fixing a Shadow: One Hundred and Fifty Years of Photography*, 31.

[6] Christopher M. Lyman, *The Vanishing Race and Other Illusions: Photographs of Indians by Edward S. Curtis*, 1st ed. (New York: Pantheon Books in association with the Smithsonian Institution, 1982), 50–51.

[7] Ibid., 107.

[8] Gerald Vizenor, "Ishi Bares His Chest: Tribal Simulations and Survivance," in *Partial Recall*, ed. Lucy R. Lippard and Suzanne Benally (New York: New Press: Distributed by W.W. Norton & Co. Inc., 1992), 66.

[9] Rick Hill, "High Speed Film Captures the Vanishing American, in Living Color," *American Indian Culture and Research Journal* 20, no. 3 (1996): 114.

[10] Lyman, *The Vanishing Race and Other Illusions: Photographs of Indians by Edward S. Curtis*, 17.

[11] Ibid., 19.

[12] Ibid., 149.

[13] Ibid., 67.

[14] Ibid., 51.

[15] Steve McDowell, "Images across Boundaries," *El Palacio*, Winter 1994, 41.

[16] Ibid., 41–2.

[17] quoted in K. Tsianina Lomawaima, *They Called It Prairie Light: The Story of Chilocco Indian School* (Lincoln: University of Nebraska Press, 1994), 4.

[18] Bush and Mitchell, *The Photograph and the American Indian*, 297.

[19] Gerald McMaster, "Colonial Alchemy: Reading the Boarding School Experience," in *Partial Recall*, ed. Lucy R. Lippard and Suzanne Benally (New York: New Press: Distributed by W.W. Norton & Co. Inc., 1992), 78.

[20] Peggy Albright, *Richard Throssel: Crow Indian Photographer*, 1st ed. (Albuquerque: University of New Mexico Press, 1996), 7.

[21] Ibid., 28.

[22] Ibid., 71.

[23] Fred E. Miller and Nancy Fields O'Connor, *Fred E. Miller, Photographer of the Crows*, 1st ed. (Missoula, Mont.: University of Montana and Carnan Vidfilm, 1985), 21.

[24] Lucy R. Lippard and Suzanne Benally, *Partial Recall*, 1st ed. (New York: New Press: Distributed by W.W. Norton & Co. Inc., 1992), 35.

[25] William Webb, Robert A. Weinstein, and Natural History Museum of Los Angeles County, *Dwellers at the Source; Southwestern Indian Photographs of A. C. Vroman, 1895–1904* (New York: Grossman Publishers, 1973), 13.

[26] Susan Sontag, *On Photography*, 1st Anchor Books ed. (New York: Anchor Books, 1990), 64.

[27] Ibid., 59–62.

[28] Charles Francis Saunders, *The Indians of the Terraced Houses* (New York: G.P. Putnam's Sons, 1912), 45–6.

[29] Lee Marmon, Interview by author, tape recording, 3 August 2000.

[30] Leah Dilworth, *Imagining Indians in the Southwest: Persistent Visions of a Primitive Past* (Washington: Smithsonian Institution Press, 1996), 79.

[31] Ibid., 110–11.

[32] Quoted in Ibid., 114.

[33]Webb, Weinstein, and Natural History Museum of Los Angeles County, *Dwellers at the Source; Southwestern Indian Photographs of A. C. Vroman, 1895–1904,* 13.

[34]Dilworth, *Imagining Indians in the Southwest: Persistent Visions of a Primitive Past,* 73.

[35]Quoted in Webb, Weinstein, and Natural History Museum of Los Angeles County, *Dwellers at the Source; Southwestern Indian Photographs of A. C. Vroman, 1895–1904,* 14.

[36]George Wharton James, "The Snake Dance of the Hopis," *Camera Craft: A Photographic Monthly* VI, no. 1 (1902): 7.

[37]Marc Gaede, Marnie Gaede, and Barton Wright, *The Hopi Photographs: Kate Cory, 1905–1912,* 1st ed. (La Canada: Chaco Press, 1986), 4.

[38]Frederick J. Dockstader, *Shadows on Glass: The Indian World of Ben Wittick* (Savage, Maryland: Rowman & Littlefield Publishers, Inc., 1990), 36.

[39]Gaede, *The Hopi Photographs: Kate Cory, 1905–1912,* 2.

[40]Kate Cory, Letter to the Bureau of American Ethnology, 24 December 1907.

[41]Dockstader, *Shadows on Glass: The Indian World of Ben Wittick,* 154.

[42]John Malcolm Gunn, *Schat-Chen; History, Traditions and Narratives of the Queres Indians of Laguna and Acoma* (Albuquerque, N.M.: Albright & Anderson, 1917), 41.

[43]John Gattuso, *A Circle of Nations: Voices and Visions of American Indians, The Earthsong Collection* (Hillsboro, Or.: Beyond Words Pub., 1993), 5.

[44]Alexandra Harris, "A Picture to Remember Them By: Photography and Community at Laguna Pueblo" (Master of Arts, University of California at Los Angeles, unpublished, 2001), 33.

[45]Dennis Tedlock, *The Spoken Word and the Work of Interpretation, University of Pennsylvania Publications in Conduct and Communication* (Philadelphia: University of Pennsylvania Press, 1983), 183.

[46]Ibid., 184.

[47]Harris, "A Picture to Remember Them By: Photography and Community at Laguna Pueblo", 5.

[48]Ibid.

[49]Paul Chaat Smith, "Every Picture Tells a Story," in *Partial Recall,* ed. Lucy R. Lippard and Suzanne Benally (New York: New Press: Distributed by W.W. Norton & Co. Inc., 1992), 97.

[50]Ibid., 98–99.

[51]Lippard and Benally, *Partial Recall,* 14.

[52]Deborah Root, "White Indians: Appropriation and the Politics of Display," in *Borrowed Power: Essays on Cultural Appropiation,* ed. Bruce H. Ziff and Pratima V. Rao (New Brunswick, N.J.: Rutgers University Press, 1997), 225.

[53]Ibid., 228–30.

[54]Jolene Rickard, "Sovereignty: A Line in the Sand," in *Strong Hearts: Native American Visions and Voices,* ed. Nancy Ackerman and Peggy Roalf (New York, NY: Aperture, 1995), 108.

[55]Hulleah Tsinhnahjinnie, "When Is a Photograph Worth a Thousand Words?," in *Native Nations: Journeys in American Photography,* ed. Jane Alison (London: Barbican Art Gallery in association with Booth-Clibborn Eds., 1998), 53.

[56]quoted in Victor Masayesva, Erin Younger, and Northlight Gallery, *Hopi Photographers, Hopi Images, Sun Tracks; V. 8* (Tucson, Ariz.: Sun Tracks & University of Arizona Press, 1983), 33.

[57]Rickard, "Sovereignty: A Line in the Sand," 54.

[58]Sontag, *On Photography,* 14.

[59]Nigel Holman, "Photography as Social and Economic Exchange: Understanding the Challenges Posed by Photography of Zuni Religious Ceremonies," *American Indian Culture and Research Journal* 20, no. 3 (1996): 96.

[60]Tsinhnahjinnie, "When Is a Photograph Worth a Thousand Words?," 55.

6

A Tour of Indian Peoples and Indian Lands

David E. Wilkins

One of the greatest obstacles faced by the Indian today in his desire for self-determination . . . is the American public's ignorance of the historical relationship of the United States with Indian tribes and the lack of general awareness of the status of the American Indian in our society today.
American Indian Policy Review Commission, 1977[1]

This chapter provides descriptions, definitions, and analysis of the most important concepts necessary for a solid foundation for the study of Indian politics. I will attempt to clarify how **indigenous** peoples, variously grouped, are defined, and discuss why such definitions are necessary. I will then analyze how the term *Indian* is defined and discuss what constitutes a **reservation** and **Indian Country.** Finally, I will conclude the chapter with a description of the basic demographic facts and socioeconomic data that applies throughout Indian lands.

WHAT IS AN INDIAN TRIBE?

American Indians, tribal nations, Indian **tribes**, indigenous nations, **Fourth World** Peoples, Native American Peoples, Aboriginal Peoples, First Nations, and Native Peoples—these are just a sample of current terms that are used to refer to indigenous peoples in the continental United States in a collective sense. Alaska Natives, including Aleuts, Inuit, and Indians, and Native Hawaiians are the indigenous peoples of those respective territories. While I will provide some descriptive details about Alaska Natives, I will have less to say about Native Hawaiians because their legal status is unique among aboriginal peoples of the United States.[2]

Reprinted from *American Indian Politics and the American Political System*, by David E. Wilkins, (2002), by permission of Rowman & Littlefield Publishers, Inc.

This was brought to light in the Supreme Court's 2000 ruling in *Rice v. Cayetano.*[3] In that case, the Court struck down restrictions that had allowed only persons with Native Hawaiian blood to vote for the trustees of the Office of Hawaiian Affairs, a state agency created to better the lives of Hawaii's aboriginal people. While *Cayetano* did not specifically address the political relationship of Native Hawaiians to the federal government, it called into question the status of the more than 150 federal statutes that recognize that Hawaii's native peoples do, in fact, have a unique legal status.

The departments of the Interior and Justice issued a preliminary report on August 23, 2000, that recommended that Congress "enact further legislation to clarify Native Hawaiians' political status and to create a framework for recognizing a government-to-government relationship with a representative Native Hawaiian governing body."[4] If Congress acts to create such a framework, and a bill was introduced on July 20, 2000 (S. 2898), by Senator Daniel K. Akaka (D-HI), then Hawaii's Natives would have a political relationship with the federal government similar to that of federally recognized tribes. The **sovereignty** movement in Hawaii is very complex, however, and some segments of the population desire more than mere federal recognition of their status because of their **nation's** preexisting sovereign status.[5]

Indigenous communities expect to be referred to by their own names—Navajo or Diné, Ojibwe or Anishinabe, Sioux or Lakota, Suquamish, or Tohono O'odham—since they constitute separate political, legal, and cultural entities. In fact, before Europeans arrived in the Americas, it is highly doubtful whether any tribes held a "conception of that racial character which today we categorize as 'Indian.' People recognized their neighbors as co-owners of the lands given to them by the Great Spirit and saw themselves sharing a basic status within creation as a life form."[6] However, when discussing Indian peoples generically, *American Indian tribes* and *Native Americans* remain the most widely used terms despite the inherent problems associated with both. For instance, America's indigenous people are not *from* India, and the term *Native American* was "used during the nativist (anti-immigration, anti-foreign) movement (1860s–1925) and the anti-black, anti-Catholic, and anti-Jewish Ku Klux Klan resurgence during the early 1900s."[7]

There is no universally agreed upon definition of what constitutes an Indian tribe, in part because each tribal community defines itself differently and because the U.S. government in its relations with tribes has operated from conflicting sets of cultural and political premises across time. Although no universal definition exists, many statutes give definitions for purposes of particular laws, federal agencies like the **Bureau of Indian Affairs** generate their own definitions, numerous courts have crafted definitions, and the term *tribe* is found—though not defined—in the Constitution's commerce clause.

For example, the Indian Self -Determination Act of 1975 (as amended) defines an Indian tribe as "any Indian tribe, band, nation, or other organized group or community . . . which is recognized as eligible for the special programs and services provided by the United States to Indians because of their status as Indians." By contrast, the Supreme Court in *Montoya v. United States* (1901) even more ambiguously said that "by a 'tribe' we understand a body of Indians of the same or a similar race, united in a community under one leadership or government, and inhabiting a particular though sometimes ill-defined territory."[8]

Broadly, the term *tribe* can be defined from two perspectives—*ethnological* and *political-legal.*[9] From an ethnological perspective, a tribe may be defined as a group of indigenous people connected by biology or blood; kinship, cultural and spiritual values; language; political authority; and a territorial land base. But for our purposes, it is the political-legal definition (since there is no single definitive legal definition) of tribe, especially by the federal government, which is crucial since whether or not a tribal group is *recognized* as a tribe by the federal government has important political, cultural, and economic consequences, as we shall see shortly.

FEDERALLY RECOGNIZED TRIBAL AND ALASKA NATIVE ENTITIES

The extension of **federal recognition** by the United States to a tribal nation is the formal diplomatic acknowledgment by the federal government of a tribe's legal status as a sovereign. This is comparable to when the United States extended "recognition" to the former republics of the Soviet Union after that state's political disintegration. It is the beginning point of a government-to-government relationship between an indigenous people and the U.S. government.[10] The reality is that an American Indian tribe is not a legally recognized entity in the eyes of the federal government unless some explicit action by an arm of the government (i.e., congressional statute, administrative ruling by the BIA, presidential executive order, or a judicial opinion) decides that it exists in a formal manner.

Federal recognition has historically had two distinctive meanings. Before the 1870s, "recognize" or "recognition" was used in the cognitive sense. In other words, federal officials simply acknowledged that a tribe existed, usually by negotiating treaties with them or enacting specific laws to fulfill specific **treaty** pledges.[11] During the 1870s, however, "recognition," or more accurately, "acknowledgment," began to be used in a formal jurisdictional sense. It is this later usage that the federal government most often employs to describe its relationship to tribes. In short, federal acknowledgment is a formal act that establishes a political relationship between a tribe and the United States. It affirms a tribe's sovereign status. Simultaneously, it outlines the federal government's responsibilities to the tribe.

More specifically, federal acknowledgment means that a tribe is not only entitled to the immunities and privileges available to other tribes, but is also subject to the same federal powers, limitations, and other obligations of recognized tribes. What this means, particularly the "limitations" term, is that "acknowledgment shall subject the Indian tribe to the same authority of Congress and the United States to which other federally acknowledged tribes are subjected."[12] In other words, tribes are informed that they are now subject to federal **plenary power** and may, ironically, benefit from the virtually unlimited and still largely unreviewable authority of the federal government. For example, recognized tribes have exemptions from most state tax laws, enjoy sovereign immunity, and are not subject to the same constitutional constraints as are the federal and state governments.

Until 1978, federal recognition or acknowledgment was usually bestowed by congressional act or presidential action. But in 1978 the BIA, the Department of the Interior agency primarily responsible for carrying out the federal government's treaty and trust obligations to tribal nations, published regulations which contained specific criteria that unacknowledged or nonrecognized tribal groups had to meet in order to be formally recognized by the United States. This set of guidelines was based mainly on confirmation by individuals and groups outside the petitioning tribe that members of the group were Indians. The mandatory criteria were the following: the identification of the petitioners "from historical times until the present on a substantially continuous basis, as 'American Indian' or 'Aboriginal'" by the federal government, state or local governments, scholars, or other Indian tribes; the habitation of the tribe on land identified as Indian; a functioning government that had authority over its members; a constitution; a roll of members based on criteria acceptable to the secretary of the interior; not being a terminated tribe; and members not belonging to other tribes.[13]

These criteria largely were designed to fit the "aboriginal" or "mythic" image of the western and already recognized tribes. They were problematic for many eastern tribes who sought recognition, since they paid little heed to the massive historical, cultural, economic, and legal barriers those tribes had to endure merely to survive as tribes into the late twentieth century, lacking any semblance of federal support or protection.

Since the late 1970s there has been tension between those who support BIA or administrative recognition versus those who believe that only the Congress has authority to recognize tribes. The debate over administrative versus legislative recognition rages on, with some advocates from each camp asserting their exclusive right to extend or withhold recognition. This raises an important question: is there a qualitative difference between the two types of recognition? There are two important differences. First, tribes that opt for the administrative variety must meet the formalized set of criteria mentioned earlier. Tribes that pursue congressional recognition, provided they can muster enough proof that they are a legitimate group composed of people of Indian ancestry, have only to make a compelling case to the congressional representative(s) of the state they reside in. The congressional sponsor(s) then make(s) the case for the tribe via legislation.

The second major difference involves the administrative law component known as "subordinate delegation." The major grant of authority the Congress has delegated to the secretary of the interior is located in title 25—*Indians*—of the *U.S. Code*. Section 1 states that the head of Indian affairs, formerly the commissioner of Indian Affairs, today the assistant secretary of Indian affairs, is "appointed by the President, by and with the advice and consent of the Senate."[14] In section 2, the head is authorized to "have the management of all Indian affairs and of all matters arising out of Indian relations."[15] As William Quinn states, this law "would arguably not authorize the Secretary or Commissioner to establish a perpetual government-to-government relationship via federal acknowledgment with an Indian group not already under the Department's aegis."[16] Nevertheless, Quinn asserts that the secretary of the interior, with the U.S. Supreme Court's approval, has historically exercised the authority to "recognize" tribes "when a vacuum of responsibility existed over decades, resulting in a gradual and unchallenged accretion of this authority."[17]

The problem, however, is not that the secretary is usurping unused congressional authority; instead, it is the manner and degree to which secretarial discretion and interpretation of federal laws have been discharged by BIA officials. As Felix Cohen said more than forty years ago, "Indians for some decades have had neither armies nor lawyers to oppose increasingly broad interpretations of the power of the Commissioner of Indian Affairs, and so little by little 'the management of all Indian affairs' has come to be read as 'the management of all the affairs of Indians.'"[18] This statement has relevance today, notwithstanding the federal government's policy of Indian self-determination and the more recent policy of tribal self-governance.

The Congress's track record is problematic as well. Generally speaking, however, tribes with explicit congressional acknowledgment have found their status less subject to the whims of BIA officials, though even that is no guarantee of smooth affairs, because BIA oversees and administers most of the government's political relationship with tribes.

A prime example involves the Pascua Yaqui tribe of southern Arizona. The Yaqui were legislatively recognized in 1978. However, in the late 1980s, when they solicited the approval of the BIA on some changes in their constitution, they were informed by bureau officials that they were limited in what governmental powers they could exercise because they were not a "historic tribe," but were instead merely a "created adult Indian community":

> A historic tribe has existed since time immemorial. Its powers derive from its unextinguished, inherent sovereignty. Such a tribe has the full range of governmental powers except where it has been removed by Federal law in favor of either the United States or the state in which the tribe is located. By contrast, a community of adult Indians is composed simply of Indian people who reside together on trust land. A community of adult Indians may have a certain status which entitles it to certain privileges and immunities. . . . However, that status is derived as a necessary scheme to benefit Indians, not from some historical inherent sovereignty.[19]

The bureau's attempt to create two categories of recognized tribes, a novel and disturbing approach to determining tribal identity, was halted by Congress, which declared that no department or agency of the government could develop regulations that negated or diminished the privileges and immunities of any federally recognized tribes.[20]

The Congress has, moreover, in recent years tried to reassert its constitutional authority in the field by introducing legislation that would transfer administrative and congressional consideration of applications for federal recognition to an independent commission.[21]

Congress's actions, along with the increasing politicization of the administrative recognition process because of Indian gaming operations and state concerns, compelled Kevin Gover, the assistant secretary of Indian Affairs (head of the BIA), in May 2000 to testify before Congress that his agency was no longer able to do the job of recognizing tribes. Gover admitted that he had been unable to streamline the recognition process, which in some cases had taken years to resolve, but he placed larger blame on the fact that Indian gaming revenues had enabled some groups to wage protracted legal battles that often involved nonrecognized tribes, non-Indian citizens and towns, and recognized tribes.[22]

As of 2001, the Department of the Interior officially recognizes 561 indigenous entities—332 are Indian nations, tribes, bands, organized communities, or Pueblos in the lower forty-eight states; 229 are Alaska Native villages or corporations—on a list annually prepared by the BIA. These constitute the indigenous peoples eligible for the special programs and services provided by the United States to indigenous communities because of their status as Indians or Alaska Natives.

The situation of Alaska Native villages and corporations is complicated not only by distinctive ethnological differences but also by their unique political and legal status. Although Alaska Natives are eligible to receive services from the BIA, their political sovereignty as self-governing bodies has been questioned and at times constrained by the federal government. A recent Supreme Court case, *Alaska v. Native Village of Venetie Tribal Government* (1998),[23] cast some doubts on the sovereign status of Alaskan villages. *Venetie* dealt with the jurisdictional status of Alaska Native villages and whether or not lands owned in fee simple by these communities—a type of ownership defined by the Alaska Native Claims Settlement Act of 1971—constituted "Indian Country."

In a major victory for Alaskan state authorities and a blow to the sovereignty of the village of Venetie, an Athabaskan community of some 350 people, Justice Clarence Thomas for a unanimous court held that Venetie's 1.8 million acres of **fee-simple** lands did not qualify as "Indian Country" because they had not been set aside by the

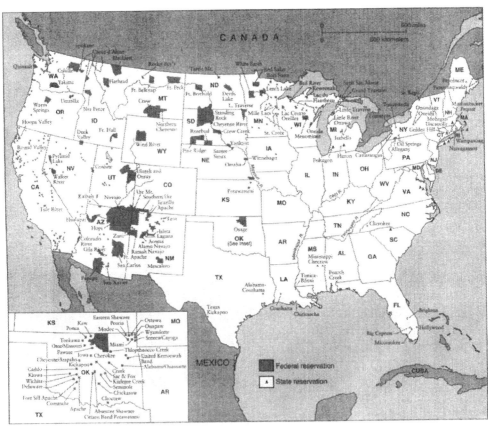

Federal and State Indian Reservation Lands, 1992.

Reprinted from *Encyclopedia of North American Indians*, by Frederick E. Hoxie, (1996), by permission of Houghton Mifflin.

federal government for tribal use and were not "under federal supervision." Thus, the tribal government lacked inherent authority to impose a 5 percent business tax on a contractor building a state-funded school in the village. In denying Venetie, and by extension every other Alaskan village, the power to tax, this ruling called into question what the actual political status of these villages was.

In addition, the indigenous people of Hawaii, who prefer to be called Hawaiians, Hawaiian Natives, or Native Hawaiians, although they are treated as Native Americans for some legal purposes, are not on the Department of the Interior's list of federally recognized tribal entities and have a unique status under federal law.[24]

But there are other indigenous people in the United States who are *not federally recognized*, who had their recognized status *terminated* by the federal government, or who have *state recognition* only. I will discuss these three categories briefly.

NONRECOGNIZED OR UNACKNOWLEDGED GROUPS

These are groups exhibiting a tremendous degree of racial, ethnic, and cultural diversity. In some cases, they are descendants of tribes who never fought the United States, had no resources desired by the federal government, or lived in geographic isolation and were simply ignored, and hence may never have participated in a treaty or benefited from the trust relationship which forms the basis of most contemporary recognized tribes' status. Despite these circumstances, some of these groups retain their aboriginal language, hold some lands in common, and in some cases have retained some degree of traditional structures of governance. These groups feel entitled to recognition status and have petitioned the United States to be so recognized.[25]

In other cases, groups have questionable genealogical connections to legitimate historical tribes but, for varying reasons, have chosen to self-identify as particular tribes and desire to be recognized by the federal government.[26] As of 2000, the BIA had received a total of 237 letters of intent and petitions for federal recognition. The acknowledgment process, established in 1978 and administered by the Branch of Acknowledgment and Research (BAR) in the BIA, proved to be an extremely slow, expensive, and politicized process that required excessive historical documentation and was greatly influenced by already recognized tribes who were reluctant to let other groups, regardless of their historical legitimacy, gain politically recognized status.[27] Because of these and other problems, the bureau surrendered its power to administratively recognize tribal groups in the fall of 2000. Between 1978 and 2000, the BIA officially recognized only fifteen tribes (e.g., Grand Traverse Band of Ottawa & Chippewa and Jamestown S'Klallam) and denied the petitions of fifteen groups (e.g., Lower Muscogee Creek Tribe east of the Mississippi, Kaweah Indian Nation, Southeastern Cherokee Confederacy).[28]

TERMINATED TRIBES

From 1953 to the mid-1960s, the federal government's Indian policy was called **"termination"** because the United States wanted to sever the trust relationship and end federal benefits and support services to as many tribes, bands, and California rancherias as was feasible in an effort to expedite Indian assimilation and to lift

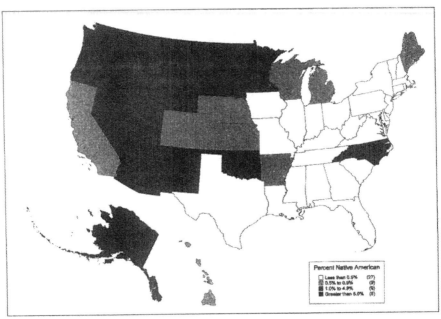

American Indians by State, 1990. Source: Larry Hajime Shinagawa and Michael Jang, *Atlas of American Diversity* (Walnut Creek, Calif: AltaMira, 1998), 104.

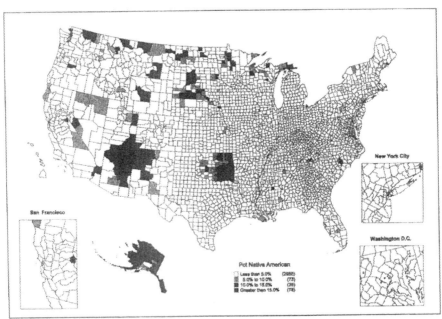

American Indians by County, 1990. Source: Larry Hajime Shinagawa and Michael Jang, *Atlas of American Diversity* (Walnut Creek, Calif: AltaMira, 1998), 104.

discriminatory practices and policies that negatively affected indigenous peoples.[29] This policy was exemplified by House Concurrent Resolution No. 108, passed in 1953. This measure declared that,

> Whereas it is the policy of Congress, as rapidly as possible, to make the Indians within the territorial limits of the United States subject to the same laws and entitled to the same privileges and responsibilities as are applicable to other citizens of the United States, to end their status as wards of the United States, and to grant them all of the rights and prerogatives pertaining to American citizenship; and Whereas the Indians within the territorial limits of the United States should assume their full responsibilities as American citizens: Now, therefore, be it resolved . . . that it is declared to be the sense of Congress that, at the earliest possible time, all of the Indian tribes and the individual members thereof located within the States of California, Florida, New York . . . should be freed from Federal supervision and control and from all disabilities and limitations specially applicable to Indians.[30]

Over one hundred tribes, bands, and California rancherias—totaling a little more than eleven thousand Indians—were "terminated" and lost their status as "recognized" and sovereign Indian communities. Termination thus subjected the tribes and their members to state law, their trust assets were usually individualized and either sold or held by banks, and they were no longer eligible for the other benefits and exemptions recognized tribes enjoy.

The terminated tribes, other tribes faced with termination, and Indian and non-Indian interest groups began to lobby Congress to end this disastrous policy, because of the economic and political hardships it was causing. By the mid-1960s, the policy was stifled. Gradually, terminated tribes began to push for "restoration" of their recognized status. The first tribe terminated, the Menominee of Wisconsin (terminated in 1954), was also the first tribe to be legislatively "restored," in 1973.

Although discredited as policy by the mid-1960s, and rejected by Presidents Nixon and Reagan in their Indian policy statements, termination was not officially rejected by Congress until 1988 in a largely symbolic gesture that declared that "the Congress hereby repudiates and rejects HCR 108 of the 83rd Congress and any policy of unilateral termination of federal relations with any Indian nation."[31]

STATE-RECOGNIZED TRIBES

Some Indian tribes have been recognized by their host states since the colonial era (e.g., Pamunkey Tribe of Virginia), although others have been recognized by state decrees (governor's action or state statute) in contemporary times. There are currently over fifty state-recognized tribes in Alabama, Connecticut, Georgia, Louisiana, Massachusetts, Michigan, Montana, New Jersey, North Carolina, New York, Oklahoma, Virginia, Washington, and West Virginia. See table 1 for a list of these tribes. Depending on the policy established by the individual state, state recognition may or may not depend on prior federal recognition. Importantly, state recognition is not a prerequisite for federal recognition, although a long-standing relationship with a state

Table 1 State Recognized Tribes

Alabama

Echota Cherokee
Northeast Alabama Cherokee
MaChis Lower Creek
Southeast Alabama Cherokee
Star Muscogee Creek
Mowa Band of Choctaw

Georgia

Georgia Eastern Cherokee
Cherokee of Georgia
Lower Muskogee Creek
Tama Tribal Town

New Jersey

Nanticoke Lenni-Lenape
Powhatan Renape
Ramapough Mountain

Michigan

Burt Lake Band of Ottawa & Chippewa Indians
Gun Lake Band of Grand River Ottawa Indians
Grand River Band of Ottawa Indians
Swan Creek Black River Confederated Tribes

North Carolina

Coharie Intra-Tribal Council
Haliwa-Saponi Tribe
Lumbee
Meherrin Tribe
Person County Indians
Waccamaw-Siouan Tribe

Virginia

Chickahominy Indian Tribe
Eastern Chickahominy Indian Tribe
Mattaponi Indian Tribe
Monacan Indian Tribe
Nansemond Indian Tribe
Pamunkey Indian Tribe
United Rappahannock Tribe
Upper Mattaponi Indian Tribe

West Virginia

Appalachian American Indians of West Virginia

Connecticut

Golden Hill Paugussett
Paucatuck Eastern Pequot
Schagticoke

Louisiana

Choctaw-Apache of Ebarb
Caddo Tribe
Clifton Choctaw
Four Winds Cherokee
United Houma Nation

New York

Shinnecock
Poospatuk

Montana

Little Shell Tribe of Chippewa

Oklahoma

Delaware Tribe of East Oklahoma
Loyal Shawnee Tribe
Yuchi Tribe

Washington

Chinook Indian Tribe
Duwamish Tribe
Kikiallus Indian Nation
Marietta Band of Nooksack Indians
Steilacoom Indian Tribe
Snohomish Tribe of Indians

Source: http://www.thespike.com/tablest.htm

is one factor in the federal recognition criteria that the BIA weighs in its determination of whether a group has historical longevity in a particular place.

For example, the Lumbee Tribe of North Carolina was legislatively recognized by the state in 1953.[32] Confident, the Lumbee leadership two years later asked Representative Frank Carlyle (D-NC) to introduce a bill before Congress that would extend federal recognition to the Lumbee. On June 7, 1956, the Congress passed an act which provided a measure of recognition to the Lumbee Nation,[33] without giving them the full range of benefits and services other federally recognized tribes received because federal policy at the time was focused on terminating the unique trust relationship between tribes and the United States. To date, the Lumbee Tribe is still not considered a federally recognized tribe by the BIA or the Indian Health Service, though they qualify for and receive other federal services as a recognized tribe.[34]

WHO IS AN AMERICAN INDIAN?

Having established the complexity of determining what an Indian tribe is from a legal-political perspective, we now turn to a brief but necessary examination of the equally if not more cumbersome question of "Who is an Indian?" This is important, as McClain and Stewart note, because "the question of who is an Indian is central to any discussion of American Indian politics."[35] The political relationship that exists between tribes and the federal government, bloated with issues of disparate power, cultural biases, and race and ethnicity, makes this so. Of course, like the concept of "Indian tribe," before Columbus arrived in 1492 there were no peoples in the Americas known as "Indians" or "Native Americans." Each indigenous community had its own name relating to the character of its people and the lands they inhabited.

With the political status of Indian nations defined, the question of deciding just "who is an Indian" would not appear to be a difficult one to answer. The decision rests with the tribal nations who retain, as one of their inherent sovereign powers, the power to decide who belongs to their nation. Unless this right has been expressly ceded in a treaty, it remains probably the most essential component of self-government. If tribes were to lose the right to decide who their citizens/members were, then it would logically follow that any government could dictate or influence what the tribe's membership should entail.

Since the identification of individuals as Indians depends upon or coincides with their association in a unique body politic and distinctive cultural and linguistic systems, historically, at least, "allegiance rather than ancestry per se [was] the deciding factor" in determining who was an Indian.[36] In other words, historically, to be considered an Indian one had to meet certain basic tribally defined criteria, including the social, cultural, linguistic, territorial, sociopsychological, and ceremonial. These criteria, of course, varied from tribal nation to tribal nation. However, as the federal government's power waxed by the late nineteenth century, with the corresponding waning of tribal power, indigenous cultural-social-territorial-based definitions of tribal identity were sometimes ignored and replaced by purely legal and frequently race-based definitions often arbitrarily articulated in congressional laws, administrative regulations, or court cases.

Congress, in particular, began to employ and still uses ethnological data, including varying fractions of **blood quantum.** See table 2, which is an official chart developed

Table 2 Chart to Establish Degree of Indian Blood

	NI*	1/16	1/8	3/16	1/4	5/16	3/8	7/16	1/2	9/16	5/8	11/16	3/4	13/16	7/8	15/16	4/4
1/16	1/32	1/16	3/32	1/8	5/32	3/16	7/32	1/4	9/32	5/16	11/32	3/8	13/32	7/16	15/32	1/2	17/32
1/8	1/16	3/32	1/8	5/32	3/16	7/32	1/4	9/32	5/16	11/32	3/8	13/32	7/16	15/32	1/2	17/32	9/16
3/16	3/32	1/8	5/32	3/16	7/32	1/4	9/32	5/16	11/32	3/8	13/32	7/16	15/32	1/2	17/32	9/16	19/32
1/4	1/8	5/32	3/16	7/32	1/4	9/32	5/16	11/32	3/8	13/32	7/16	15/32	1/2	17/32	9/16	19/32	5/8
5/16	5/32	3/16	7/32	1/4	9/32	5/16	11/32	3/8	13/32	7/16	15/32	1/2	17/32	9/16	19/32	5/8	21/32
3/8	3/16	7/32	1/4	9/32	5/16	11/32	3/8	13/32	7/16	15/32	1/2	17/32	9/16	19/32	5/8	21/32	11/16
7/16	7/32	1/4	9/32	5/16	11/32	3/8	13/32	7/16	15/32	1/2	17/32	9/16	19/32	5/8	21/32	11/16	23/32
1/2	1/4	9/32	5/16	11/32	3/8	13/32	7/16	15/32	1/2	17/32	9/16	19/32	5/8	21/32	11/16	23/32	3/4
9/16	9/32	5/16	11/32	3/8	13/32	7/16	15/32	1/2	17/32	9/16	19/32	5/8	21/32	11/16	23/32	3/4	25/32
5/8	5/16	11/32	3/8	13/32	7/16	15/32	1/2	17/32	9/16	19/32	5/8	21/32	11/16	23/32	3/4	25/32	13/16
11/16	11/32	3/8	13/32	7/16	15/32	1/2	17/32	9/16	19/32	5/8	21/32	11/16	23/32	3/4	25/32	13/16	27/32
3/4	3/8	13/32	7/16	15/32	1/2	17/32	9/16	19/32	5/8	21/32	11/16	23/32	3/4	25/32	13/16	27/32	7/8
13/16	13/32	7/16	15/32	1/2	17/32	9/16	19/32	5/8	21/32	11/16	23/32	3/4	25/32	13/16	27/32	7/8	29/32
7/8	7/16	15/32	1/2	17/32	9/16	19/32	5/8	21/32	11/16	23/32	3/4	25/32	13/16	27/32	7/8	29/32	15/16
15/16	15/32	1/2	17/32	9/16	19/32	5/8	21/32	11/16	23/32	3/4	25/32	13/16	27/32	7/8	29/32	15/16	31/32
4/4	1/2	17/32	9/16	19/32	5/8	21/32	11/16	23/32	3/4	25/32	13/16	27/32	7/8	29/32	15/16	31/32	4/4
1/32	1/64	3/64	5/64	7/64	9/64	11/64	13/64	15/64	17/64	19/64	21/64	23/64	25/64	27/64	29/64	31/64	33/64
3/32	3/64	5/64	7/64	9/64	11/64	13/64	15/64	17/64	19/64	21/64	23/64	25/64	27/64	29/64	31/64	33/64	35/64
5/32	5/64	7/64	9/64	11/64	13/64	15/64	17/64	19/64	21/64	23/64	25/64	27/64	29/64	31/64	33/64	35/64	37/64
7/32	7/64	9/64	11/64	13/64	15/64	17/64	19/64	21/64	23/64	25/64	27/64	29/64	31/64	33/64	35/64	37/64	39/64
9/32	9/64	11/64	13/64	15/64	17/64	19/64	21/64	23/64	25/64	27/64	29/64	31/64	33/64	35/64	37/64	39/64	41/64
11/32	11/64	13/64	15/64	17/64	19/64	21/64	23/64	25/64	27/64	29/64	31/64	33/64	35/64	37/64	39/64	41/64	43/64
13/32	13/64	15/64	17/64	19/64	21/64	23/64	25/64	27/64	29/64	31/64	33/64	35/64	37/64	39/64	41/64	43/64	45/64
15/32	15/64	17/64	19/64	21/64	23/64	25/64	27/64	29/64	31/64	33/64	35/64	37/64	39/64	41/64	43/64	45/64	47/64
17/32	17/64	19/64	21/64	23/64	25/64	27/64	29/64	31/64	33/64	35/64	37/64	39/64	41/64	43/64	45/64	47/64	49/64
19/32	19/64	21/64	23/64	25/64	27/64	29/64	31/64	33/64	35/64	37/64	39/64	41/64	43/64	45/64	47/64	49/64	51/64
21/32	21/64	23/64	25/64	27/64	29/64	31/64	33/64	35/64	37/64	39/64	41/64	43/64	45/64	47/64	49/64	51/64	53/64
23/32	23/64	25/64	27/64	29/64	31/64	33/64	35/64	37/64	39/64	41/64	43/64	45/64	47/64	49/64	51/64	53/64	55/64
25/32	25/64	27/64	29/64	31/64	33/64	35/64	37/64	39/64	41/64	43/64	45/64	47/64	49/64	51/64	53/64	55/64	57/64
27/32	27/64	29/64	31/64	33/64	35/64	37/64	39/64	41/64	43/64	45/64	47/64	49/64	51/64	53/64	55/64	57/64	59/64
29/32	29/64	31/64	33/64	35/64	37/64	39/64	41/64	43/64	45/64	47/64	49/64	51/64	53/64	55/64	57/64	59/64	61/64
31/32	31/64	33/64	35/64	37/64	39/64	41/64	43/64	45/64	47/64	49/64	51/64	53/64	55/64	57/64	59/64	61/64	63/64

Source: Department of Interior, Bureau of Indian Affairs, Phoenix area office. Tribal Enrollment (Washington: Government Printing Office, 1980).

Note: To determine the degree of blood of children, find degree of one parent in left column and the other parent in the top row; read across and down. For example, if a child has parents with 11/16 and 5/8 degrees of blood, then that child would be 21/32 degree Indian.

*Non-Indian.

by the BIA describing the fractionalization of Indian identity. In fact, blood quantum remains one of the most important criteria used by the federal government and tribal governments to determine Indian status, despite the fact that its continued use "poses enormous conceptual and practical problems" since blood is not the carrier of genetic material and cultural traits as was thought in the nineteenth century.[37]

When blood quantum was first used in the Indian context in the early part of the twentieth century as a mechanism to reduce federal expenditures for Indian education, it "was meant to measure the amount of Indian blood possessed by an individual. Because racial blood types could not be observed directly, Indian blood quantum was inferred from the racial backgrounds of parents. If both parents were reputed to have "unadulterated" Indian blood, then the blood quantum of their children was fixed at 100 percent. For children of racially mixed parents, their Indian blood quantum might be some fractional amount such as, ¾, ½, or ⅛."[38]

The federal government's principal function in formulating definitions of "Indian," since like the concept "tribe" there is no single constitutional or universally accepted definition, is to "establish a test whereby it may be determined whether a given individual is to be excluded from the scope of legislation dealing with Indians."[39] The most widely accepted "legal" definition of "Indian" is from Felix Cohen, who wrote in 1943 that:

> The term "Indian" may be used in an ethnological or in a legal sense. Ethnologically, the Indian race may be distinguished from the Caucasian, Negro, Mongolian, and other races. If a person is three-fourths Caucasian and one-fourth Indian, it is absurd, from the ethnological standpoint, to assign him to the Indian race. Yet legally such a person may be an Indian. From a legal standpoint, then, the biological question of race is generally pertinent, but not conclusive. Legal status depends not only upon biological, but also upon social factors, such as the relation of the individual concerned to a white or Indian community. . . . Recognizing the possible diversity of definitions of "Indianhood," we may nevertheless find some practical value in a definition of "Indian" as a person meeting two qualifications: (a) That some of his ancestors lived in America before its discovery by the white race, and (b) That the individual is considered an "Indian" by the community in which he lives.[40]

Because of the Constitution's silence on the issue of who is an Indian, Congress, the BIA, and the federal courts have had great latitude in developing specific meanings for specific situations which only sometimes reflect the definitions of particular tribes. But because of the plenary power doctrine and the **trust doctrine**, these federal actors, but especially the Congress, have vested themselves with the right to define "who an Indian is" for purposes relating to legislation and have sometimes established base rolls which actually identify who a tribe's members are. This was done in the case of the so-called Five Civilized Tribes of present-day Oklahoma. Congress, in 1893, enacted a law that all but secured to the federal government the right to determine the membership of these tribes.[41]

Over thirty "legal" definitions have been promulgated by various agencies, departments, and congressional committees and subcommittees that explain who is and is not an Indian eligible for federal services.[42] These definitions can be grouped into six categories. First, and most common, are those definitions that require a specific blood quantum, with one-fourth being the most widely accepted fraction. Second, there is a set of definitions clustered under the requirement that the individual be a member of a federally recognized indigenous community.

A third category includes definitions that mandate residence "on or near" a federal Indian reservation. A fourth class includes definitions grouped under descendancy. These entail definitions that extend eligibility not only to tribal members but also to their descendants up to a specified degree. For example, the definition of Indian found in a 1998 bill, Indian Trust-Estate Planning and Land Title Management Improvement Act, declares that "the term 'Indian' means any individual who is a member, or a descendant of a member, of a North American tribe, band, pueblo, or other organized group of natives who are indigenous to the continental U.S., or who otherwise has a special relationship with the U.S. through a treaty, agreement, or other form of recognition." The bill's sponsors described an "Alaska Native" as "an individual who is an Alaskan Indian, Eskimo, Aleut, or any combination thereof, who are indigenous to Alaska."

Under the fifth grouping are several definitions that rely on self-identification. The U.S. Census Bureau, for example, allows individuals to simply declare that they are Indian. Finally, the sixth class is a miscellaneous category that includes definitions which do not easily fit in the other categories.[43]

Defining "Indian" and "tribe" are not simple tasks in part because of the political and economic resources involved and because of the number and power of the respective actors: tribal governments, individual Indians, Congress, the president, the Department of the Interior, the BIA, federal courts, and, increasingly, state governments and the various agencies and individuals who constitute those sovereigns. But who does the defining and how these emotionally laden terms are defined are crucial in expanding our understanding of the politics of individual tribes, intertribal relations, and intergovernmental relations.

For example, in terms of identity, high outmarriage rates, steadily decreasing federal dollars, and an intensified tribal-state relationship have prompted questions about "whether the rules defining Indianness and tribal membership should be relaxed or tightened—that is, made more inclusionary or more exclusionary."[44] For instance, some tribes are eliminating blood quantum and adopting descent criteria, while others are pursuing an "ethnic purification strategy" by adopting a stricter set of blood quantum rules concerning tribal enrollment. These decisions impact tribes and their political relationship with the federal government.

While tribes retain the right to establish their own membership criteria, the BIA in August 2000 published proposed regulations on the documentation requirements and standards necessary for Indians to receive a "certificate of degree of Indian blood" (CDIB), which is the federal government's way of determining whether individuals possess sufficient Indian blood to be eligible for certain federal programs and services provided exclusively to American Indians or Alaska Natives.[45]

But a number of Indian leaders, like W. Ron Allen, chairman of the Jamestown S'Klallam Tribe of Washington, charged that the federal government should not be in the business of determining who is Indian. The proposed regulations, he argued, by requiring applicants to show a relationship to an enrolled member of a federally recognized tribe, would potentially exclude members or descendants of terminated tribes, state-recognized tribes, and nonrecognized tribes.

Since the BIA's standard blood quantum is one-fourth, and with the high rates of outmarriage, Russell Thornton, an anthropologist, suggests that sometime in this century the proportion of the Indian population with less than one-fourth blood quantum will rise to 60 percent. If this trend is correct, from the federal government's standpoint "decreasing blood quanta of the total Native American population may be perceived as meaning that the numbers of Native Americans to whom it is obligated have declined."[46] This will not mean the extinction of Indian tribes, but it will mean a new form of federal termination of Indians who are eligible for federal aid and services.

Questions around whether a tribe is federally recognized, state-recognized, nonrecognized, or terminated have direct bearing on the internal and external political dynamics of tribes, and directly affect intergovernmental relations, since only recognized tribes may engage in gaming operations that are not directly subject to state law, may exercise criminal jurisdiction over their members and a measure of civil jurisdiction over nonmembers, and are exempt from a variety of state and federal taxes.

WHAT ARE INDIAN LANDS?

The first and most obvious difference between Indian peoples and all other groups in the United States is that Indians were here before anyone else. All the land in the continental United States, Alaska, and Hawaii was inhabited and revered by the over six hundred distinctive indigenous peoples who dwelt here. Gradually, however, from 1492 forward, various foreign nations—Russia, Holland, Spain, Great Britain, France, Sweden, and later the United States—competed for an economic foothold in North America. For the three most dominant European states, France, Spain, and Great Britain (and later the United States, as Britain's successor), this usually included efforts to secure title to indigenous lands through formal treaties, which were sometimes coercive and occasionally fraudulent, while some were fairly negotiated.[47]

When the United States declared independence in 1776, it wisely opted to continue the policy of negotiating treaties with tribes, which it continued to do until 1871, when Congress unilaterally declared that "hereafter no Indian nation or tribe within the territory of the United States shall be acknowledged or recognized as an independent nation, tribe, or power with whom the United States may contract by treaty."[48] However, this stance proved unworkable and within a short period the United States was again negotiating *agreements* with tribal nations that were often referred to and accorded the legal status of treaties. The negotiation of agreements continued until 1912.

Many of these documents were primarily viewed as land cession arrangements by the federal government, in which the United States purchased varying amounts of tribal lands in exchange for monies, goods, and services. In addition, tribes "reserved" their remaining lands, or agreed to relocate to new lands, which were usually designated as reservations. These reserved lands were to be held "in trust" by the United States on behalf of the tribe(s), who were deemed the beneficiaries. As the tribes' "trustee," the federal government theoretically exercised the responsibility to assist the tribes in the protection of their lands, resources, and cultural heritage and pledged that it would hold itself to the highest standards of good faith and honesty in all its dealings with the tribes.

For example, article 1 of a treaty the Kickapoo signed on October 24, 1832, contained a cession of land:

> The Kickapoo tribe of Indians, in consideration of the stipulations hereinafter made, do hereby cede to the United States, the lands assigned to them by the treaty of Edwardsville, and concluded at St. Louis . . . and all other claims to lands within the State of Missouri.[49]

The second article, however, described the lands the tribe secured for their land cessions:

> The United States will provide for the Kickapoo tribe, a country to reside in, southwest of the Missouri river, as their permanent place of residence as long as they remain a tribe . . . [and] it is hereby agreed that the country within the following boundaries shall be assigned, conveyed, and forever secured . . . to the said Kickapoo tribe.[50]

In this case the Kickapoo agreed to relocate to a little over 700,000 acres of new lands in Kansas that were to serve as their permanent "reservation."

In short, a reservation is an area of land—whether aboriginal or new—that has been reserved for an Indian tribe, band, village, or nation. Generally, the United States holds, in trust for the tribe, legal title to the reserved territory. The tribe in these instances holds a beneficial title to the lands, or, in other words, an exclusive right of occupancy. Of course, reservations were not all created by treaty. Congress has established a number of reservations by statute.

The president, through the use of executive order power, established many other reservations. For instance, the state of Arizona has twenty-one reservations—twenty of which were created by presidents. The core foundation of the Navajo Reservation (the largest in the country), was treaty-established in 1868, though the many additions to it were mostly by executive orders. In 1919, Congress forbade the president from establishing any more reservations via executive order. Finally, the secretary of the interior is empowered under the 1934 Indian Reorganization Act to establish, expand, or restore reservations.

As of 1998, there were 314 reservations and other restricted and trust lands in the United States. These reserved lands are located in thirty-one states, mostly in the West. There are also twelve state-established reservations in Connecticut, Massachusetts, Michigan, New York, New Jersey, South Carolina, Georgia, and Virginia. Despite the large number of federally recognized Alaska Native groups, there is only one reservation, the Annette Island Indian Reserve.[51]

At the present, the indigenous land base in the United States, including Alaska, is approximately one hundred million acres—fifty-six million in the continental United States, forty-four million in Alaska. This represents approximately 4 percent of all lands in the United States. The map on page 141 graphically shows the rapid and

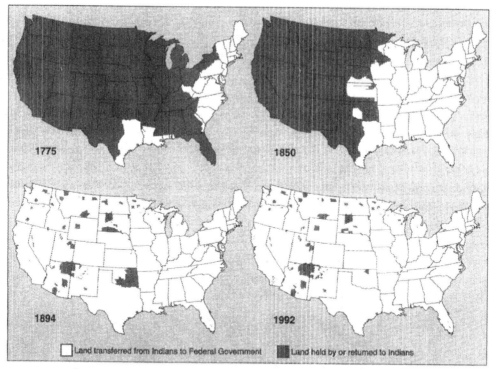

American Indian Land Losses. Source: *Encyclopedia of North American Indians,* edited by Frederick E. Hoxie. Copyright © 1996 by Houghton Mifflin Company. All rights reserved.

enormous loss of aboriginal territory to the United States from the birth of the American republic to the present day.

The roughly one hundred million acres constitutes territory over which tribal governments and Alaska Native villages and corporations exercise varying amounts of governmental jurisdiction, and where state laws are generally inapplicable, with exceptions.

In 1999, 1,397,931 Indians were identified in a BIA report out of the total U.S. Indian population in 2000 of 2,475,956 (individuals self-identifying as single-race American Indian or Alaska Native).

WHAT IS INDIAN COUNTRY?

For an indigenous government to be able to exercise criminal or civil jurisdiction over their territory, their own members, and, in some limited cases, non-Indians, the land in question must be designated as *Indian Country.* In the colonial era, Indian Country encompassed all the lands beyond the frontier, lands "populated by tribes and bands of Indians who rejected contact with 'civilized' populations."[52] Today, however, the concept "has been elevated by federal law above other ideas because it transcends mere geographical limitations and represents that sphere of influence in which Indian traditions and federal laws passed specifically to deal with the political relationship of the United States to American Indians have primacy."[53]

INDIAN COUNTRY: BEYOND THE RESERVATION

Broadly, the term "Indian Country" means land within which Indian laws and customs and federal laws relating to Indians are generally applicable. But it is also defined as all the land under the supervision and protection of the federal government that has been set aside primarily for the use of Indians. Federal law defines it, first, as all land within the boundaries of an Indian reservation, whether owned by Indians or non-Indians. Second, it includes all "dependent Indian communities" in the United States. These are lands—pueblos of New Mexico, Oklahoma Indian tribal lands, and California rancherias—previously recognized by other European nations and now by the successor government, the United States, as belonging to the tribes or as set aside by the federal government for the use and benefit of the Indians.

Pueblo lands, because they were previously recognized as belonging to the pueblos under Spanish, Mexican, and later U.S. law, are not, strictly speaking, reservations, but are considered Indian lands and are held in trust by the federal government because they are held in communal ownership with fee-simple title residing in each pueblo. Some Pueblo Indian lands are held in equitable ownership by various pueblos, with the United States holding legal title. These lands include reservations created by congressional statute and executive order reservations established by the president.

Oklahoma's numerous Indian tribes also have a distinctive history, though their lands also constitute Indian Country. It is important to note that the tribes in the eastern part of the state, what was called "Indian Territory," home of the Five Civilized Tribes, have a somewhat different history from tribes in the western part of the state, or what was called "Oklahoma Territory," home of the Cheyenne, Arapaho, Kiowa, Comanche, etc. Although the BIA and the Bureau of the Census have asserted that there are no Indian reservations in Oklahoma, except for the Osage, John Moore argues that the reservation status of Oklahoma tribes persists, notwithstanding allotment and other policies designed to terminate Indian communal land holdings.[54]

Some California tribes, because of heavy Spanish influence dating from 1769, live on **rancherias**, a Spanish term meaning "small reservation" and originally applied to Indians who had not been settled in Christian mission communities. The history of death and dispossession visited upon California's indigenous population may well be the worst of any aboriginal peoples in the United States. From a population of well over 300,000 at the time of contact, California Indians experienced a staggering rate of decline from diseases, outright genocide, and displacement.[55] That they have retained any lands at all is a remarkable testimony to their fortitude.

Finally, the Indian Country designation includes all individual Indian allotments (I will discuss the **allotment policy** shortly) that are still held in trust or restricted status by the federal government—whether inside or outside an Indian reservation.[56]

For political and legal purposes, the designation of Indian Country is crucial because the reach of a tribal nation's jurisdiction is generally restricted to lands so designated. And it is Indian Country where most jurisdictional disputes arise between tribes and their members, tribes and non-Indians, and tribes and the local, county, state, or federal governments.

For example, this was the central question in the recent U.S. Supreme Court case involving indigenous people, *Alaska v. Native Village of Venetie Tribal Government*

(1998). In this case, the court had to decide whether the village of Venetie constituted Indian Country. If so, then the tribal government had the right to impose a tax on a construction company; if not, then it lacked such taxing power. In a harmful ruling for Alaska Native sovereignty, the Supreme Court held that the village's fee-simple lands did not constitute Indian Country, thus depriving Alaska villages and corporations of the power to exercise a number of governmental powers that tribal nations in the lower forty-eight states exercise routinely. The Supreme Court, however, need not have relied so exclusively on the question of whether or not Venetie constituted "Indian Country" since the statutes articulating this concept clearly did not encompass Alaska at the time they were enacted.

DEMOGRAPHY AND INDIAN COUNTRY

According to a report, *Changing America,* prepared by the Council of Economic Advisers for President Clinton's Race Initiative in 1998, the population of the United States is increasingly diverse. In recent years the four major racial/ethnic minority groups—Latinos, Asian Americans, African Americans, and American Indians—have each grown faster than the population as a whole. Whereas in 1970 the combination of these four groups represented only 16 percent of the entire population, by 1998 this had increased to 27 percent.[57] The Bureau of the Census, the report noted, projects that by 2050, these groups will account for "almost half of the U.S. population." Early data from the 2000 U.S. census, which shows a total population of 281,421,906, indicate the continuing transformation of race and ethnicity in America. While the categories of white (211,460,626), Hispanic or Latino (35,305,818), black or African American (34,658,1901), American Indian or Alaska Native (2,475,956), Asian (10,242,998), and Native Hawaiian or other Pacific Islander (398,835) were familiar, for the first time in history individuals could choose to self-identify as having more than one race. Some 6,826,228 people, 2.4 percent of the total population, claimed affiliation with two or more races.[58]

While this projected growth has potentially staggering political and economic implications, the fact is that the total indigenous population, despite the large number of indigenous nations—561 and counting—is comparatively quite small (see figures 1–6). In 2000, there were a reported 2,475,956 self-identified Indians and Alaska Natives, a 26 percent increase since 1990. This is a drastic decline from pre-European figures of over seven million, but it is far more than the nadir of perhaps only 250,000 around 1900.[59] The 2000 figure represents only 0.9 percent of the total U.S. population of 281,421,906.

Although the overall population of self-identified American Indians and Alaska Natives is still quite small, because of the new category allowing individuals to identify as belonging to more than one race (sixty-three racial options were possible), the 2000 census data are not directly comparable with data from the 1990 census or previous censuses. Thus, while approximately 2.5 million individuals identified themselves as American Indian and Alaska Native alone, an additional 1.6 million people reported themselves as being indigenous and belonging to "at least one other race." Within this group, the most common combinations were "American Indian and Alaska Native *and* White" (66 percent of the population reported this); "American

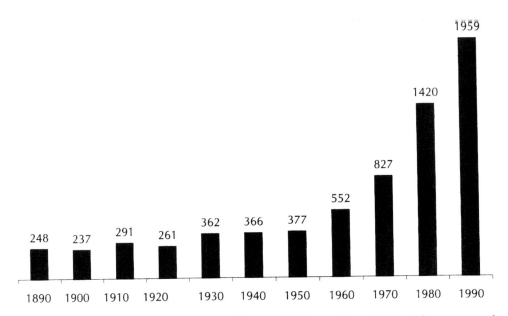

American Indian Population, 1890–1990 (thousands). Source: Larry Hajime Shinagawa and Michael Jang, *Atlas of American Diversity* (Walnut Creek, Calif.: AltaMira, 1998), 107–8. Notes: 1900, partially estimated; 1930 Eskimo and Aleut populations are based on 1939 counts.

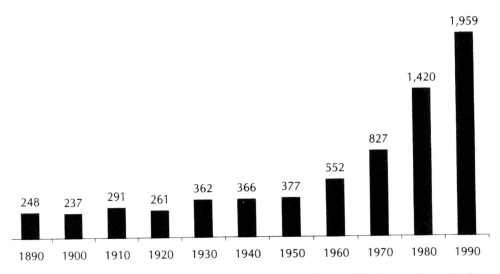

American Indian Population Growth Rate, 1980–1990 (thousands). Source: Larry Hajime Shinagawa and Michael Jang, *Atlas of American Diversity* (Walnut Creek, Calif.: AltaMira, 1998), 107–8.

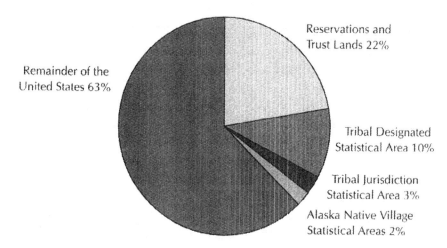

American Indian Population by Type of Area, 1990 (percent). Source: Larry Hajime Shina-gawa and Michael Jang, *Atlas of American Diversity* (Walnut Creek, Calif.: AltaMira, 1998), 107–8.

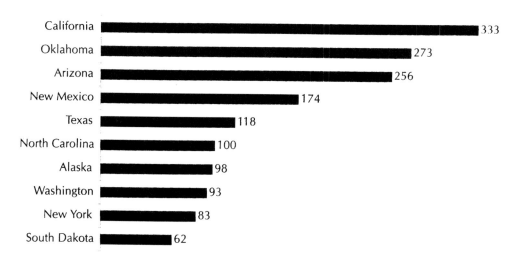

States with the Ten Largest American Indian Populations, 2000 (thousands). Source: www.census.gov/clo/www/redistricting.html

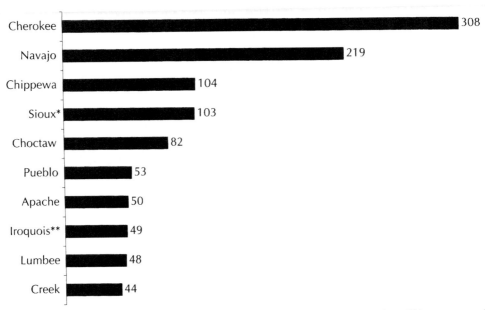

Ten Largest American Indian Tribes, 1990 (thousands). Source: Larry Hajime Shinagawa and Michael Jang, *Atlas of American Diversity* (Walnut Creek, Calif.: AltaMira, 1998), 107–8. *Any entry with the spelling "Siouan" was miscoded to Sioux in North Carolina. **Reporting and/or processing problems have affected the data for this tribe.

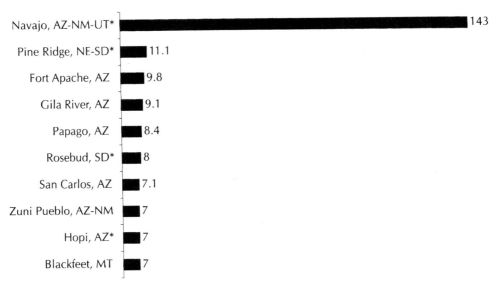

Reservations with the Largest Numbers of American Indians,1990 (thousands). Source: Larry Hajime Shinagawa and Michael Jang, *Atlas of American Diversity* (Walnut Creek, Calif.: AltaMira, 1998), 107–8. *Includes trust lands.

Indian and Alaska Native *and* Black or African American" (11 percent of the population); and "American Indian and Alaska Native *and* White *and* Black or African American" (7 percent). In sum, approximately 4.1 million people reported themselves as being American Indian and Alaska Native "alone or in combination with one or more other races."[60] The wide diversity within this population will be discussed in greater detail in forthcoming Census reports not yet available.

Suffice it to say, the amount of racial mixing acknowledged in the American Indian context is extreme when compared to that of other racial/ethnic groups. As Russell Thornton, a Cherokee anthropologist, noted in his analysis of the 2000 census data, American Indians have a racial mixture of 37 percent, which "far exceeds percentages for other groups." Thornton noted that only about 5 percent of African Americans reported mixed ancestry.[61]

In Alaska, there is only one small reservation, Annette Island Reserve, though for census purposes lands are designated as "Alaska Native Village Statistical areas" that are inhabited and recognized as indigenous areas. Approximately 47,244 Alaska Natives live on these lands. In sum, more than 60 percent, over one million, of all Indian people do not live on Indian reservations.[62] A majority of indigenous peoples, in fact some 56.2 percent, live in metropolitan or suburban areas. And roughly half of all urban Indians can be found in as few as sixteen cities, largely as a result of the 1950s and 1960s termination, relocation, and educational programs of the federal government.

In the early days of relocation, the BIA generally helped send Indians to Chicago, Los Angeles, Denver, or Salt Lake City. By 1990, Indians had migrated to a number of other metropolitan areas. Cities with the largest Indian populations in 1990 were Tulsa, Oklahoma (48,348); Oklahoma City, Oklahoma (46,111); Los Angeles-Long Beach, California (43,689); Phoenix, Arizona (38,309); and Seattle-Tacoma, Washington (32,980).[63] The vast majority of Indians still live in the western half of the United States.

The states with the ten largest indigenous populations are shown in figure 4. The District of Columbia had the fewest Indians, 1,466. See maps 2 and 3 for details about Indian population by county and state.

There is also great variation in the population of individual tribes (see figure 5). The largest tribe is the Cherokee Nation of Oklahoma, with 369,035 members. The smallest tribes have fewer than one hundred members. The indigenous population is also a young population, with more than 35 percent younger than age seventeen. In fact, the median age for reservation Indians is more than ten years younger than that of the general U.S. population (see figures 7 and 8). The Indian population, like that of the Jews and the Japanese Americans in Hawaii, is also one that experiences an extremely high level of intergroup marriage (marriage between persons of different races). Although intergroup married couples accounted for only 4 percent of all married couples in the United States in 1990, American Indians had a 53 percent intergroup marriage rate. Potentially, this figure could have severe cultural and political implications for indigenous nations.[64]

As Snipp mused:

> The extraordinarily high level of racial intermarriage for American Indians provides a good reason to expect that growing numbers of American Indians and

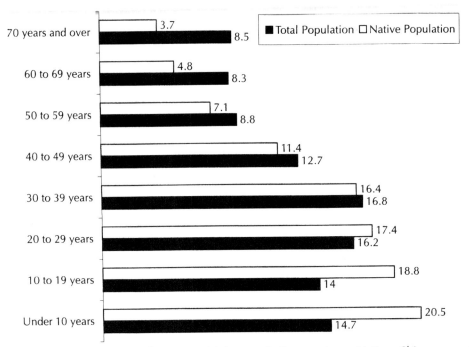

American Indian Age Distribution, 1990 (percent). Source: Larry Hajime Shinagawa and Michael Jang, *Atlas of American Diversity* (Walnut Creek, Calif.: AltaMira, 1998), 107–8.

American Indian Median Age, 1990. Source: Larry Hajime Shinagawa and Michael Jang, *Atlas of American Diversity* (Walnut Creek, Calif.: AltaMira, 1998), 107–8.
*Includes trust lands.

their descendants will choose non-Indians for spouses and to a greater or lesser degree become absorbed into the dominant culture. Some of these Indians will abandon their cultural heritage altogether, while others may make only minor accommodations as a result of having a non-Indian spouse. This raises a question that is extremely controversial within many quarters of the American Indian community: Are American Indians assimilating so quickly through racial intermarriage that they will eventually, in the not too distant future, marry themselves out of existence?[65]

Predicting the future is an impossible task and I will not hazard a guess as to whether this intermarriage rate will continue. Suffice it to say, this is viewed as a serious predicament by some tribes and raises some important questions. For instance, will Indians, like many intermarried Jews, be able to show a propensity for combining extensive intermarriage with a surge in ethnic and religious pride? For while the rate of Jewish intermarriage is higher today than at any earlier point, American Jewish culture and community life appear to be flourishing, including a resurgent interest in Yiddish.[66]

Other questions confront tribes as well. Will they continue to use blood quantum as their primary definitional criteria? Will the federal government claim that its legal and moral obligations to Indians dissipate if a tribal nation's blood quantum falls below a certain percentage? Will tribes be able to exercise jurisdiction over a multiracial citizenry? These are questions some tribes are beginning to address as we begin the new millennium.

CONCLUSION

The power to define—what is a tribe, who is an Indian, what constitutes Indian Country, which group gets recognized—along with the power to decide whether or not to act in a colonial capacity in relation to indigenous nations are important means by which the federal government has gained and retains a dominant position vis-à-vis tribal groups. While on one hand supporting the right of indigenous polities to exercise self-determination, the United States on the other still insists that it has the power and the right to trump important tribal governmental decisions regarding identity and has shown throughout its history that it will so act if it deems it necessary to further its own economic, political, and cultural interests.

The demographic data presented glaringly show that diversity and uncertainty are hallmarks of Indian Country, with more than half the indigenous population living off reservations and Indians outmarrying at increasing rates. What the impact of such movement and marriage rates will be on tribal national identity, federal Indian policy, and the government-to-government relationship is, however, impossible to predict.

END NOTES

[1]U.S. Congress, *American Indian Policy Review Commission: Final Report,* vol. 1 (Washington, D.C.: Government Printing Office, 1977), 3.

[2]See, e.g., Haunani-Kay Trask, *From a Native Daughter: Colonialism and Sovereignty in Hawai'i* (Monroe, Maine: Common Courage, 1993) and Roger MacPherson Furrer, ed., *He Alo á He Alo* (*Face to Face*): *Hawaiian Voices on Sovereignty* (Honolulu, Hawaii: American Friends Service Committee-Hawai'i, 1993).

[3]528 U.S. 495 (2000).

[4]Http://www.doi.gov/nativehawaiians/.

[5]See, S. James Anaya, "The Native Hawaiian People and International Human Rights Law: Toward a Remedy for Past and Continuing Wrongs," *Georgia Law Review* 28 (1994), 309–64.

[6]Vine Deloria Jr: "The American Indian Image in North America," *Encyclopedia of Indians of the Americas,* vol. 1 (St. Clair Shores, Mich.: Scholarly Press, 1974), 43.

[7]Paula D. McClain and Joseph Stewart Jr., *"Can We All Get Along?" Racial and Ethnic Minorities in American Politics* (Boulder, Colo.: Westview, 1998), 6, citing John Higham, *Strangers in the Land: Patterns of American Nativism, 1860–1925* (Westport, Conn.: Greenwood, 1963).

[8]180 U.S. 261 (1901).

[9]Felix S. Cohen, *Handbook of Federal Indian Law,* reprint ed. (Albuquerque: University of New Mexico Press, 1972), 268.

[10]Jack Utter, *American Indians: Answers to Today's Questions* (Lake Ann, Mich.: National Woodlands, 1993), 30–31.

[11]William Quinn Jr., "Federal Acknowledgment of American Indian Tribes? The Historical Development of a Legal Concept," *American Journal of Legal History* 34 (October 1990): 331–63.

[12]56 *Federal Register* 47, 325 (1991).

[13]25 Code of Federal Regulations 83.7 (a)–(g) (1991).

[14]25 *U.S.C.* chapter 1, section 1, 961.

[15]25 *U.S.C.* chapter 1, 962.

[16]William W. Quinn Jr., "Federal Acknowledgment of American Indian Tribes: Authority, Judicial Interposition, and 25 C.F.R. Sec. 83," *American Indian Law Review* 17 (fall 1992): 48.

[17]Quinn, "Federal Acknowledgment of American Indian Tribes," 52.

[18]Felix Cohen, "The Erosion of Indian Rights, 1950–1953: A Case Study in Bureaucracy," *Yale Law Journal* 62 (February 1953): 352.

[19]Letter from Carol A. Bacon, acting director of the Office of Tribal Services, Bureau of Indian Affairs, 3 December 1991. The author has copy of the letter.

[20]108 Stat., 709.

[21]See U.S. Congress, House, "A Bill to Provide for Administrative Procedures to Extend Federal Recognition to Certain Indian Groups, and for Other Purposes," 105th Cong., 2d sess., 1998, H. Rept. 1154. As of this writing—May 1999—none of these bills has become law.

[22]Ellen Barry, "Agency Willing to Relinquish Power to Recognize Tribes," *Boston Globe,* 26 May 2000, B1.

[23]118 U.S. 948 (1998).

[24]See, e.g., Trask, *From a Native Daughter,* and Anaya, "The Native Hawaiian People," 309.

[25]Allogan Slagle, "Unfinished Justice: Completing the Restoration and Acknowledgment of California Indian Tribes," *American Indian Journal* 13, no. 4 (fall 1989): 325–45.

[26]William W. Quinn Jr., "The Southeast Syndrome: Notes on Indian Descendant Recruitment Organizations and Their Perceptions of Native American Culture," *American Indian Quarterly* 14, no. 2 (spring 1990): 147–54.

[27]Jackie J. Kim, "The Indian Federal Recognition Procedures Act of 1995: A Congressional Solution to an Administrative Morass," *The Administrative Law Journal of the American University* 9, no. 3 (Fall 1995): 899–932.

[28]See http://www.doi.gov/bia/bar/indexq.htm for statistical details of the acknowledgment project's efforts.

[29]Donald Fixico, *Termination and Relocation: Federal Indian Policy, 1945–1960* (Albuquerque, N.Mex.: University of New Mexico Press, 1986).

[30]67 Stat., B132.

[31]110 Stat., 130.

[32]N.C. Public Laws, 1953, chapter 874, p. 747.

[33]70 Stat., 254.

[34]David E. Wilkins, "Breaking into the Intergovernmental Matrix: The Lumbee Tribe's Efforts to Secure Federal Acknowledgment," *Publius: The Journal of Federalism* 23 (Fall 1993): 123–42.

[35]McClain and Stewart, *"Can We All Get Along?"* 6.

[36]Bart Vogel, "Who Is an Indian in Federal Indian Law?" in *Studies in American Indian Law,* ed. Ralph Johnson (Pullman, Wash.: Washington State University, 1970), 53.

[37]C. Matthew Snipp, *American Indians: The First of This Land* (New York: Russell Sage Foundation, 1989), 34.

[38]Snipp, *First of This Land,* 33.

[39]Cohen, *Handbook,* 2.

[40]Cohen, *Handbook,* 2.

[41]29 Stat., 321.

[42]Abdul C. Kahn, *Report on the Indian Definition Study* (Washington, D.C.: Department of Education, 1980).

[43]Kahn, *Indian Definition Study,* 56.

[44]Joane Nagel, *American Indian Ethnic Renewal: Red Power and the Resurgence of Identity and Culture* (New York: Oxford University Press, 1996), 243.

[45]Brian Stackes, "Planned Bureau of Indian Affairs Regulations Stir Concerns Among Tribal Leaders," *Indian Country Today,* 18 August 2000, 1.

[46]Russell Thornton, "Tribal Membership Requirements and the Demography of 'Old' and 'New' Native Americans," in *Changing Numbers, Changing Needs: American Indian Demography and Public Health,* ed. Gary D. Sandefur, Ronald R. Rindfuss, and Barney Cohen (Washington, D.C.: National Academy Press, 1996), 110–11.

[47]See, e.g., Francis Paul Prucha, *American Indian Treaties: The History of a Political Anomaly* (Berkeley, Calif.: University of California Press, 1994) and Robert A. Williams Jr. *Linking Arms Together: American Indian Treaty Visions of Law and Peace, 1600–1800* (New York: Oxford University Press, 1997).

[48]16 Stat., 566.

[49]7 Stat., 391.

[50]7 Stat., 391.

[51]Cesare Marino, "Reservations," in *Native America in the Twentieth Century: An Encyclopedia,* ed. Mary B. Davis (New York: Garland Publishing, Inc., 1996), 544–56.

[52]Vine Deloria Jr. and Clifford M. Lytle, *American Indians, American Justice* (Austin: University of Texas Press, 1983), 58.

[53]Deloria and Lytle, *American Indians,* 58.

[54]John H. Moore, "The Enduring Reservations of Oklahoma," in *State & Reservation: New Perspectives on Federal Indian Policy,* ed. George Pierre Castile and Robert L. Bee (Tucson: University of Arizona Press, 1992), 92–109.

[55]See, Robert F. Heizer, *The Destruction of California Indians* (Lincoln: University of Nebraska Press, 1993) for a first rate account of what these nations experienced from 1847 to 1865.

[56]Title 18, U.S. Code, section 1151.

[57]Council of Economic Advisers, *Changing America: Indicators of Social and Economic Well-Being by Race and Hispanic Origin* (Washington, D.C.: Government Printing Office, 1998), 4.

[58]www.census.gov/prod/2001pubs.

[59]Russell Thornton, *American Indian Holocaust and Survival: A Population History Since 1492* (Norman: University of Oklahoma Press, 1987).

[60]www.census.gov/prod/2001pubs.

[61]Russell Thornton, "What the Census Doesn't Count," *New York Times,* 23 March 2001, A21.

[62]C. Matthew Snipp, "The Size and Distribution of the American Indian Population: Fertility, Mortality, Migration, and Residence," in *Changing Numbers, Changing Needs: American Indian Demography and Public Health,* ed. Gary D. Sandefur, Ronald R. Rindfuss, and Barney Cohen (Washington, D.C.: National Academy Press, 1996), 42–43.

[63]Snipp, "The Size and Distribution," 39.

[64]Snipp, *The First of This Land,* 171.

[65]Snipp, *The First of This Land,* 165.

[66]Lawrence H. Fuchs, *The American Kaleidoscope* (Hanover, N.H.: Wesleyan University Press, 1990), 329.

7

Native American Literary Analysis, Poetry, and Prose

Separated from Mother Earth: Self-loathing and Sexual Brutality in Leslie Marmon Silko's Almanac of the Dead

Henrietta Moore

Vine Deloria, Jr., writes in his introduction to *The Metaphysics of Modern Existence*, "The fundamental factor that keeps Indians and non-Indians from communicating is that they are speaking about two entirely different perceptions of the world" (vii). These differing perceptions of the world are based on their differing perceptions of the earth and their relationships to the earth. While both Native Americans and European Americans have creation myths that include a metaphoric genesis from the very soil of the earth, they differ in their characterizations of the earth. European Americans traditionally view the earth as acted upon: the creator exerts his power upon the earth and creates life. American Indians traditionally view the earth as living spirit and matter, and therefore changing and responding to its environment; this perception is an underlying tenet of their relationship to the earth.

Jace Weaver notes in his book, *That the People Might Live*, that Silko has been strongly influenced by Vine Deloria, Jr.,: "Many of the same themes that run through the work of Vine Deloria propel the writing of Leslie Silko. Sovereignty, community, and the vitality and power of a tradition that is constantly evolving are fundamental categories for the Laguna author" (132). Vine Deloria, Jr., when writing about Indian religion in *God is Red*, says, "[. . .] all inanimate entities have spirit and personality so that the mountains, rivers, waterfalls, even the continents and the earth itself have intelligence, knowledge, and the ability to communicate ideas" (152).

Leslie Marmon Silko's novel, *Almanac of the Dead,* reflects a Native American perspective and perception in her plot, structure, characterization, language, and writing style; in her depiction of time, space, place, life/death cycles; and in relationships to nature. In an interview with Ray Gonzalez, Silko discusses the way she wrote *Almanac of the Dead:* "It's done in a way that narrative can have a narrative within a narrative, and where past/present/future can really be experienced. It is actually the way in which a lot of tribal people see and measure time—past, present, and future at once" (103). Silko's novel is a collection of short intense sketches, which creates for the reader a sense of skipping through time and place, stopping a few minutes here and there to observe, in a god-like manner, the crazy and tragic humans. The energy and pacing of the narration condenses time and morphs past, present and prophecy. The novel touches upon all aspects of the conflict between European world-view and Native American world-view: the relationship of humans to earth and nature, the relationship of men and women, and the relationship of the seen to the unseen.

Many of Silko's Native American characters possess extrasensory abilities to understand animals and the natural world. Silko says in an interview with Laura Coltelli, 1993, "As children we are taught what we are allowed to see; Western European culture does not allow us to see the spirit and being in rocks, water, and trees and other plants. Therefore, the spirit and being of rocks and water and plants remain invisible to most of us" (124).

Silko's plot and characters illustrate the imbalance that occurs when humans become alienated from their earthly origins. In a conversation with Thomas Irmer and Matthias Schmidt, 1995, Silko says "So we are natural, we are part of the natural world, we are not separate. There is some yearning, some longing; we know that we are part of the trees, and the earth, and the water" (152).

Silko's characters react instinctively, both physically and socially, in order to survive, and these reactions reveal their natural animal natures. The various ways her characters seek to satisfy their physical and social needs are metaphors for their relationship to the earth, and because they are part of the earth, their relationship to themselves. Silko explores the various and sometimes extreme mutations that occur when those needs are perverted.

Silko's characters express their relationship to their natural origins through their actions; they express their essential personalities through their physical behavior. For example, sexual behavior is intrinsically linked to the ideology of the characters. Silko says in an interview with Thomas Irmer and Matthias Schmidt, 1995, "Human beings have deluded themselves, fooled themselves to think that they can control nature, that they can control the human body which is a part of nature" (156).

The brutal sexual behavior of many of the characters is symptomatic of their unhealthy relationship with the earth and their own corporeal bodies, which are incarnations of the earth. There is an imbalance within the characters; they are at war with their own physical beings in much the same way they are at war with the earth. Silko exposes the visceral driving force at the center of her characters by observing their sexual desires and behaviors. When the sexual behavior of individual characters is compared and analyzed with those of the entire cast of characters, it becomes clear that characters alienated from the land are also alienated from their bodies and exhibit the most perverse and destructive sexual behavior.

The wide range of sexual behaviors depicted in Silko's characters can be understood by comparing the extremes: El Feo and Angelita, who are depicted as most closely connected to the land, and Serlo and Max Blue, who are depicted as most disconnected from the land.

El Feo and Angelita, Native Americans with close ties to the land, are the only characters in the novel who enjoy what can be described as mutually satisfying, non-exploitive sex: they "have food and sex together twice a day [. . .]" (471). Sexual behavior is juxtaposed with eating; it is depicted as a natural, energizing function. The relationship is not coercive or possessive. They believe the earth is their elemental mother, and that all of life will be in balance if they have their land. "El Feo did not believe in political parties, ideology, or rules. El Feo believed in the land. With the return of Indian land would come the return of justice, followed by peace" (518). When Angelita speaks to her followers she says, "To hell with the Marxists! To hell with the Capitalists! To hell with the white man! We want our mother the land!" (519). Silko depicts these native characters, with their close connection to the land, as the most balanced and harmonious and with an appreciation and acceptance of their earthiness.

The Indians tease Angelita that she is in love with Marx, and she admits to El Feo that it is true. Angelita believes that "Marx had been inspired by reading about certain Native American communal societies, though naturally as a European he had misunderstood a great deal" (519). Silko speaks through the character of Angelita to explain to the reader some of Marx's theories on capitalism. Silko shows that Angelita is drawn to Marx because his views are closer to the indigenous view that communities are more important than individuals and because Marx writes against the capitalist system that has caused such harm to Native Peoples.

Serlo is the extreme opposite of Angelita. He is unable to engage sexually with other humans, or indeed, to relate to any of the earth's creatures. He is obsessed with cleanliness and sterility. His sexually abusive grandfather has taught him that sexual contact with a woman is repulsive and filthy. Serlo feeds his distorted theories by reading racist psychological writing, which promulgates that "even the most perfect genetic specimen could be ruined, absolutely destroyed, by the defects of the child's mother" (542). Serlo has "fetishes of purity and cleanliness; there were insinuations his sex organ touched only sterile, pre-warmed stainless steel cylinders [. . .]" (547). He believes himself to be one of the few pure-blooded people in the world, and he saves "all his sperm in a freezer for use in future generations" (547). Serlo expects in the future the earth will be totally contaminated with "swarms of brown and yellow human larvae called natives" (545). To Serlo, mothers are contaminated, and mothers have contaminated the earth by spawning progeny of impure blood. To protect himself from what he believes will be a revolution of the "degenerate masses" (546), he has built an underground chamber or "Alternative Earth" unit that is completely self-contained. But this underground refuge will only be temporary because he believes that inevitably the earth will be uninhabitable and he plans to construct Alternative Earth Modules that will orbit in colonies "where the select few would continue as they always had, gliding in luxury and ease across polished decks of steel and glass islands where they looked down on earth [. . .]" (542). The colonies will be "self-sufficient, closed systems, capable of remaining cut off from earth for years [. . .]" (543).

Silko's rendering of Serlo's character depicts the European male as filled with disgust and hate for his mother and all things associated with the maternal. The references to the unclean earth are reminiscent of Biblical text reflecting the Judeo-Christian attitude toward women. The language "alternative earth" and "cut off from earth" indicate Serlo's alienation from the earth. In addition, the use of the word "colonies" is a clear indicator that Serlo is representative of the Euro-American white male intentions to dominate and exploit the earth and forge further in search of new worlds to conquer and exploit. The new all-male and motherless world Serlo dreams of creating will finally free him from his dependency on the maternal.

Silko has created Serlo as the extreme opposite of the Native American female. The Native female is close to the earth and lives in harmony with the earth and her own earthly nature, whereas the European male is furthest removed from his connection to the earth and therefore lives in a state of conflict, even war, against the earth and his own earthly nature. Vine Deloria, Jr., writes in *God is Red*, "Developing a sense of ourselves that would properly balance history and nature and space and time is a more difficult task than we would suspect and involves a radical revelation of the way we look at the world around us" (61).

Consistent with Silko's non-linear approach, Max Blue is a black hole in the center of a vortex where all light is trapped. He has relinquished all sexual desire. After narrowly escaping death, Max lives in constant fear of death. He spends most of his time on the golf course, his only satisfaction watching the golf ball fly into the blue Arizona sky. He has detached himself from the earth and tries to quell his fear of death by focusing his attention on the bright white sphere as it hangs above the earth. "He loved to watch the arc of the ball and the way wind currents held the ball aloft perfectly suspended as if time no longer existed" (637). He struggles to free himself of earth and time. Max fears the low gray clouds that remind him of a coffin lid, and he finds relief only when he is looking into the sky, especially when he follows the white round golf ball propelled into the sky. Max "[. . .] watched the arch of the ball against the sun. Max thought of the great cathedrals he had seen in Europe where light was celebrated as the presence of God" (356). Once again, the reader is reminded of the European male's Judeo-Christian heritage—one of a powerful white male God. Max momentarily feels power over earth and time when he drives the small white globe (like a small white earth) into the sky. Max worships the sky as a symbolic power above the earth. His desire is to dominate the earth (and implicitly, the female).

Characters of mixed-blood are conflicted about their indigenous heritage and so can reject or embrace their connection to the earth. Mernardo is a mixed-blood character, who denies his indigenous heritage. He tries to be white by sexually possessing white bodies. Mernardo learns of his Indian heritage when his classmates call him "flat nose" and rejects his Indian ancestry after the "teaching Brothers had given them a long lecture about pagan people and pagan stories" (258). He stops listening to his grandfather's stories and makes excuses for his facial features by telling people that his nose was broken in a boxing match. When he meets blond, slender, Alegria he thinks that "millions (of dollars) might raise him to her level and he and she might possibly be considered social equals" (268). Mernardo tries to become part of the white dominant society by possessing a blond body. As he goes further and further into the white world, he becomes paranoid and obsessed with protecting himself. When a white man gives him a bulletproof vest, he puts all his trust in the power of white technology and wears the vest continually. He even wears the vest during sex with Alegria, perhaps thinking the white man's vest would make him appear white to Alegria. The sexual behavior of this character represents the imbalance that occurs when a person rejects his Native heritage and is therefore in conflict with himself.

Mernardo tells himself that Indians are superstitious and stupid, but it is to Tacho, his indigenous chauffer, that he goes to for interpretation of his troubled dreams. Characters like Mernardo self-destruct in Silko's novel. He actually commits a kind of suicide-by-indigenous-person when he insists that Tacho fire a bullet into the bullet-proof vest to prove that modern technology has made him invincible. Mernardo wears the bulletproof to protect himself from an outside attack, but the enemy is within; the inner conflict ultimately kills him. After Mernardo's death Tacho thinks, "A great many fools like Menardo would die pretending they were white men; only the strongest would survive" (511).

Native American characters are portrayed as more connected to the land and also more natural about their bodies. Only the indigenous characters are able to understand the voice of the earth and other earth creatures. Zeta can hear the snake; Lecha can hear the spirits of the dead; Rosa can hear the spirits of her brothers and sisters; Tacho can hear the Macahs; El Feo and Tacho can see into the Opal.

Sterling is Native American, but he has drifted away from his people and his land. After working away from his people for most of his adult life, he has lost connections, so when he comes back to his tribe he fails to protect the image of the giant snake and is banished. Sterling is portrayed with a lack of initiative, which indicates self-determination has been taken from him by the dominant society. His best sex is the "deluxe" that Janey, the prostitute, gives him. Janey does all the work and makes all the decisions. Sterling lays back and closes his eyes, and the sex happens to him, like a dream.

Throughout the novel Silko has woven the concept that a balanced, healthy world is a mother-centered, earth-centered world, and that concept is emphasized when Sterling is the only character to arrive at a healing place. He has been raised with some maternal nurturing; therefore, he is able to connect to others and to the land. However, Sterling's self-identity is damaged, and he wanders in search of his identity and his place in the world. Once back on his land, he feels a great sense of relief and begins to understand the importance of his connection to place. He thinks of his aunts. He sees the snake revealed within the rocks and soil where the earth has been split open to mine the uranium. He feels the spirit of the snake and of the land. He envisions a future where indigenous people take back their land and people return to an earth-centered life, bringing human life and earth-life back into balance.

The land is a strong character in the novel. It has strength and power; it has memory; it has voice. The novel starts with the land and the fact that Sterling has not protected the spirit of the land from the Hollywood camera crew. The novel ends with Sterling back on his land with an understanding of his relationship to the land and to the spirits of the land.

In *The Sacred Hoop*, Paula Gunn Allen eloquently describes the Native American perspective on relationship of people to earth.

The earth is not a mere source of survival, distant from the creatures it nurtures and from the spirit that breathes in us, nor is it to be considered an inert resource on which we draw in order to keep our ideological self functioning, whether we perceive that self in sociological or personal terms. We must not conceive of the earth as an ever-dead other that supplies us with a sense of ego identity by virtue of our contrast to its perceived nonbeing. (119)

Silko's *Almanac of the Dead* exemplifies imaginative literature with a Native American perspective. She has assimilated ideas, theories and predictions from the best minds of contemporary Native American scholars and elders, as well as traditional indigenous knowledge, and she has synthesized Native American observations, insights and world-views into an epic novel dense with implications, imprecations and prescience.

WORKS CITED

Allen, Paula Gunn. *The Sacred Hoop: Recovering the Feminine in American Indian Traditions.* Boston: Beacon Press, 1992.

Deloria, Vine Jr. *God is Red: A Native View of Religion.* Golden: Fulcrum Publishing, 1994.

———, *Custer Died for Your Sins: An Indian Manifesto* New York: Avon Books, 1971.

———, *The Metaphysics of Modern Existence.* San Francisco: Harper & Row Publishing, 1979.

Silko, Leslie Marmon. *Almanac of the Dead.* New York: Penquin Books, 1992.

———, Interview with Florence Boos. "An Interview with Leslie Marmon Silko." *Conversations with Leslie Marmon Silko.* Ed. Ellen L. Arnold Jackson: University Press of Mississippi, 2000. 135–145.

———, Interview with Laura Coltelli. "Almanac of the Dead: An Interview with Leslie Marmon Silko." *Conversations with Leslie Marmon Silko.* Ed. Ellen L. Arnold. Jackson: University Press of Mississippi, 2000. 119–134.

———, Interview with Ray Gonzalez. "The Past is Right Here and Now: An Interview with Leslie Marmon Silko." *Conversations with Leslie Marmon Silko.* Ed. Ellen L. Arnold. Jackson: University Press of Mississippi, 2000. 97–106.

———, Interview with Thomas Irmer and Matthias Schmidt. "An Interview with Leslie Marmon Silko." *Conversations with Leslie Marmon Silko.* Ed. Ellen L. Arnold Jackson: University Press of Mississippi, 2000. 146–161

Weaver, Jace. *That the People Might Live: Native American Literatures And Native American Community.* New York: Oxford University Press, 1997.

All the following poems and prose are by Henrietta Moore (Cherokee)

Cherokee Granddaughter

The grass is itching on my ankles
as I step through the thick growth
in my California sandals.

According to Frank's directions
it should be near.
Frank . . . daddy, father,
What to call him.
Nothing felt right.

The air is hot and muggy
like an Oklahoma August.

There it is.
. . . ANAWEGA
The letters carved in the old stone
are worn down and barely readable.
I don't know what it means.

I stand awkwardly for a few minutes,
feeling the air,
watching a hawk,
listening to the insects.

"Hello great-grandmother."

Cry to the Universe

We desire to hear ourselves,
to know that we are real.

We growl, whine, howl.
gurgle, wheeze, snort, wail.

Our sounds travel
into the atmosphere
until they bump into matter.

and we believe that we matter.

Words are sound waves
traveling forever.

Our cry to the universe.

H. Moore
2/2000

Prayers for Roadkill

Driving hours and hours
each week, month, year,

I pass dead mangled animals
on the road.

Many little souls
violently torn from their bodies.

Their bodies
hit again and again.
Blood, bones and flesh
ground into the earth and asphalt,

until they are a part
of the place they died,
part of the road
I travel on.

When I see a fresh kill,
the animal still
recognizable,
the blood still red,

a sudden sharp sadness
hits me
and I'm compelled
to speak.

Please, may the
little soul transfer into
a painless other world.

The words fall
from my speeding car,
swirl in the traffic
and litter the roadside.

April 24, 2000

Instinctive Hero

Coiled in the pale dirt beside the paved road,
the snake is like a twisted twig,
no threat to the drivers in big fast machines.

I see him only for a few seconds,
his head raised, fangs exposed,
rattles blurring in the sunlight.

He can't know the invisible force before him.
Hot air hits him, dense with foreign smells;
He strikes into the wind and heat.

He strikes again and again,
a writhing spring-loaded coil of life,
like the DNA of survival.

I imagine his fangs touching a tire
and his long body unraveling
as it is dashed to the pavement,
again and again,
and flung to the side of the road.

No medal nor marker
for this instinctive hero.

Ultimate Insult to Intellect

Intellect, I've had faith in you,
rejecting myth, magic and
superstition.

I've been a true disciple,
pushing past primal fears
of oozing, slimy, putrid death

and fantasies of gods, demons,
heavenly wars and
everlasting life.

I accept that I will end,
cease to be, stop,
disappear.

My biggest fear is
at the end of mortal thought
the universe is not
rational and impersonal.

But,
really is controlled
by an egotistical,
emotional,
irrational,
entity.

and,
I never had a chance.

FOUND AND LOST

Tree people stood along the far edge of the front field. They were short sturdy people with gray gnarled trunks and thick, twisted limbs, tapering into thin, brittle fingers; their leaves round and leathery, dusty green with serrated edges. The trees were called hedge trees or Osage Orange. Grandmother told me the Osage Indians used the wood for bows.

It seemed a strange name for the trees because there was nothing orange on them. They had round green fruit we called hedge apples. The fruit was about the size of a large apple, puffy and pebbly, with deep lines criss-crossing all over it; it looked like a small green brain. When bruised it bled a sticky, milky substance. They were not poison, but were bitter and not good to eat. Sometimes the cows ate them and ruined their milk.

I had heard people say hedge trees could withstand high winds, even tornadoes. The trees held to their ground. They were compact, and when the wind hit, the trunks barely moved, but their small leaves rattled and whistled. The people in that area said that if caught in the open during a tornado, head for the nearest hedge tree. A low spot in the land, like under a bridge, was best, but the next best was a hedge tree.

Grandma said I could play in the front field but not to go to the row of hedge trees. There were no hedge trees next to the house, only cottonwood trees, elms, and one pine tree. Grandpa painted the trunks with white paint. It kept the ants from the trees and made them look clean and kind of dressed up. In the winter, the leaves fell off and they looked naked and cold.

In Kansas the wind nearly always blows. It blows gentle, medium and fierce, but it is a rare moment when there is no wind. One of those rare moments might be just before a big storm. At these times, it is like the wind is holding its breath, gathering all its strength so it can blow everything off the face of the earth.

The constant wind made all the trees talk. Every tree had a voice. The leaves of the cottonwoods made a soft rattle. If I closed my eyes it sounded like rain. The elms sounded like muffled laughter. The pine tree whispered in gentle wind, but in a strong wind it sounded like a very hoarse voice trying to scream. Even in winter, after the leaves were gone, wind on the bare limbs made sounds. The wind hissed, growled, wailed and whistled as it moved against and around each thing in its path. The wind caused everything to have a voice.

Sometimes Grandma and I went for a walk looking for wild flowers. We walked across the open prairie, and as far as I could see the grass moved in waves and ripples like a giant gray-green billowing blanket. The grass made fluid sounds like wind-rivers. If we stood quietly and the wind died down near us, I could hear gusts of wind on the distant grass. Like a far away wind world where nothing but invisible wind existed and wind people flew out into the visible world and hit on things and yelled at things because no one could see them.

Certain spots in those fields of prairie grass seemed to vibrate with some unseen remains of ancient life. In some places the rocks and soil that held the grass in place were undisturbed for thousands of years. I knew Indians had lived on the land long before we lived there. I picked up rocks and examined them closely for signs of past life. If a rock seemed special, I held it in my hand, ran my fingers over all the surfaces and edges. I lay its smooth surface against the side of my face, smelled it, sometimes tasted it. They were cool and smooth, smelled of dirt and moisture, and tasted of minerals.

One day, when Bobby was playing at my house, we both wandered into the field in back of the farm looking for arrowheads. We played in the field for most of the morning, picking up rocks, carrying them around for a while, then throwing them down when something more interesting caught our attention.

At first Bobby ran around, talking loud and fast about each rock he found. He said one orange rock was part of a tomahawk. He claimed there was still blood on the rock. Then he kept trying to scare me by yelling that he saw a snake. Finally, I ignored him. Even if he had seen a snake, I wouldn't have believed him.

He picked up a rock with something shining in it and declared it was gold. I was pretty interested in that at first and wanted to see the rock. Bobby laughed and ran away from me saying the gold was his, and he would never tell where he found it. I chased him for a while, but I was pretty sure it wasn't gold, and anyway I didn't want to let Bobby know I was interested. He could keep up a game like that for hours. I sat down in the high grass and caught my breath. Bobby kept calling to me that he had found gold, but I didn't answer him.

It was a different world below the tops of the grass. I put my face next to the dirt. The grass grew out of thick round clumps, like little islands and the tall skinny blades were like little trees. It was cool in the shade of the grass, and the smell of dirt was strong. I could see rocks and dirt clods scattered among the grass islands. Small brown ants roamed around; a sow bug crawled past. I poked the sow bug, and he rolled up in a ball. I threw the ball a few feet. I bet he would wonder what happened when he uncurled and saw he was in a different place. Maybe he would think God moved him. Was there a God for bugs? I guessed it was the same God, but maybe the bugs didn't know that. What if tiny people lived in this place? I wished I could see one. They probably all ran when Bobby and I came into the field. They might be hiding behind the rocks, or even in tiny cellars, like we had for storms. It was quieter close to the ground. The wind sounded far away. Bobby had stopped talking.

Then I heard rustling in the grass. Maybe there really was a snake. I froze trying to hear where the sound was coming from. Suddenly a loud yell broke the silence, and Bobby jumped into the grass beside me. I screamed.

Bobby rolled on the ground and laughed and laughed. My heart was racing; my eyes watered.

"I got ya. Ya looked so funny. Your eyes were big as pumpkins."

I sat quietly. I felt like he had destroyed a whole world. He was smashing down the little palm trees, scraping out holes with his elbows and shoes, and pushing the rocks around. I wished something would bite him. If there were tiny people, I hoped they got away.

"Do ya want to see my gold?"

"No."

"Well, that's good, 'cause I hid it. No one will ever find it."

Bobby was silent for a few moments, probably thinking up his next prank. It seemed that when Bobby was around trouble was not far away. He was the only person near my age who lived close enough to visit. His mother sometimes came over to visit Grandma, and he and I played outside. Grandma didn't let me go to his house. She said they ran around like a bunch of wild Indians over there.

Bobby rose up on his knees and pointed at the ground in front of him.

"Hey, look at this."

I glanced in his direction, but did not move.

"It's one of them cow ants."

I saw a red ant as big as a beetle crawling through the grass. It looked like red velvet.

"They're strange. They don't live in ant hills like other ants."

I had seen ants like this before and they were always alone, sort of wandering around, like they were looking for something.

"They must have an ant family somewhere."

"Nah, they're not like regular ants."

"You don't know. Maybe he is going home to his family right now."

Bobby picked up a rock.

"Maybe he will go to ant heaven right now."

"No!"

Bobby held the rock over the ant. The ant was moving pretty fast.

I said, "Let's follow him."

The ant moved out of sight into the grass.

Bobby said, "Okay. We'll follow him to his home and kill the whole bunch of em."

We crawled along behind the ant. Bobby kept the rock in his hand. The ant seemed to have no clear direction, but weaved back and forth over dirt clumps and rocks, through the tall grass. What if the ant knew we were following him and he was trying to throw us off his trail? After about fifteen minutes of crawling around, we were both tired of the cow ant. I was hoping Bobby wouldn't kill the ant. It was only an ant, but I had begun to think of his ant family. I looked around for something to distract Bobby.

I noticed something orange in the dirt to my right. I crawled over to the color and saw that it was on the surface of a flat rock. I brushed dirt off the rock and more orange color appeared.

I called to Bobby. "Look at this."

He crawled over to me. I had uncovered a flat rock about a foot wide with orange and black marks on it. We stared at it, and, suddenly, I saw it was a picture.

I said, "It looks like a stack of heads."

Bobby stared. He brushed more dirt away and dug around the rock.

"It looks like a totem pole."

I looked again. There were black outlines of faces, painted in with orange and some green. The faces were stacked on top of each other. I had never seen a real totem pole, but I had seen pictures in books.

"It's a picture of a totem pole."

Bobby said, "I bet there is a whole totem pole buried here. We can dig it out."

He continued to dig around the edge of the rock. I found a stick and helped dig. After we dug down about six inches, Bobby tried to move the rock, but it didn't even wiggle. Bobby was deeply engrossed in his latest adventure. He searched around until he found a sharp flat rock to use as a digging tool.

"We gotta dig deeper."

We both dug another six inches. The rock seemed to go straight down. Bobby again tried to move the rock, but it was solid.

Bobby stood up.

"Let's go get shovels."

He started running for the house. I ran along with him.

"Don't tell anyone where this is. We'll get the shovels and dig it up and it will be ours. Well, I'll keep it at my house, but you can come see it anytime."

I didn't like the sound of that. I was the one who found it, and besides Grandma wouldn't let me go to his house.

In a few minutes we were at the barn and were about to go for Grandpa's tools when Bobby's mother came out of the house and called out.

"Come on Bobby. It's time to go home."

Bobby stomped his foot. "No, Ma. I can't go now. I gotta get something first."

"It's time to go home. Your father is expecting us."

Bobby whined. "Ma!"

"Now, Bobby."

Bobby turned to me.

"Don't tell anyone about this. Next time I come over, we'll dig up that totem pole."

I agreed, but I was glad he had to go. I wasn't sure I wanted my totem pole dug up, much less taken to Bobby's house. Bobby and his mother drove off and then Grandma noticed me.

"What in the world have you two been doing? Look at your clothes."

I looked down at my dress and shoes. I was covered in dirt and grass stains. My shoes were full of dirt.

"Grandma, we found an Indian totem pole in the field. It was painted orange and green."

Grandma didn't hear me. "Come in the house and take those clothes off. I'll fix a tub of warm water. You must have been crawling in the dirt. You're probably covered with chiggers and ticks."

I followed Grandma into the house and took off my dirty clothes. The bath water was warm, then she added hot water from the stove and the bath water was hot.

"Grandma, the water is too hot."

Grandma scrubbed me good and washed my hair. I held a towel over my face to keep soap from getting in my eyes while Grandma poured warm rinse water over my hair. Soap got into my eyes anyway.

"Grandma, I have soap in my eyes."

Grandma didn't hear me. She was talking to herself.

"Every time that boy comes over here, there is trouble."

Bobby didn't come back for a long time, and when he did, we couldn't find the totem pole rock again. We walked around and around in the field, but could never find that flat rock with the painting on it again. There were lots of rocks with orange in them. Finally, Bobby got tired of looking, and he declared it was all just my imagination.

RED FLOWERS

One hot summer morning, I woke up sweating, climbed out of bed and walked out on the front porch searching for a breeze. I knew it was going to be what my grandmother called a "scorcher."

Around noon, Grandmother brought out the brown metal fan, set it in a window and plugged it in. It was a stout little fan, with a heavy base and a wire cage around the blades. She switched the black arrow on the base to "on" and the blades made one slow turn, then picked up speed with a soft growl until the blades became a fuzzy circle inside the wire cage. It settled into a low rumble and swung its head back and forth, as if looking around the room. I sat directly in front of it and the sound of the spinning blades changed pitch slightly as the fan moved from side to side. A tunnel of air moved across my sweat-covered skin. The fan trembled for an instant, as if it were straining against the end of an invisible chord, then it whirred back towards me with another cooling stream of air.

I sat in front of that fan, with nothing on my mind except the next puff of air on my skin. The sound and vibrations from the fan created its own atmosphere, like the beginning of a small, lazy wind cloud. I thought of the cotton-ball clouds that sometimes appeared in the hot summer sky. They never amounted to anything. No rain came from them; they appeared and disappeared like cloud-thoughts.

I watched a few flies that had slipped in through a hole in the screen door. Grandmother would be in with the fly swat and punish them properly for sneaking into the house. A fly bumped into a window and buzzed against the glass. He pushed against the glass with a determined buzz for a few seconds, then walked along the edge of the wood pane. I thought about getting the fly swat; he would be easy to kill against the glass. The dead fly would leave a smear of blood, black slime, and pieces of wing on the window. The fly didn't mean any harm. He was just walking along on the giant, see-through road.

Was the glass hot to the fly's feet? Was it hot, like the hard-packed clay between the chicken coop and the house? I had to run fast across that stretch of ground to keep my bare feet from burning. The bottoms of my feet were fairly tough from going barefoot. I could walk on gravel and little stickers didn't hurt, but it hurt when I stepped on thorns from under the locust tree. Once, I stepped on a hornet. That stung like fire. I sat down and examined the bottom of my foot, looking for the thorn, or whatever was in my foot that hurt so. I saw what looked like a tiny thorn with a round end. I grabbed the thing and pulled it out of my foot and saw that it was moving, pulsing. I took it to Grandmother and she told me it was a stinger, probably from a hornet. I asked where the hornet was and she said he was most likely smashed on the ground where I had stepped on him. I went back and looked, but couldn't find him.

Grandmother came in with the fly swat. She went to the window and killed three flies, swap, swap, swap.

"Grandpa better fix that screen door. No tell'in what will come in that hole. It's gett'n big enough to let in a buzzard."

A buzzard! I saw one of those land in a field once. It looked as big as Grandma. Grandma said they ate dead things and they circled over something if it was going to die, I always watched them carefully. I wondered how the buzzards knew. Maybe they could see inside of you, or maybe a person about to die smelled different. I figured if one of them circled over me, I would die soon.

"Come on in the kitchen. We better have a bite to eat."

"I'm not hungry, Grandma."

"The heat's taken your appetite. Just eat a little and drink some water."

I was what Grandmother called a "picky eater." I didn't like meat, mostly because I had seen it alive. I liked most anything sweet, but we didn't often have candy, cake or pie. Sometimes, on a special occasion, Grandma baked a cake. She said it was from "scratch." When a cake was in the oven, Grandma cautioned us not to slam the door because the cake would "fall." That meant after it cooled the middle sunk down. She fussed about it, but I thought it was great because it meant more frosting in the middle.

I followed Grandma into the kitchen. She had made a potted meat sandwich and cut it in four pieces. I ate two of the pieces and drank a few sips of water. She put a little bit of plum jam on some bread for desert.

After lunch we sat on the back porch. In the morning, the front porch had the shade; in the afternoon the back porch had the shade. Grandmother sat with the fly swat in her hand, like a warning to the flies. We sat in green painted metal chairs that bounced a little when we moved. I liked to bounce mine a lot. Sometimes Grandma would tell me to stop bouncing or the chair would break. I think she just got tired of me bouncing.

In the evening, after a very hot summer day, Grandma and I went for a walk. We walked down our dirt driveway and out onto the gravel road that went into town. It was exciting to be on this road because occasionally cars drove past us. It might be a truck with hay stacked in the back or a tractor, or it might be a slow-moving sedan filled with people on their way to town. We could see any cars coming toward us, and if we heard the sound of a car motor behind us, Grandma and I stepped off the dirt road and into the weeds. We stood beside the road until the car passed. Sometimes they waved and Grandma would nod back.

We tried to stay out of the weeds because of ticks and chiggers. Grandma always checked my skin after our walks. Usually there would be a few ticks; the worst ones were called "seed ticks," and they were so small they looked like little freckles. Grandma pulled them off my skin. If they were left on the skin, they could grow big and fat with blood. I had seen large ticks on the dogs that looked like brown speckled marbles. Grandpa pulled them off the dog, then threw them on the ground and squashed them with his boot.

We walked all the way to a place where people dumped their trash. It was a pile of old, broken things: a piece of sofa with the springs and stuffing sticking out, a bed springs twisted and half buried in dirt, rusted cans, papers, and bottles, pieces of chair, a doll's head, part of an old shoe, a burlap bag with a lump of something inside. It was a hill of things lying, twisted and torn, scratched and broken.

Grandma would not let me rummage around in the trash, but I saw a piece of bright blue glass sparkling in the sun and ran to it. Grandma picked up a stick, dug around the blue piece and uncovered a glass bottle. She put it in her apron pocket.

On the way back, we walked across the pasture behind the chicken coop. It was fenced with barbed wire and cattle grazed there, but the land stretched out as far as I could see, and most of the time the cattle were far away in another area of the pasture. We crawled through the fence. Grandma held the wires apart for me to crawl through and I held them for her. We walked along the "cow trail," with Grandmother keeping a sharp eye for snakes.

Hedge trees bordered the pasture where it met the road, and out in the middle of the flat grassland stood one or two trees, alone in the distance, isolated from the other trees. I looked around for cows. I had seen cows up close when they came to the edge of the fence. They were always busy eating. They stood one place a long time and ate the grass all around their feet, then moved a little way and began eating again. Lots of flies sat on the cows and they tried to get the flies off by twitching their skin. I wondered how they were able to make their whole skin wriggle like that. The most I could do was make the skin wrinkle between my eyes. Once in a while, they turned their heads and watched me for a long moment. They had big brown eyes and long lashes and they never stopped chewing.

Cows had horns growing out the sides of their heads. Grandma said the devil had horns. I wondered if the cow horns were like devil horns. Cows had long tails that flipped around like whips to brush off flies. Grandma said the devil had a tail. I imagined the devil with cow horns and cow tail. But the devil had two legs and looked like a man, and he was red, the same color as the fire in hell.

There were cows and bulls. They both looked about the same to me, except bulls were bigger and hated the color red. They hated it so much they charged people wearing red.

The path was smooth and hard under my bare feet. The grass had been worn away where cows traveled the same route over and over. I picked flowers that grew near the trail. I gathered a handful of blue and yellow flowers and looked in the distance for more flowers. I wanted to get a lot of different colors. We walked all the way to the tree and I discovered red flowers. I was busy choosing only the prettiest flowers when Grandma said, "Let's go back now."

I didn't want to go yet and picked another flower. Grandma took my hand. "That's enough now. It's time to get on back." She seemed to be in more of a hurry than usual. Then, I saw in the distance, a group of cows moving in our direction. They looked little, but they were growing bigger.

I walked on the side of Grandma away from the cows. I whispered, "Grandma, are there bulls there?"

"No, that's just some cows. They won't bother us if we don't bother them."

"Grandma, I have red flowers."

"That's nice," she said.

The red flowers were the prettiest. I peeked around Grandma at the approaching cows. One of them might be a bull. We were only halfway back to the fence. What if the bull saw my red flowers and started running after us?

I dropped my flowers on the ground.

I walked fast to keep up with Grandma and neither of us spoke until we reached the fence. Once on the other side of the fence Grandma noticed my flowers were gone.

Grandma said, "Where are your flowers?"

I looked back across the pasture. "The bull was after them."

"Bulls don't like flowers."

"They were red. Bulls don't like red."

Grandma looked at me for a long moment. "Good heavens. You needn't have thrown away the flowers. A bull couldn't see that good, even if there was a bull . . . and I don't think there was a bull."

My chin started to tremble. I had been stupid to throw my flowers away.

"Now, never mind about the flowers; there will be more flowers. Let's go have some Kool-Aid."

Back in the kitchen, Grandma made a pitcher of red Kool-Aid. She washed the blue bottle until it sparkled and set in it the window. It cast a blue shadow on the floor. I carried my glass of Kool-Aid to the window and it cast a red shimmering shadow beside the blue one. I took a sip and wondered if bulls hated red Kool-Aid.

GOD OF THE CLOTHESPINS

On Sundays my grandparents listened to the radio preachers. The voice in the radio always started out calm and gradually built to an emotional, shouting pitch. By the end of the sermon, the rasping voice was frantic, rhythmic, louder and louder. Most of the time I couldn't understand the words, but I understood the sound, foreboding and threatening. The voice wheezed and sputtered and gasped for breath between shouts. Grandpa blew small puffs of smoke from his pipe and stared at the radio. Grandma sat still except for an occasional soft drumming of her fingers on the arm of her chair. The radio preacher broadcast the wrath of God, and yet, my grandparents sat quietly, soberly, barely moving.

I sat on the living room floor tracing paths and trails in the rug, my mind surrounded with images of a vengeful old man sitting on a golden throne in the sky while people burned in a lake of fire.

Our lives were full of thoughts of God and sin and the devil. Grandma told stories of how God could see everything we did, how the devil was always out to trick us and lead us into damnation. She told stories of how spirits communicated after death, of how she or someone she knew was warned of impending disaster or of a loved one in danger. When I said my prayers at night, I imagined God, devil, evil spirits, angels, and thousands of ghosts all floating invisibly in the sky. The prayer always ended with, "If I should die before I wake, I pray the Lord my soul to take."

Grandma sometimes was awakened from her sleep in the middle of the night "knowing" that someone in her family was in trouble. She would be moved by "the Spirit" to get out of bed and pray hard for that person. The night her sister died, Grandma knew to the minute. There was no doubt in my mind that Grandma had magical powers.

Although Grandma had powers, I understood that God was at the top of the power ladder and He could do absolutely anything. It boggled my mind. There was no way out. He could even read my thoughts. I struggled to find some logic behind it all, and often wondered if there was any way out of Hell.

Maybe there was a little tunnel just big enough for me, a path overlooked in all the commotion and fire of hell. Maybe a path like the paths among the circles and swirls in the rug. The rug was a wonderland of color, shades of red and blue outlined with black. Places in the rug were worn so thin I could see the wood floor. I lay my face on the rug and looked out on the landscape of "rug" country.

Grandma's wooden clothespins scattered onto the rug became people. There were two kinds of clothespins: one of solid construction with a round top and the other made of two pieces held together with twisted wire. I separated them into two "tribes," and they immediately began a war. Some of them died on the battlefield. On the rug I marked off a light blue area for heaven a red spot for hell. Some clothespins floated over to heaven, but others were cast into hell. I was God of the clothespins.

OLD, OLD PEOPLE

We did not take many car trips, but one time we went to visit my grandmother's family in Oklahoma. Grandma made lunch to eat on the way. Grandpa got the car ready.

Grandpa checked the oil and water in the car. He checked the spark plugs and the tires. He washed the windshield and checked the windshield wipers. Then, he started the car and let it run for a while to "warm up" the engine. Grandma put in the box of food, towels, and a blanket. Even though it was August, we always had to have a blanket in the car—"for emergencies." Wrapping a blanket around someone had healing power.

We started our trip just after daylight. The early morning air seemed filled with excitement and adventure. I wore one of the new dresses Grandma had made me and the vinyl seat cover was cool against my bare legs. I looked out the window and watched the familiar landscape move past. I turned in the seat and looked out the back window to see the road disappear behind us.

I wondered about the people who lived in the houses beside the road. Sometimes a boy or girl was standing beside the road watching us pass by. We would stare at each other flickering by. I thought: Who are you? Who are you? I wondered how long the trip would take, but I knew better than to ask a lot of questions. I looked down the road in front of the car and wondered how far the road went. Did it ever end?

We drove through little towns, places with just a few buildings clustered near the road. The sun rose higher and it got hot in the car. Grandma rolled her window down a bit and hot dry air blew in on me. After a while, Grandpa stopped the car at little store with two gas pumps in front. A man came out of the store and said to Grandpa, "What can I do for you?" Grandpa got out of the car and started talking to the man. They walked around the car and checked the tires. Grandpa lifted the hood of the car and they both looked at the engine.

Grandma asked me if I had to go to the bathroom. I didn't, but I wanted to get out of the car. She took me to the outdoor toilet in back of the store. I went in the toilet and looked around, stood for a minute, and then came out.

We then went in the little store. I was thirsty and asked for a drink of water. Grandma did an unusual thing and said I could have a soda pop. The soda pops were kept in a large red cooler filled with cold water and ice. The store manager lifted up the lid on the boy and asked me which flavor I wanted. I looked in at the bottles. There was red, orange, clear and brown. I started to ask for red and then I noticed the little purple bottle. I pointed to that one and the man pulled the bottled out of the ice water. It was called a "grapette" and it was smaller than the other bottles. It was such a pretty color and it seemed child size. The man opened the bottle using a bottle opener on the side of the cooler and handed the drink to me.

I took a swallow and it was wonderful—cold, sweet and fruity. It smelled like grapes. I took the soda pop to the car with me. The man was putting gas in the car. The gasoline flowed out of a glass bottle set on top of round cast-iron stands. The stands were red and the gasoline was clear red and bubbled as it flowed out. It looked like strawberry soda pop. The man washed the windshield. Grandpa got in the car, adjusted the mirror and slowly pulled out on the main road.

I finished the grapeette, hating to drink the last drop. I examined the bottle for a while, then looked through the bottle at the fields and houses. The curved glass made everything distorted and wavy. The movement of the car and the wavy glass made me feel a little sick. It was getting hotter in the car. Then I felt a lot sick. Then, I threw up.

Grandma turned around as soon as she heard me. Quickly, she grabbed one of the towels and began to clean me up. "Good Heavens. I shouldn't have let you have that sweet drink in this heat."

Now, the car was hot, my sweaty legs stuck to the vinyl seat cover and the air smelled like vomit. I concentrated on not throwing up again. Grandma wet a cloth with water from a jug of water in the front and handed it to me. I kept the wet cloth pressed to my mouth and nose. How far away did we have to go? I wished we were home. I leaned my head against the window and looked at the dotted line on the asphalt road until the lines blurred. I fell asleep.

The sound of gravel beneath the tires woke me up. I looked out the window and saw a different place. The trees grew close together, like weeds. Mailboxes stood beside dirt roads that were visible for a short distance before being swallowed up by the trees. Shadows covered the road, making it darker but not cooler. The air was heavy.

Grandma pointed to a mailbox and said, "That's their mailbox." Grandpa turned the car onto a narrow dirt road with grass growing between the tire ruts. The road curved sharply and tree branches hung over the road. I wondered what kind of animals lived in the woods.

In a few minutes the car pulled into a clearing and before us sat an old wood house with a porch all along the front. The wood was weathered with little patches of paint here and there. The front porch sagged and the porch posts leaned. Steps to the porch were made of orange and red rocks. Some rocks had fallen out and lay on the ground.

Several dogs ran up as our car approached. When Grandpa got out, the dogs surrounded him, all barking and baying. Presently, an old man came out on the porch. He hollered at the dogs, then at us. "Come on in."

By the time we reached the porch an old woman came out to join the old man. I had never in my life seen such old, old people. The man wore loose-fitting overalls and he was barefoot. He had thick white hair that stood up off his forehead and looked electrified. His eyes were light blue and sunk back in his face, his mouth caved in and when he smiled there were no teeth. The old woman had long gray hair wound in a bun on the back of her neck. She was wearing a faded floral print dress, shapeless and hanging nearly to her ankles. She had on shoes, but no socks. "Come in and sit down a spell. You must be tired. Are you hungry?" She looked at the old man. "For crying out loud, Dad, put some shoes on."

The inside of the house was faded and smelled like old clothes, old bodies, pipe smoke, and burnt oatmeal. It was not tidy like my grandparent's house. Shoes lay on the floor, a blanket lay in a pile on the sofa. Every table and shelf was stacked with objects: bottles, figurines, photographs, pipes, screw drivers, pieces of machinery, bolts, springs. "Excuse the place," the old woman said. "My back has been out and I haven't been able to keep a clean house." Grandma said, "It looks just fine. Don't bother about it." I looked at Grandma. What did she mean, it looked just fine? Her face was set in her "company smile," and her eyes warned me not to say anything about the house.

My grandparents sat down. Grandma leaned back, but her fingers tapped lightly on the arm of her chair and from time to time she pulled and patted her hair net. I sat quietly in a chair near Grandma and looked at the many strange objects in the room, then out the screen door at the dogs lying on the porch.

The old woman said, "So this is your granddaughter."

Grandma nodded. "Yes, this is Ellen."

The old woman looked at me closely. "She doesn't look Indian."

Grandma stopped her fingers in mid tap. "Well, her father is only one quarter. So, Ellen is only one eighth."

I wondered which part of me was Indian. Probably my hair. It was dark and long. Grandma braided it each morning. I wished my hair were yellow like Mother's. My dream of blond hair was interrupted when two cars drove up to the house. Three women and a whole bunch of kids piled out of the cars. The kids ran up to the porch. The women followed, carrying large bowls of food.

Grandma stood up to greet the visitors. The women looked like Grandma. One of them ran to Grandma and hugged her.

"Sister, I'm just so glad to see you. It's been too long."

Grandma stepped back and looked at the woman. "You look tired, Violet. You've been working too hard."

The other women took the food to the kitchen. The children stood in the living room and stared at me. I thought: Who are you? Who are you?

Violet said, "This is Ellen. She's Aunt Maud's daughter's girl." She laughed. "Sort of a cousin."

All of the kids were older than me. One of the girls said, "You wanna play?" I nodded my head. They all started for the door. "Well, come on," the girl said. I looked at Grandma. "Go ahead and play," she said.

The oldest girl was Sandra. I never did get the names of all the children. I tagged along with Sandra and tried to figure out what game we were playing. Sometimes it was hide and seek, sometimes, "house," or jacks, or "red rover." We climbed trees and pretended to be at sea, the wind moving the tree limbs like waves tossing a boat. We picked wild flowers until someone saw a bull in the pasture and everyone screamed and ran. We ran, climbed, tumbled and laughed until dark. We stopped only when the women called us to eat. The grownups filled their plates first; then we kids put food on our plates and took them outside and sat on the porch to eat, giving the dogs our leftovers.

After dark, the adults were still visiting and we caught lightning bugs and put them in jars. Some of the kids smeared the florescent bug bodies on their fingers and it looked like they wore glowing rings. In the dark, only the glowing spots could be seen from a distance. When the kids ran, they made light swirls and streaks.

Finally, we were all put to bed on quilts on the floors. The floor was covered with kids. Gradually, everyone stopped talking, and the house was full of sleeping sounds, adults snoring in the other room, children making sounds like a pile of puppies. I could see out the screen door and there were still lots and lots of lightening bugs. Above the dark outline of trees, the sky was full of stars. The stars and lightening bugs looked the same, as if the stars came near the ground and were floating and twinkling. I could hear katydids buzzing and the dogs howled every once in a while. I wanted to stay awake forever.

GRANDMOTHER'S BIRTHDAY from novel *THE DESCENDENT* by Henrietta Moore

It was nearly 10:00 P.M. when they arrived at Pala reservation. John turned left at the mission and tried to remember where the Cord had overheated and Waneeta had appeared. She had pointed down the road saying her house was nearby.

There was no moonlight. Beyond the perimeter of the headlight beams everything was dark and flat. He was tired and kept blinking his eyes to clear his blurred vision. After a few miles, he felt sure he had gone past the turnoff to Waneeta's. He stopped the car and turned off the lights.

Neither of them said a word. They both sat staring into the blackness. John was desperately trying to collect the pieces of his memory and decipher where he was and what to do next. Gradually, he became aware of an unusual sound. Apart from the rustling leaves and night insects, he could hear the rhythmic sound of human voices—singing voices. He peered into the darkness to his right where the singing seemed to come from. As his eyes became more accustomed to the dark he could see a small fire through the trees. He guessed about a half mile away. Then he noticed a narrow dirt road going that direction.

He started the car and turned down the dirt road. In a few minutes they came into a clearing. The headlights shown onto the faces of a group of Indian men at the edge of a campfire. The singing stopped. Several men started toward the car. John could see behind the men a large group of Indian people—men, women and children. On each side of the fire a row of five or six Indian men kneeled on the ground with a blanket laying across their knees. For a second he glimpsed a man standing at the head of the fire between the two rows holding a bundle of strings with something attached to the ends.

Halfway to the car one of the Indian men shouted. "Turn those lights off."

John turned off the car lights, but kept the engine running.

When the men reached the car one of them looked into the car. "What are you doing here? This is reservation land."

One of the men in back of the group came forward. "I saw this car before." He looked in at John. "I remember you. Your car was broke." He looked over at Lilly. "Same car—different woman." He laughed.

John's heart was beating so hard he could hardly talk. "I'm looking for Waneeta." He was greeted with stony silence. "She invited me out to her house. I thought this was the road."

A large man with an unfriendly expression said. "Waneeta's not here. You better be on your way."

Lilly spoke up. "Please, my son is with Waneeta. Teresa brought him to her."

The man seemed to soften a little.

Lilly continued, "I know it's late, but we must find Waneeta quickly. My son may be in danger."

The man who recognized John said. "Hey, Leon, come here a minute. Let's talk."

All the men stepped back from the car. They stood in a group and spoke in low tones. The glow of cigarettes moved in the air and they discussed what should be done. John noticed the rest of the people were still standing near the fire silently watching to see the outcome of this disruption of their gathering.

In a few minutes, the men moved back to the car. Leon said. "Waneeta is not here, but we will tell her about you."

John stammered. "When will you tell her? Can you tell her tonight?"

"No, not tonight. She is not close."

"But we have no place to go. It's miles back to a place to stay for the night. Isn't there something . . ."

John was interrupted by a young man who pushed his way between John and Leon. "Leon, Grandmother wants to see them."

"These people? She wants to see these people?"

"Yes, and she said to remind you it is her birthday."

Leon stood as if unable to force himself to move for a moment, then he motioned to John. "Turn your car off. Come with us. Both of you."

John hesitated and wondered for a second if he should gun the engine and escape from whatever fate awaited them.

Leon said. "Don't worry. It's Grandmother's birthday party and she wants to see the unexpected guests."

John looked at Lilly. Lilly said, "Let's go."

"Okay," John sighed. He shut off the car engine and they both followed Leon and the other men to the fire.

Many sets of dark eyes watched them with curiosity. When they reached the fire and the rest of the group, John saw a very old woman sitting on a chair. The old woman was small with deeply wrinkled skin, white hair and black eyes. Her eyes sparkled from the firelight; but John had the impression they sparkled in any light. She wore a brightly colored shawl around her shoulders. Several women were sitting around her, some with small children asleep in their laps.

John and Lilly stood before the old woman. Lilly said, "Happy birthday. My name is Lilly and this is John. Forgive us for interrupting your party."

Grandmother smiled. "Maybe you knew it was my birthday."

Lilly looked at John and a thought seem to come to her. She smiled at Grandmother.

"Maybe we did." She reached into her purse and pulled out a small silver pocket watch with red jewels on the back. "For your birthday."

Grandmother laughed. "Bring food for John and Lilly. Go on with the games."

Leon said. "But Grandmother, is it right?"

Grandmother looked seriously at Leon. "Yes, Leon, it is right." She laughed. "And, it is my birthday."

Beans and rice with a piece of fried bread were brought to John and Lilly along with glasses of water. They sat on the blanketed ground with the plates on their knees. No eating utensils were brought, so they scooped the beans up with the fried bread. Later, they each were brought a piece of birthday cake.

Immediately the "games" resumed. Two rows of men on each side of the fire faced each other. Each side had a blanket covering their hands. The man at the head of the fire seemed to be a score keeper. This man handed to one of the teams of men a bunch of strings with small black and white objects, like bones, attached. These men held the blanket in their teeth so they could move the black and white objects from person to person unseen by the row of men on the other side of the fire. As the men worked under the blanket, they and the group of people behind them sang. The songs were repetitive and the volume rose and fell. After a while the men uttered a series of grunts that signaled they had stopped shifting the objects from person to person. The other side called out numbers and colors pointing to each person. The score keeper then took the black and white objects from each man's hands under the blanket. It seemed to be a guessing game and after a while it was obvious that it was also a gambling game. As the games went on the players would laugh and tease back and forth.

John got the impression the songs were meant not only to encourage their own team but to intimidate the opposing team. As the games continued, the voices increased in pitch and volume and made his heart beat faster. The sounds were ancient and hypnotic, yet at times full of tension and excitement.

The games went on for hours. John and Lilly fell asleep on the blankets with firelight flickering on their faces and songs in the air. From time to time John would awaken and notice Grandmother still watching the games; her eyes bright.

8

Indigenous Communities, Spiritualities, and New Age Commercialism

Gabriel S. Estrada, Indiana Rogers, and Rob Blair

Nahuatl (Aztec) women's actions and bodies have kept Indigenous vision alive through difficult times. Ines Hernandez-Avila, a Nimipu-Chicana author, finds she can best understand her relationship to earth and her own role as a Indian activist through Aztec Dance. In "An Open Letter to Chicanas: On the Power and Politics of Origin," Ines proclaims:

> Within the dance tradition of the Concheros of "la Gran Tenochtitlan," la Malinche is a path-opener, an abrecaminos, who cleanses and blesses the path with the smoke of the incense in her sahumador . . . my role as a Malinche within a ceremonial context has helped me to understand how I am a Malinche in a social and intellectual context. We should consider the possibility that each Mexicana/Chicana could become a Malinche in the sense of being a path-opener, a guide, a voice, a warrior woman, willing to go to the front to combat the injustices that our people suffer. In this way our indigenous mother will be revindicated as well" (244–245).

In Hernandez-Avila's words, community action is the key to healing the devastation of colonization. To affirm justice for "people" as a group is the goal of her spiritual path.

Perhaps the greatest contrast to the Indigenous communal focus of spirituality is the individual empowerment focus of non-Indigenous New Age spiritualist who claim "shaman" or "Medicine Person" status independent of any traditional Indigenous community upon which their medicine is supposedly based. Without a link to Native American communities, New Agers often try to lift fragments of Indigenous medicines in order to personally evolve. From many Indigenous perspectives, the pursuit of individual power at the expense of group welfare is antithetical to spirituality. Indigenous healers are usually bound to serve Indigenous communities. In contrast, individual empowerment is a catch phrase in American popular culture and the New Age movement. At worst, the all-powerful individual becomes a reflection of the Great Chain of Being philosophies of Western tradition in which a small elite claim the spiritual right to dominate the masses because of the presumed spiritual superiority of that elite group. In this system, the Truths of individuals such as the The Pope, The King, the Father, or, eventually, The Scientist, are held up as laws that all others are forced to follow or at least integrate into their way of being. Sometimes, individual spiritual empowerment does little more than move one up in the hierarchy at the expense of others, the result being narcissistic self-glorification of half truths.

The irony of the current Western focus on individual empowerment is that White people come from tribes which often had a more community and relationship oriented cosmology. In *The Death of Nature: Women, Ecology, and the Scientific Revolution,* Carolyn Merchant documents the rise of Eurocentric wars, patriarchy, colonialism, and technology throughout the last millennium which formed a hierarchy in which Nature increasingly became linked with femininity and powerlessness. In effect, she demonstrates that violence against tribal peoples in the Americas is a continuation of the genocide of tribal cultures in Europe at the hands of Christianity and Western patriarchal empires. She affirms, "Historically, holistic presuppositions about nature have been assumed by communities of people who have succeeded in living in equilibrium with their environments. The idea of cyclical processes, of the interconnectedness of all things, and the assumption that nature is active and alive are fundamental to the history of human thought. No element from an interlocking cycle can be removed without the collapse of the whole" (293). For example, one interpretation of the Celtic Knot is just that, the sacredness of an interconnected universe. While many ancient Indigenous ideas of the world's continents involve respect for the elements of wind, fire, air, earth; metal or spirit, differences in language, geography, and customs create important differences among various groups.

As tribal Europeans, Africans, or Asians became colonized to various degrees, many were forced from their ancestral lands to carry on their legacy of colonization in the Americas, often under the guise of Christianity. The Christian religion's genocidal attempts to destroy Indigenous peoples and beliefs are still met with resistance by traditional Indigenous peoples, non-Christians, and many reformed Christians themselves. For example, Leslie Marmon Silko's "Storyteller" recounts an evil, genderless, nationless witch who curses "white" people with a self-fulfilling prophesy:

Then they grow away from the earth
then they grow away from the sun
then they grow away from the plants and animals.
They see no life

> When they look
> they see only objects.
> The world is a dead thing for them. (73)

Here, progress, objectivity, religions of the "heavens" and colonization are an evil curse. The myth that European peoples bring morally objective religion, science and culture as justification of colonization of the Americas is grotesquely discounted as mere witchery. Again, the source of this curse is unknown and not attributed to the White race itself; at times Silko hints that this curse originates from Native American witches on a self-destructive mission. Whatever the origin, the sickness is clear: to lack relationships is a self-destructive path that can endanger all life. Ecological crisis, colonial wars, and genocide are but manifestations of people who are ungrounded in the spirit of the earth and living without communities that extend beyond the boundaries of human kind and individual egos.

If Silko offers a Pueblo critique of white spirituality, then Luci Tapahonso shares its complement, a blessing for new life into a thriving community and cosmos of the Navajo. Luci Tapahonso's "Blue Horses Rush In" gives a taste of women's power to give birth in a context of Navajo cosmology. Chamisa Bah Edmo receives the dedication and it is Chamisa's mother who "clenched her fists and gasped./ She moans with ageless pain and pushes: This is it!" In using the modifier "ageless," Tapahonso allows the reader to recognize the vast history Navajo women that stretches all the way to creation itself and the first woman to give birth. Her power of creation impacts the husband who is praying for both the mother and the child and leaves him "stunned" (438). While the mother is physically active, the husband is physically immobile. After the baby Chamisa "slips out," horses from the four directions of a Navajo cosmos enter the room announced from afar by the "thundering of hooves on the desert floor" (438). The act of birth and the four directions structures the poem's stanzas. The first stanza feature pre-birth, the second, the birth process, and the third, the completion of birth. For each color of horses, a new stanza begins. In this birthing situation "white horses" arrive first "from the west". Their whiteness has an affinity to the moonlight that glows on the golden chamisa that will share the child's name. Next, "Yellow horses arrive from the east" bringing a scent of prairie grass (439). As "Blue horses rush in" from the south, another element of history becomes evident as Tapahonso describes "It is possible to see across the entire valley to Niist'áá from Tó,/ Bah, from here your grandmothers went to war long ago" (439). The fact that "grandmothers" went to war shows that women have an important role in protecting their families, and a long history of doing so. Finally, "Black horses . . . from the north" arrive to complete the fourth direction and color and strike the balance of which the Navajo cosmos is made. The fact that all four colored horses from all four directions arrives seems to indicate that Chamisa has a good spiritual foundation as a female.

The speaker is more than witness, she is a spiritual part of Tapahonso who will look after the child as a female role model and make sure the child knows her rich Navajo history. The speaker wishes Chamisa growth saying ". . . we will celebrate each change you live" (439). And she promises strength in Chamisa's future with the conclusion "You will grow strong like the horses of your past./ You will grow strong like the horses of your birth," again emphasizing the ancient Navajo path for women that involves the four directions, sacred mountains, seasons, ages, and colors. While Chamisa's mother physically embodies perhaps the ultimate creative act of giving birth, she is not alone. The speaker is also actively participating and aiding that creation with a prayer and vision for Chamisa, whose birth is very much community and woman oriented in Tapahonso's poem. In the anthology, the poem is prefaced with a reference to another one of Tapahonso's poems, "1864," that "tells of the notorious Long Walk that the Navajo people endured and survived at the hands of the United States troops" (438). So it is in the context of the forced march, loss of lands, and high death toll that Chamisa is born, again reference in grandmothers who "went to war" (439). While the US expected Navajos to pass away or give up their ancestral homeland, Chamisa's birth symbolizes the hope for the continued survival and flourishing of Navajos on their traditional lands. Chamisa will "grow strong" spiritually despite the historical threats to her nation, a positive message both to Navajos as well as the general US public who may have assumed that Navajos were passing away without their traditions, language, and beliefs.

While many Native American writers share their spirituality in writing to a general public, part of the danger of presenting venerable beliefs of the female creative spirit in Western influenced writing is that readers might take the writing to be a summation of all that the spirit is. Readers unfamiliar with Navajo customs may not be aware of the strict ceremonial cycles that Navajo women must endure in order to birth or be a part of a birth. As always, written language is but an approximation of the oral tradition and living ceremonies that are the foundation for the complex reality of any peoples. Another danger might be that non-Navajos might try to claim those ways as their own, an action that would probably hurt the "borrowers" more than anyone else. And finally, some traditionalist will always feel strongly that sacred aspects of culture should not be written. But, again, given the context of Western education and the Navajo need to see culture reflected in books, Tapahonso seems justified in her artistic choices in representing her own creative tradition of Navajo women spiritually linked with community and sacred geography.

As I have considered the spiritual voices of Nahuatl, Pueblo, and Navajo peoples as expressed by members of those groups, I thought it only fair to provide the same courtesy to Euro-American writers in relation to New Age commercialism of Native American beliefs. Indiana Rogers and Rob Blair are two of my AIS 100 students who are also a couple. Future editions of this book may feature the works of other students as well. I asked Indiana and Rob to submit their paper to this text not only because they are articulate and critical writers, but also because I believe that those who make intellectual and spiritual discourse an important part of a relationship are interesting models for others. Together, both have made substantial critiques of New Age beliefs based upon their own cultural and spiritual expectations.

IN SEARCH OF NATIVE TRUTHS IN A WORLD OF FIFTEEN MINUTE SHAMANS

Indiana Rogers and Rob Blair

Throughout history religious organizations, and/or religious people, have in some form or another often sought monetary gain by peddling merchandise, metaphysical absolutions, and enlightenment. For example, during the Dark Ages, priests and other religious persons would sell penance to patrons of the church, basically selling redemption to people who felt that they had sinned against God and wanted to purchase their salvation and forgiveness. With the modern-day phenomenon of the internet, this trend has only increased in frequency and absurdity. Within the context of cosmology, cultural tradition, and spiritual learning or knowledge, there exists an obvious division between those groups that practice legitimate and original methods and those groups that take many liberties with original methods in order to sell a certain concept to make a profit. The term "shaman" has almost become a clichéd notion that practically anyone who maintains limited understanding of native practices can easily claim as a description of self, and they can thereby offer this "miracle" to everyone else at a fantastic price. In reality, shamans don't provide their services over the internet, nor do they consider it a business that allows for fiscal benefits. Are human beings so desperate for guidance that they fail to be discriminating in their search for understanding? Or do they simply not know any better so they take the easiest route? I discovered three different web pages on the internet that reflect these conflicting views; two of which suggests that the visitor to the site prepare their checkbook for greatness, and the other suggests that the visitor read further and learn about a culture in order to appreciate and experience its practices.

The first, and most suspect, web page I found was for the "Native Pathways Church" that seems to imply that all you need is a church member packet that can teach anyone to be a shaman. The future member will be able to advance through "ten levels of shamanship" while participating in "tribal ceremonies and community developments" although the type or origin of the tribe is never specified. This site also insists that the members, in order to find happiness, provide funds for an actual church to be built for their "ceremonies" to guarantee that everyone have the "proper" opportunity to become a shaman. There is also a pastor, named Jane Fowler, and the church member packets include a vaguely labeled "tenets of faith" section, and all of these elements sound largely Christian based and not "native" or "tribal" based at all. A "Shaman Support Group" is also an added benefit of the members who join the church, and although the final portion of the site boasts "You Are Not Alone" it continues to explain that all members are responsible for their own "copying, mailing costs, black vest purchasing/making, book acquisition, drum purchasing/making, medicine bundle creation, and integrity."

Although this site does not mention UFOs or charge expensive hotline prices, I found it to be offensive and outrageous because it attempts to create the guise of authenticity but does not offer any actual information as to what tribe their methods are based on, what their overall purpose is beyond helping everyone to become a shaman. The site neither explains why shamanism is significant, nor does it provide any history on the subject. The only goal they mention is "happiness" and the only two books you need for reference are books by a white man named Ken Wilber, one of them being a book entitled "A Brief History of Everything." This seems like another way in which to profit from the vulnerability of "lost souls" without offering any original teachings whatsoever.

The second website features Rowland Anton Barkley, the self-proclaimed "deep *trance*forming shaman." Barkley's website neither offers clues to his lineage nor does it state any of his degrees or qualifications for shamanism. The site does, however, heavily emphasize the fact that Barkley offers workshops on a slue of pedantic metaphysical treatments such as "soul retrieval counseling workshops, holographic healing, dynamic natural activation counseling, and 6-day shamanic workshops," the last class being an instructional course on how to become a shaman. Barkley's website brandishes many pedantic new-age phrases but does not once stop to clarify what these treatments or terms mean, offering no definitions to his spiritual procedures. For example, here is a passage from Barkley's web page section concerning the *Eight Keys to Your Holographic Healing:* "People habitually leave soulparts back in old traumatic incidents, swap them as co-dependent "love", or just not even fully incarnate in the first place. What would happen if all that you are as a Divine Spirit were to fully incarnate, integrate, and create here, now? With Soul Retrieval and Holographic Timeline Clearing attain presence in the present!" This overly esoteric passage is vague and tells the reader next to nothing about the spiritual cleansing Barkley is selling. Barkley offers no explanation of his metaphysical theory or theological credo; he is purposefully vague in order to sell his product, his seminars, to the person browsing his website.

The contrasting website that I found was one for the Native American Church. The leader, a man by the name of Little Crow, offers meetings, for those who would like to attend, at a casino gathering room and does not charge money for this community experience. It is stated that "all are welcome," but nowhere is it stated that all will become shamans and find inner happiness. Little Crow provides a detailed history of his heritage as a Sioux descendant on the website, and recommends a book to his visitors entitled "The Sacred World Within, a Dakota/Lakota World View." Little Crow's philosophy and theological standpoint leans close to that of pantheism and his primary message is that everything is a part of God and that everything in the world is interconnected. He also offers gatherings based on oral traditions, and the "Declaration" of the church is stated as having the purpose of "preservation of an all-inclusive Oral Tradition anchored in the concept of 'the sacredness of all things of Creation.'" Items such as the recommended books can be purchased on the website, but nowhere on the website does it insist that you need these books in order to find enlightenment—you are only encouraged to attend the seminars at your own pace. This website seemed most authentic, especially compared to the other website that offered inner peace if you pay for a church in which to find this inner peace. An actual native descendant teaching the oral traditions of his people seems more trustworthy than a white person teaching unspecified "tribal methods" to fifty people who expect to leave as shamans.

There are obviously various approaches to spirituality and modes of spiritual thought, but your own enlightenment should not come at a material price. If one finds it necessary to seek happiness, then why would shamanism or any other type of spiritual leadership operating as pop-psychology among Euro-Americans be the answer? If I wanted to learn more about native rituals, lifestyles, or methods, I would want to consult someone who belongs to a specific culture, not someone who has read a brief history of all cultures and therefore assumes they know the way. There may or may not be a right or wrong strategy for finding enlightenment or spiritual growth/information, but it seems that some ways might provide better assistance in your search—and most likely these ways do not include those that cost money, involve white missionaries that want to convert hundreds by the minute, UFOs, or any unnecessary materials. In the current era of widespread internet accessibility, the individual needs to take it upon themselves to separate the earnest from the flamboyant, the authentic from the salesman. To find roots, you should seek and return to roots, not seek someone who, for a price, will tell you what those roots once represented.

PERSONAL PERSPECTIVES ON NAHUATL SPIRITUALITY, DANCE, AND ORAL TRADITIONS Gabriel S. Estrada

Dance is an important way that we learn who we are as Nahuatl peoples. My sense of who I am as Nahuatl through my family's oral tradition resonates with traditions I learned from Aztec Dance teachers from Tlacopan, Mexico City. Because I grew up on the Washington Idaho border near the Coure D'elaine reservation, I experienced my Nahuatl culture in a way that would have differed from growing up in our ancient settlements in central Mexico. In the San Francisco group Teokalli, the Aztec dances of the Old Old Coyote and the White Eagle reflected the stories I had heard as a child from my father. The "50,0000–100,000" Aztec dancers in the U.S. and Mexico are a reflection of the "1,319,848" fluent speakers of Nahuatl and the large portion of tens of millions of Mexican Indians who maintain aspects of their Chichimec-Nahuatl roots (Tezozomoc 69). Since the 1970's Aztec Dance is increasingly popular in Mexico and the US, after suffering centuries of repression under the Catholic Church.

The general timing of this cultural regeneration is long predicted by Cuauhtemoc in a Nahuatl language of mathematics and poetry. Through oral tradition, the words of the Nahuatl speaker and leader, Cuauhtemoc, predict a sunrise of regeneration for Nahuatl and Indigenous cultures after the long night of colonization. As the last leader of the early central Nahuatl confederacy resistance to Spanish colonization in 1521, Cuauhtemoc draws upon a cyclical notion of Nahuatl time and space to prophesize that Nahuatl peoples would eventually rebuild what they would lose in the short term. I provide an English translation of the Nahuatl/Spanish version of the beginning of Cuauhtemoc's last message that has been retold throughout centuries by Nahuatl peoples.

Totonaltzin ya omotlatihtzinoh/ Our sacred collective energy does well to hide itself.
Totonaltzin ya omixpolihuitih/ Our sun now does well to disappear from the eye.
Ihuan zentlayohuayan otechmocahuilih/ In this manner, in the a time of total darkness,
    it does well to hide itself.
Mach tictomachitiah oczeppa hualmohuicaz/ with certainty it dignifies us to know
    that in another time it will find it well to come again

Ma oczeppa hualmoquixtiz/ that another time it will come to us

Ihuan yancuican techmotlahuiliquiuh/ and again come to enlighten us . . .

Axcan tehuantzitzin tiquintotequimaquiliah in topiltzitizinhuan/ today, it dignifies us to give the responsibility to our beloved children

Ca totlahcuiloliztzin ihuan totlamatiliztzin ma pixquilli/ take care of our venerable writing and sow our illustrious cosmovision

Ipanpa nemilioliztli in totlazohtlalnantzin Anahuac/ for cause of the permanence of our collective of our Beloved Mother Earth, Water Surrounded Land!

Yei Kalli Makuiltochtli/ 12 of August, 1521

Mexico-Tenochtitlan

Kuauktemotzin/Cuauhtemoc

(Stivalet Corral 40–42, 2001)

Cuauhtemoc is known for being an eagle warrior in the style of a direct attack, but he is also less commonly known as a jaguar warrior who fights from subconscious, nocturnal, and interior level that tekpatl, the obsidian knife, represents. In his last message, he says that the overt battle is over and that the battle must now become more subtle and interior. He does not say to give up as he tells Nahuatl people to pass on traditions to the youth in secret until the dark period of colonization is over. It is such a Nahuatl oral tradition that my father told to me, as his father told to him, as his grandfather told to him, and his grandfather told to him, etc. In a sense, Cuauhtémoc proposes a training of warriors that is also part of the Nahuatl tradition, that of the jaguar and the night. As he uses the sun and its disappearance and reappearance, he sets in motion the idea that periods of eagle and jaguar warriors will always follow one another. Spanish colonization is the night of training for jaguars. It is difficult, but cannot be avoided or rejected, just as one cannot avoid the night itself, the lessons that force us to evolve. Drawing upon central Nahuatl elders, Stivalet explains that days and nights do not just refer to single days and nights, but rather to bundles of years that alternate with solar and lunar qualities in a ratio of 13:9, the night being the shorter of the two. Each bundle consists of 52 years. 9x52 = 468 years which, when added to the date of 1521 equals 1989, a time in which decolonization for Indigenous people was beginning to ferment as the date for 500 years of Indigenous and Popular Resistance in 1992 came closer. According to Stivalet, people have the opportunity to transform back into solar beings within the 676 years of day that will transform and balance the old darkness of the jaguar. Stivalet explains Cuauhtémoc's words to show that Native Americans will be able to use their experience and memory to recreate cultures and societies with greater ease in the first part of this millennium than was possible in the last half of the last millennium. Again, the idea is cyclical like the relative movements of the earth and sun. Like the seasons, the darkness that colonization represents will never go away, although there are times when it will recede like a tide leaving its pockets of water behind so that people can have balance and memory. It is only when humans can comprehend the full violence and misunderstandings of the past that they can have the insight and courage to change old patterns that have become extreme to a destructive degree.

Internal balance must occur in order to circulate to outside relationships, just as a heart must internally pump out blood in order for it to return to be renewed. The night of internal activity balances the day of outside activity. To further explain the Nahuatl concept of duality, I translate the words Hue Teopixki, a Nahuatl elder, healer, and speaker of central Nahuatl people: "Our cosmic medicine . . . bases itself in . . . a dual opposition of opposites . . . anger and peace; cold and heat; sky and earth; above and below; man and woman; strength and weakness; light and darkness; rain and drought are, at the same time, attractive and repulsive couples, related . . . in an alternating sequence of power" (Hue Teopixque qtd. in Vío 107). He continues to explain that it is only recently, with the theories of relativity and energy, that Western sciences can even begin to understand cosmic dualisms and relativities that Nahuatl peoples have understood for thousands of years (152). Duality is the representation of two, ome, and creative energy, teotl, together known as "Ometeotl," in Nahuatl, a concept that Anzaldua (1987) integrates throughout her writings about mediations of internal complements of male and female.

Cuauhtemoc's cyclical sense of Ometeotl is evident in the circular path in which knowledge, language, and stories are passed from one generation to the next, from old to young in a cosmic regeneration. The need for Nahuatl youth to learn about Indigenous culture and language is a kind of message that, until recently, many academics did not realize or report. Even after a colonial period of Spanish Inquisition and colonization, Mexican Independence, and Revolution, the formulators of Mexican education and history continued to establish texts that viewed Nahuatl and other Indians as backwards and contrary to the religious, linguistic, social, and racial "progress" of the Mestizo or Mexican nation. In a Post-Revolutionary Mexico of 1925, José Vasconcelos posits in *La Raza Cosmica* that a Euro-centric Mestizo culture is racially superior to that of the Indigenous cultures of Mexico, writing ". . . the mixture of very distant types, as in the case of Spaniards and American Indians, has questionable results . . . even the most contradictory racial mixtures can have beneficial results, as long as the spiritual factor contributes to raise them . . . A religion such as Christianity made the American Indians advance, in a few centuries, from cannibalism to a relative degree of civilization" (5). In subsequent years, his theories were critiqued for their obvious "anti-Indianism" which predicated that Indians must permanently forfeit their culture to "survive the advance of progress" rooted in old Christian intolerance (Socoto qtd. in Vasconcelos 1979), a clear contrast to a return to Nahuatl culture that Cuauhtemoc speaks of and is repeated through generations of oral tradition in Stivalet's analysis. Even key words of Cuauhtemoc's speech tell all. When he says, "Totlazohtlalnantzin Tlalli" he is saying that we must live to see our understanding of "Our Beloved Mother Earth" revive yet once again. In the Nahuatl language, the sense of hope is very strong and repeated with every generation, just as an ancient tree flowers each spring. In Nahuatl language, flower is xochitl, which also symbolically represents a poetry. As Nahuatl culture flowers, poetry is abundant. So I end with poetry, a more traditional form of expression that I use to reflect on sacred spaces.

Xuchipillán

Being in Xuchipillán,
my grandfather's pueblo,
is like being under clear water.

I don't mean to say that it is humid,
even though summer monsoons turn the air
into a thick soup of mesquite.

I mean to say
that the time is different
like a pulsing ocean
that pulls you in and out and under
with a rhythm of a strange womb.

The highway from Guadalajara burns blackly
through the cornfields and guava groves
in which buses, VCR's, and watches all function
with their usual ticks and bangs.
Even as I leave on that highway south,
I see the earth drop into an unexpected canyon
where a leaf twists and falls forever
into the white rush of river below.
Small orange flowers, cempoaxuchitl, line the roadside.
And so my name envelops me.
I am Caxcán from Xuchipillán,
the Flower Child's Land.

Time is liquid there
like braids of twisting currents
in the river Xuchipillán.
There is
five-color corn time,
crow-flower time,
red sun time,
black mountain time,
and even VCR clock time
all braided and writhing
like a river woven of hissing snakes.

Ella

You sit still like a mountain
above the waves of desert heat.
Clouds clean your heavy face and neck
like damp grey hankerchiefs.
Your feet are hard
like sleeping boulders.
You do not let go of the earth.

We talk in my car on the way to Nogales
lined with yellow palo verde blooms.
You ask to put in a cassette of strumming Conchero music.
"This is from my friends in Xochimilco," you explain.
The strings and rattle make the car seem home made.

Your tongue is an obsidian blade.
You dream of saying "I'm sorry,"
but your wide teeth cage the words when you wake.
Sometimes, I see your lips bleed red
when you spread rumors about the ones you really love.
You are more careful when you are singing.
You should never be a nun
with that tongue of obsidian.

Seeds flow from your hands
and into my bird's open orange beak.
My green parrot runs back and forth
in search of your red painted nails
even though I've long returned from vacation
to find that my parrot turned greener.

Your mother's words of caution fall onto your head,
wrap around your neck,
roll down your back
and slowly seep into your thick skin.
There is no escape.
It looks like you are caught kneeling
in a sudden monsoon
of yellow and orange marigolds.

In the ceremony's sun,
you are a red strawberry with skinny legs.
You grimace and curse
when warm red juice appears between your unbelieving thighs.
You are salty and spilling over,
too bitter to eat and too dangerous to be around the men.

You are new underwear, practical, necessary,
So like your mother
you are 100% cotton and stitched with flowery detail,
So like your father
you are picked and made in the white hot sun.

You dream that
you are crying and barefoot
as you walk backwards
across the glittering glass and broken black asphalt
at midnight
under a new cradle of stars.
You will arrive at your bed
in the safe light of
dawn.

Grandma's Blue Sky

By indigo night,
I weight my black hair
with the bright iron of seven stars
and plunge headfirst
into the whirling birth of sparkling space

You retrieve me, My Friend.
You ignite my orange skin.
I warmly rise from the belly of the desert
like sweet sap from deep mesquite roots.
Your slanting light sometimes strikes me
like the shkshkshkshk of a rattlesnake's tail
or the whirrrrrrrrrrrrrrr of a hummingbird's wings
I open my eyes and shake out my hair
as you lift me like water vapor
through soft yielding petals
of Grandma's blue sky.

WORKS CITED

Anzaldúa, Gloria. *Borderlands: La Frontera : the New Mestiza*. San Francisco: Spin-sters/Aunt Lute, 1987.
Stivalet Corral , Stivalet. Asociacion Cultural Mascarones. *Agenda Tolteca 2002*. Eds. Maria Isabel Quevedo Plascencia, Mariano Leyva Acamatzin, Tlacatzin. Oco-topec, Morelos, Mexico: Asociacion Cultural Mascarones, A. C., 2001.
Hernández-Ávila, Inés. "An Open Letter to Chicanas: On the Power and Politics of Origin." *Reinventing the Enemy's Language: Contemporary Native Women's Writings of North America*. Eds. Joy Harjo and Gloria Bird. New York: W.W. Norton and Company, 1997, 235–246.
Merchant, Carolyn. *The Death of Nature: Women, Ecology, and the Scientific Revolution*. New York: Perennial/Harper and Row, 1980.
Silko, Leslie Marmon. *Ceremony*. New York: Viking, 1977
Tapahonso, Luci. "Blue Horses Rush In." *Writing As Revision: A Student's Anthology*. Eds. Beth Alvarado and Barbara Cully. Needham Heights, MA: Simon & Schuster, 1996.

Tezozomoc. "Revernacularizing Classical Náhuatl Through Danza (Dance) Azteca-Chichimeca." Teaching Indigenous Languages. Ed. Jon Reyhner. Flagstaff: Northern Arizona University, 1997.

Vasconcelos, Jose. *The Cosmic Race/La Raza Cosmica.* Trans. Dider T. Jaen. Baltimore: John Hopkins University Press, 1979

Vio, Victor. *Chitontiquiza: reportaje del silencio mexicano.* Mexico: Grijalba, 1998.

9

Indigenous Rights in Contemporary Mexico and Central America

Gabriel S. Estrada

INDIGENOUS SOVEREIGNTIES: CHANGING INTERNATIONAL LAWS OF ECONOMICS

Indigenous cultural movements utilize international mediums to bolster their diverse community welfares and to protect Indigenous rights. The broadest statement of cultural movement is that of the United Nations Commission on Human Rights whose sub-committee of mostly Indigenous representatives prepared a Draft Declaration on the Rights of Indigenous Peoples. "Welcoming the fact that indigenous peoples are organizing themselves for political, economic, and social and cultural enhancement and in order to bring an end to all forms of discrimination and oppression wherever they occur," the Draft includes Article 31's assertion that "Indigenous peoples, as a specific form of exercising their right to self determination, have the right to autonomy or self-government in matters relating to their internal and local affairs, including culture, religion, education, information, media, health, housing, employment, social welfare, economic activities, land and resource management, environment and entry by non-members, as well as ways and means for financing these autonomous functions" in U.N. document 34 I.L.M. 541 (1995). A central claim that I will honor throughout this work is the idea that Indigenous peoples seek to autonomously operate for their own best interests, making alliances with non-Natives or other Natives when necessary. An implicit message in the above quote is that Indigenous people will be able to adapt the science and technologies involved in "health" and "resource management" while maintaining control of their own "economic activities." Clearly, Indigenous peoples are capable of making the most advanced kinds of scientific and social decisions as they impact their own cultures, especially given the history of genocide and ecocide that non-Indigenous policies have helped to foster in recent history.

The lack of U.N. ratification of the Draft Declaration is part of a long genealogy in which States such as the United States of America, the United States of Mexico, and the Republic of Guatemala have used their economic, colonial based hegemony to legally deny Indigenous peoples specific autonomous rights that include accepting or rejecting technological projects that impact Native culture and land. In a contemporary context of the last forty years, these States have used organizations such as the World Bank (WB) and International Monetary Fund (IMF) to forge scientific studies and enterprises that support their exclusionary multinational politics and support their own State economies. One tactic that they use is to look at the Gross National Product (GNP) of a State as an indicator of their economic success, regardless of genocidal or ecocidal consequences of producing that GNP. Medical anthropologist Nancy Scheper-Hughes suggests an alternative method to a simple GNP analysis. She suggests counting the number of infant deaths as an indicator of how an increase in multinational and State capital impacts poor, gendered and racialized populations (280). Her application of this methodology shows a country like Brazil, which had a rising GNP, actually experienced extreme poverty, evidenced by incredible class divisions fueled by corrupt handling of the GNP. She terms this as a "macroparasitism" of market forces that are centered in the First World and wealthy corporations worldwide.

In the context of the Americas, U.S. macroparasitic policies of economic domination fund government suppression of Indigenous movements while supporting military operations of social suppression as LeFeber reports in *Inevitable Revolutions: The United States in Central America.* 1992 Nobel Peace Prize laureate Rigoberta Menchu states "I continue to think that the IMF [International Monetary Fund] and World Bank have a direct responsibility for the extreme poverty that plagues the majority of the world's population" (175). To leave the science of economics to multinational corporate interests is to be implicit in the deaths of Indigenous and poor populations. The Draft's adamant assertion of Indigenous economic rights is a necessary response to a history of affluent First World misuse of money and technological ventures on Indigenous lands. It is for these rights that Tonatierra, an Aztlán Xicano organization, published the 2000 Treaty of Teotihuacan via the pan-Indigenous group of Consejo de Organizaciones y Naciones Indigenas del Continente (CONIC). Referencing that "the financial policies imposed by the International Monetary Fund (IMF), the World Bank, and the InterAmerican Bank for Development have been complicit with the government states in establishing economic policy . . . that . . . has increased the levels of dependence, oppression and poverty of the Indigenous Peoples and other popular sectors of society," the Treaty enlists full support for a continuance of Native American traditions and calls for the passing of the U.N. Declaration of the Rights of Indigenous Peoples that will effect Xicano and Mexican Indians in the U.S. and Mexico (http://www.tonatierra.com/index.html/conic/treaty.htm).

In the Indigenous focused *Naked Science (1996)*, Laura Nader momentarily grants that "science may refer to a body of knowledge distinguishable from other knowledge by specific methods of validation . . . science . . . embodies empiricism . . . [and] . . . rationality" but focuses on the power dynamics behind scientific claims (1). Part of what upholds Indigenous Sovereignty is the scientific belief that humans embody universal qualities that an international language of science can express. Internationally recognized and codified methodologies of science and demography shape an understanding of how Indigenous people count in the modern world. "How many Indigenous people are there? Who counts as Indigenous? What is the status of health based upon age, ethnicity, class, and gender?" are central questions that effect international policies. "Population" is a key word within the discourse of international humanism that intersects Indigenous Rights and the scientific methodologies that support those multiple interests. States that undercount Indigenous populations do so to avoid the responsibility of consulting those populations about policies that affect them. At worst, States do not accurately count Indigenous peoples and compile realistic demographics on them in order to render any proof of genocide unavailable to Indigenous and human rights interests. It is easier for States to assimilate and murder people who do not have any scientific proof of existence.

It is because of Indigenous and human rights international activism that Indigenous peoples are gaining poli-economic recognition worldwide. S. James Anaya reports that the International Labour Organization's (ILO) recognition of Indigenous People's demands for rights led to the passing of "Convention No. 169 Concerning Indigenous and Tribal Peoples in Independent Countries, June 27, 1989" which recognizes "the aspirations of [indigenous] peoples to exercise control over their own institutions, ways of life and economic development and to maintain and develop their identities, languages and religions, within the framework of the States within which they live". Anaya asserts that the ILO Convention No. 169 has already benefited groups in Bolivia, Mexico, Columbia, and Norway (2). Under the United Nations, the Organization of American States (OAS) has yet to pass the Proposed American Declaration on the Rights of Indigenous Peoples which would further protect Native Americans, although the Indigenous Rights resolutions were passed in the 1994 UN Conference on Population and Development, the Fourth World Conference on Women in 1995, the 1996 World Summit for Social Development, the second United Nations Conference on Human Settlement in 1996, and the 2001 World Conference against Racism (Anaya 4–5). In "The 2002 Tribal, State, and Federal Judges Conference: Protection of Indigenous People's Human Rights: United States, International, and Comparative Law Perspectives," Zion concludes that international law is gaining importance within States as companies increasingly permeate State boundaries and as international wars between multiple States become more common. He argues that internet technologies also facilitate monitoring of remote areas of the world for human rights violations and new changes in law, making State violations of Indigenous rights more difficult.

Based upon increasing Indigenous and human rights pressures, OAS, IMF, WB, and States are forced to come up with new policies on development in Indigenous lands. The World Bank's Draft Operational Policies (OP 4.10) on Indigenous People gives a limited definition of who they can accept in their demographics of Indigenous Peoples: "(a) close attachment to ancestral territories and the natural resources in them; (b) presence of customary social and political institutions; (c) economic systems primarily oriented to subsistence production; (d) an indigenous language, often different from the predominant language; and (e) self-identification and identification by others as members of a distinct cultural group." Ideally, this allows protection for those such as the Yanamami who face the military and encroaching logging ventures into their areas of the rainforests of South America, a plight that Donna Haraway politicizes in "The Promises of Monsters." Raramuris of the Southwest who practice subsistence farming would also benefit as economic pressure could slow the destruction of their ancestral forests in the Tarahumara Mountains and Copper Canyon in the northern Mexican state of Chihuahua. Both logging and drug trafficking interests use violence to steal resources and lives from Raramuris (Rubio 192). Of course, the immediate question is whether or not any Latin State is willing to enforce WB sanctions should they become ratified. Even so, ratification is a first and necessary step from an international perspective.

The main limitations of the WB proposals are that the requirements of this policy do not apply to groups who (a) have left their communities of origin and (b) moved to urban areas (c) and/or migrated to obtain wage labor. What that limitation does not account for is the vicious cycle of a lack of Indigenous rights. Natives face oppression from State and multinational corporate interests that force them to permanently or seasonally vacate their ancestral homes. Many times, to stay is to die or starve, yet to leave is to lose international standing as Indigenous. Euro-American Ted Downing notes that the World Bank's identifiers violate numerous aspects of the proposed Indigenous Rights stating:

> Impoverishment has led many of the world's indigenous people to leave their communities, move to urban areas, and find temporary jobs as laborers. Although absent, many of these people maintain close links with their communities, hold rights to ancestral lands, and provide financial support for civil and cultural services. Such is the case of tens of thousands of Oaxacan indigenous migrants who are working in the United States and Mexico City. The proposed policy unjustifiably excludes these and millions of other indigenous peoples from eligibility. It creates an international definition that governments may use to justify claims that indigenous peoples within their borders are not really indigenous. And worse, the proposed policy thrusts an external policy wedge deep into indigenous social structure, creating two classes of people who are eligible for benefits and risk mitigation . . . This exclusionary clause is a direct affront to the sovereignty, traditional rights and the body politic of indigenous people. It should be immediately removed and not replaced with compromise language.

Part of his critique is that the World Bank does not mandate a review of the economic projects that Indigenous peoples themselves draft. A need for Native consultation is built into Article 31's assertion that Indigenous peoples create their own economic plans. To consult Indigenous Peoples is critical as the WB and IMF find increasing criticism as their missions to "develop" Indigenous lands often leave the First World of "developing" companies with great profits that do not reach Indigenous peoples themselves, creating a greater division of capital that feeds race, class and gender oppression. For example, IMF and WB plans for poor populations to plant non-dietary "cash crops" often leave people even hungrier without the edible food they would have usually planted. Menchu writes about the Guatemala's unfortunate circumstance of raising coffee instead of corn in a Maya context in *I, Rigoberta Menchu*. Should the OP 4.10 draft be implemented and adversely affect Native populations, Indigenous critiques on those documents will appear from various Indigenous nations.

Migration is an increasing factor in Indigenous economies and politics. As Downing notes, migratory tribes such as those from Southern non-U.S. lands also exercise rights in the U.S. *El Estado del desarollo economico y social de los pueblos indigenas de Mexico* reports that Mixtecos were able to gain monies for programs from the Instituto Nacional Indigena to fund programs in the nineties on both sides of the U.S./Mexican border. Funds for these programs came from both U.S. and Mexican sources. Alfaro suggest that Zapoteco and Mixteco border-crossing organizations are positive model for other Indigenous groups that migrate across the border (313). What neither Mexican nor U.S. States recognize is the long history of Mexican Indian migrations in pre-columbian, colonial, Mexican, and U.S. eras to lands now split by the U.S.-Mexican border. The Peace and Dignity Run in 2000 comprised of Indigenous peoples that included self-identified Xicanas/os was an effort to resist State borders, culminating in a meeting at Teotihuacan, Mexico.

Given the Latin American countries of great Indigenous populations, how can it be possible that there aren't any significant mass of Indian diasporas in the U.S.? Bolivia is 71% Indian; Guatemala is 66% Indian. Ecuador is 41%; Peru is 47% Indian. The Mexican Indigenous population over five that speaks an Indigenous language is numbered at around 5.5 million in 1995 (Rubio 49). The Indigenous population is 14% at 12,000,000, although some sources report 23,000,000 Indians, or 29% of Mexico's population. At least 42,000,000 Indians, or 6.33% of pan-American populations are Indian, a number that would easily quadruple if one considers mixed blooded Mestizos/as, as Indigenous too (Ordenez Cifuentes 21-20). Ewen notes that "using an ethnic basis for the number of Indians who belong to a distinct cultural range as high as forty percent of the total Mexican population. Using the wider criteria of the United States, almost ninety percent of Mexico's population that has some Indian blood and might well be considered Indigenous if they desired" (101). Auto-identification will be a key factor as Mexican Indian movements increase and decrease activity. A continuing aspect of Native American efforts for sovereignty is to utilize the methodologies of demography to count themselves as nations and individuals, including populations that were previously uncounted or even presumed dead within official State records. Clearly, Indigenous peoples can adapt the laws of economies and scientific methodologies to answer their own cultural questions, tabulate demography, and inform their own political agendas at the home, community, pueblo, nation or international level.

INDIGENOUS LIBERATIONS FROM WAR AND SEXUAL VIOLENCE

In terms of military service, Indigenous peoples in Latin America are often the ones who most disproportionately serve in the "patriotic" role of soldier or its opposite, the rebel defending Indigenous land from State intrusion. As Eduardo Galeano documents in *Century of the Wind*, throughout the Americas, poor Native and Mestizo men disproportionately serve as soldiers in and targets of State military forces, a trend that is rooted in colonial legacies. These populations also wound, kill, and rape communities that are often Indigenous or mixed-blooded, in contrast to more European and richer populations in the U.S., Costa Rica, or other Latin American States. That is, wars tend to concentrate on the poorest areas which are often the most racially marked as Indian, and the soldiers that serve State programs of genocide tend to be racially identifiable as Indian. Throughout the twentieth century, States manage to divide Indigenous populations through war and press males into service through a variety of means that range from economic pressures, to prison, torture, and death threats (LeFeber). Violence from previous eras of colonization and wars does not merely dissipate once wars officially end. Instead, that sexualized violence tends to implode within Indigenous populations whether that population can remain at home in already oppressed communities or migrate to face a status of illegal or non-citizen in new States such as Mexico or the U.S. In *Worlds of Hurt,* Kali Tal argues that Viet Nam soldiers, Jewish Holocaust survivors, and American sexual abuse victims all suffer from post traumatic stress syndrome, an epidemiology that critiques a patriarchal American system that values suffering in male dominated wars above the trauma of women and children of any race or gender who face sexualized violence in a domestic sphere (4). Article 22 of the Indigenous Right Draft partially recognizes sexual violence when it states that "Particular attention shall be paid to the rights and special needs of indigenous elders, women, youth, children and disabled persons" which is an honest but unfortunate grouping of peoples who tend to lack power in international and community politics. Clearly, both male and female Indigenous soldiers, as well as Indigenous women and children who experience domestic, sexualized violence, share a state of trauma that warrants international and internal community concern. Scientific methodologies can help identify engendered violence in a manner that works with complex community goals as opposed to singling out "sexist" traits of "machismo" as further evidence of racial and cultural inferiority and further fueling racialized oppression that often targets women the most.

At the National Indigenous Congress of 1996, Indigenous women from various regions of Mexico, including Nahuatl lands, made an intellectual and social statement of their own specific rights in "Propuestas de las mujeres indigenas al Congreso Nacional Indigena" that I translate.

> We, Indigenous women, have the right to live in a society that bases itself in relations of respect, cooperation, equality, and equilibrium in the diverse cultures that form the nation; that is to say, no discrimination for our condition as Indigenous women, and no exclusion for being Indigenous women, and no sexual violations (physically, sexually, mentally, and economically) for being Indigenous women. (Rubio 224)

While Indigenous women of INI struggle for their rights, they do not consider leaving their culture. Instead they seek to modify practices within their own traditions, languages, lands and customs. "The customs we have shouldn't harm anyone" added Indigenous women organizers.

Among Indigenous women activist, Maya author Rigoberta Menchu is without doubt the most famous. When she won the 1992 Nobel Peace Prize, U.S. journalism begin to cover the genocide of Maya in Guatemala that relied upon a military trained by the C.I.A and funded by U.S. agricultural interests for over thirty years (LeFeber 359). Menchu's testimony and other human rights documentations of massacres offer scientific proof of State terrorism. Manz assures readers that Falla's *Massacres in the Jungle: Ixcan, Guatemala* has high "ethical standards and exceptional scholarship" (*xiii*) as Falla lists names of deceased in various massacres. The Guatemalan government heightened massacres in the 1980's, a period influenced by Reagan's strong right wing influence in Central America.

Like Menchu, Zapatistas of southern Mexico also used a variety of media to draw international attention to their quest for Indigenous rights. They used internet and FAX communications to report deaths and Mexican government attacks in Chiapas communities. The 1994 North American Free Trade Agreement (NAFTA) that promised to lower Mexican prices, privatize Indigenous lands, and increase poverty, sparked the revolt. Media coverage and international support of Zapatistas that included mass protests in Mexico City, the U.S., and Europe prompted Mexico to avoid the scorched earth policies that were prevalent in Guatemala (Carrigan 439). It was this reporting of facts to international Indigenous and human rights groups and media that put pressure on the Mexican government to begin negotiations. Part of Zapatista international support comes from writers like Carrigan who report an astounding 10% infant mortality rate and 70% poverty rate in a Chiapas state that produces 47% of Mexico's gas along with high productions of oil, wood, corn, bananas, and meat.

Lindau and Cook note that the Zapatista San Andreas Accords that demanded a cease-fire and greater autonomy from the Mexican State show that Natives work on international, community and State levels. However, because the State did not end their attacks against the Zapatistas, its signing by both parties in 1996 meant too little in terms of actual State policy. In Acteal, 45 Indigenous peoples were massacred by State troops in 1997 (33). In an attempt to subside continuing violence, the Commission of Pacification and Agreement (COCOPA) outlined a proposal that was to reform the Mexican Constitution. Zapatistas showed initiative in approving the 1996 COCOPA proposal, but the Mexican State refused, eventually offering a weaker version in 1998 that has never been passed by Congress. The Zapatista version of the 1996 COCOPA is worth quoting as it reflects the interests of various Indigenous groups that include Nahuatl peoples who had originally had input into the document through the 1996 National Congress of Indians (Stavenhagen 83). I copy first two parts of the 1996 COCOPA revision of the 1992 Constitution Article 4, a revision that had more vaguely promised to protect Indigenous customs:

> The indigenous peoples have the right to free determination and, as an expression of this, to autonomy as part of Mexican State, such that they may:
> I. Choose their internal forms of social, economic, political, and cultural organization;
> II. Apply their traditional [judicial] systems of regulation and solution for internal conflicts, respecting individual guarantees, human rights, and, in

particular, the dignity and integrity of women; their proceedings, trials, and decisions will be validated by the jurisdictional authorities of the State; (Landau and Cook 32)

Other sections of the revised article 4 include rights to vote, Indigenous land, language, and communication, once again affirming that technology, economics, law, and other rational ventures will find their appropriate places within autonomous Indigenous groups without State dictatorship.

Both COCOPA and the Zapatistas are but the more visible outcomes of a long history of extremely varied activisms by Indigenous peoples. What occurs with one group may differ in the next. For example, violence and repression have not stopped in Chiapas, and the signing of an Indigenous Rights Bill that reflects the input of Mexican Indian communities has not occurred even as privatization of Indigenous lands and eviction of Indigenous peoples in the Chiapan Lacondon forest persists. In contrast, Oaxacan Indians have managed to pass state laws that give limited autonomy to its many groups at the smaller state level (Rubio).

The anti-terrorist increases in border regulation augments the State's abilities to terrorize those who suffer most from U.S. support of anti-Indigenous terrorism in Latin America. Not surprisingly, immigrants fleeing from U.S. funded Indigenous based wars in Latin America are not granted political asylum in the U.S. The sometimes subtle and not so subtle violent U.S. terrorism of "illegality" continues for many and is bilaterally supported by U.S. and Latin American States. Grimes reports that "the state, as arbitrator of disparate interests, can maintain those structures that support the advanced capitalist enterprise, managing the contradictions and dislocation associated with its penetration and using migration as an escape valve" (18). Instead of social reforms, Latin American States exile or economically force immigration with capitalistic interests that the U.S. facilitates. Bustamante demonstrates that Mexican migrants in the U.S. are political scapegoats in times of increasing unemployment, even when they have "filled specific labor shortages within the United states at these times" (Grimes 15). In fact, Grimes asserts that the U.S. state and federal policy makers routinely exaggerate the levels of economic drains that Latin American diasporas bring to the U.S., while suppressing information on the net economic gains in such industries as farming and industry that boost the U.S. economy.

From colonial times to the present, transnational economies have impinged upon Indigenous rights through genocidal and economically oppressive actions. However, the tens of millions of Indigenous peoples left in Latin America are testimony that communities will survive. An important development towards the beginning of this new millennium is the international recognition of Indigenous rights through work in the U.N. and other international organizations that include Pan-Indigenous political groups. As transnational businesses gain power over State international policies, more attention might focus on economic rights of Indigenous peoples that are inherent in pursuing rights as Indigenous Nations. Women's contributions are not left behind in organization, although sexual issues are still hard to press. As international migration increases due to changing world markets, Indigenous issues become more complicated as many leave traditional land to settle or migrate elsewhere, sometimes returning with renewed efforts to secure Indigenous rights in their homeland. Perhaps documents such as the Draft Declaration on the Rights of Indigenous People can impact and stabilize these communities.

UN Draft Declaration on the Rights of Indigenous Peoples

Preamble:

The *United Nations (UN)* affirms that Indigenous peoples have the same rights, including the right to be different as any other peoples in the world.

All peoples in the world including Indigenous peoples contribute to humankind and no one people in the world is superior to any other. All policies or practices which are based on this idea are racist, illegal and unjust;

Indigenous peoples should be free from discrimination of any kind.

Through colonization Indigenous peoples have been dispossessed of their lands and resources and were not allowed to develop as they wished which is a violation of their human rights;

There is an urgent need to respect and promote the inherent rights of Indigenous peoples, especially lands, territories and resources;

The UN recognizes that Indigenous peoples are organizing themselves to improve their rights and to end discrimination and oppression;

Indigenous peoples can only maintain and strengthen their cultures, traditions and institutions by exercising control over the developments affecting their lands and resources based on their needs;

The UN recognizes that respect for indigenous peoples knowledge and traditional practices contributes to the proper sustainable management of the environment;

The presence of the military must be removed from First Nations lands which will in turn lead to peace, understanding and progress among peoples and Nations in the world;

The UN recognizes that First Nations families and communities have a shared responsibility for the upbringing, education and well-being of their children;

The UN recognizes that Indigenous peoples have the right to freely decide what relationship they will have with other governments based on co-existence, mutual benefit and full respect;

First Nations treaties and agreements with other governments are an international concern and responsibility;

Several important UN documents, including the UN Charter, recognize the right of self determination of all peoples which means indigenous peoples can freely decide their own political status and pursue their own economic, social and cultural development;

Nothing in this document can be used to deny Indigenous peoples of their right of self determination;

Government members of the UN should follow and put into place all international laws, especially human rights standards as they apply to Indigenous peoples in consultation with Indigenous peoples;

The United Nations has an important and ongoing role in protecting and promoting the rights of Indigenous peoples;

This declaration is an important step in recognizing and protecting Indigenous peoples rights;

Part 1

Article 1. Human Rights

Indigenous peoples have the full right to all human rights recognized under international law;

Article 2. Equality with Other peoples

Indigenous peoples have equal rights and dignity with all other peoples including freedom from any kind of negative discrimination;

Article 3. Self Determination

Indigenous peoples have the right to self determination. This means they can freely determine their political status and identity and pursue their own economic, social and cultural development;

Article 4. Strengthen Cultures

Indigenous peoples have the right to maintain and strengthen their cultures and systems while at the same time having the right to participate in the Canadian society if they so choose;

Article 5. Belong to a Nation

Every Indigenous person has the right to belong to a Nation;

Part 2

Article 6. No Genocide

Indigenous peoples have the collective right to live in freedom, peace and security and to be protected from the total destruction of their nation or any act of violence including the removal by Canada of Indigenous children from their families for any reason;

Article 7. No Ethnocide Or Assimilation

Indigenous peoples have the right to continue to live as distinct peoples and to be protected from any act which would take away this right including taking Indigenous peoples' lands and resources, forced removal from homelands, the imposition of other cultures on them or lies directed against them;

Article 8. Indigenous identities

Indigenous peoples have the right to their collective and individual identities including their identities as indigenous peoples

Article 9 Belong to Community

Indigenous peoples have the right to belong to indigenous communities or nations according to their own traditions and customs;

Article 10 Forceable Removal

Indigenous peoples have the right not to be removed from their lands by force. No relocation shall take place without their free and informed consent and only after adequate compensation is paid or the option to return is provided;

Article 11 Protection During Armed Conflict

Indigenous peoples have the right to special protection and security under international law during armed conflicts especially against other indigenous peoples. They shall not be recruited for military purposes against their will, forced to abandon their lands, forced to work under discriminatory conditions and under no circumstances shall indigenous children be recruited for the armed forces.

Part 3

Article 12 Return of Artifacts

Indigenous peoples have the right to maintain, protect, develop and revive their customs and traditions in the past, present and future including sacred sites, artifacts, ceremonies, visual and performing arts and literature. Indigenous peoples also have the right to the return of their cultural, spiritual or religious property taken without their consent;

Article 13 Practice Own Religions

Indigenous peoples have the right to practice, develop and teach their own spirituality and religious traditions, customs and ceremonies including the right to use their sacred sites, ceremonial objects and the right to the return of human remains of their ancestors; Governments shall help indigenous peoples to ensure that indigenous sacred places, including burial sites are preserved, respected and protected.

Article 14 Transmit Histories and Understand Proceedings

Indigenous people have the right to use, develop, revive and teach their indigenous histories, languages, philosophies, writing systems and literature and to their own place names. Governments are required to ensure that indigenous rights are protected. Indigenous citizens have the right to use their own languages in any court or administrative proceedings including indigenous interpreters.

Part 1

Article 15 Education Rights

Indigenous children have their right to the same education provided to other non-indigenous children. Indigenous peoples have their right to establish and control their educational systems and schools, in their own languages and cultures, using indigenous teaching methods. Dominant governments shall provide appropriate resources to indigenous peoples.

Article 16 Public Information

Indigenous peoples have the right to have their cultures and histories appropriately reflected in all forms of education and public information. External governments shall strive to eliminate prejudice and promote tolerance, understanding and good relations among indigenous peoples and all segments of society.

Article 17 Media

Indigenous people can establish their own media in their own languages. They also have the right to equal access to all forms of non-indigenous media.

Article 18 Labour Law

Indigenous peoples have the rights to under national and international labour law including a right against discrimination in employment, salary and conditions of labour issues. Indigenous peoples have the right if they so choose to fully participate in all decisions affecting them, through representatives chosen by them, and to maintain and develop their own decision making institutions;

Part 5

Article 19 Participation in Decision Making

Indigenous peoples have the right if they so choose to fully participate in all decisions affecting them, through representatives chosen by them, and to maintain and develop their own decision making institutions;

Article 20 Legislation Participation

Indigenous peoples have the full right to participate through their own procedures in policy or lawmaking if it affects them;

Article 21 Own Economic Systems

Indigenous Peoples have the right to their own political, economic and social systems including their own means of subsistence. Anyone deprived of their means of subsistence is entitled to fair compensation.

Article 22 Special Measures

Indigenous Peoples have the right to special measures for the immediate improvement of their socio-economic situation. The needs of elders, women, youth, children and disabled should get special attention.

Article 23 Right to Plan

Indigenous peoples have the right to set their own priorities for development. They can develop their own programs on health, economic development using their own institutions.

Article 24 Traditional Medicines

Indigenous Peoples have the right to their own traditional medicines and health practices including the protection of plants, animals and minerals. We also have the right to access without discrimination to all medical institutions, health services and medical care.

Part 6

Article 25 Spiritual Ties to Land

Indigenous Peoples have the right to maintain and strengthen their spiritual relationship with their traditional land, waters and resources for future generations.

Article 26 Environment

Indigenous Peoples have the right to own, develop and control the total environment of their traditional territories. This includes the use of their own laws, traditions and customs and lands and resource management systems.

Article 27 Return of Lands

Indigenous peoples have the right to the return of their traditional lands and resources taken, used or occupied without their consent. If not they should be fully compensated in land of equal quality, size and legal status.

Article 28 Environmental Protection

Indigenous Peoples have the right to the conservation, restoration and protection of their lands and resources including assistance to do this. Indigenous lands will not be used for military purposes or for the storage or disposal of hazardous materials.

Article 29 Intellectual Property

Indigenous Peoples have the right to own and control their intellectual and cultural property including indigenous sciences, technologies, genetic, seeds, medicines, flora and fauna, languages, literature, designs and visual and performing arts.

Article 30 Resource Development

Indigenous people have the right to determine their own priorities for the development of their traditional lands and resources including environmental assessment on projects affecting indigenous lands. Fair compensation will be paid to indigenous peoples where damage has been done or to lessen the effects of development.

Part 7

Article 31 Self Determination

Indigenous Peoples have the right to self determination which they can exercise through their right to self government including matters relating to culture, religion, education, health, housing, employment, social welfare, economic activities, land and resources management, environment and financing self government.

Article 32 Citizenship

Indigenous Peoples have the collective right to determine own citizenship according to their own customs and traditions including the structure membership of their institutions.

Article 33 Justice Systems

Indigenous peoples have the right to maintain, develop and promote their own justice systems including traditional practices, structures and procedures in accordance with international human rights standards.

Article 34 Individual Responsibilities

Indigenous Peoples have the right to determine the responsibilities of individuals in their communities.

Article 35 Cross Border Rights

Indigenous peoples have the right to maintain their relationships, customs, contacts, and spiritual, cultural, economic and social activities with other peoples across international borders.

Article 36 Treaty Enforcement

Indigenous peoples have the right to the recognition and enforcement of their treaties and agreements with external governments according to their original spirit and intent. Conflicts should be submitted to competent international bodies.

Part 8

Article 37 Declaration Implementation

Governments shall take effective action in consultation with Indigenous peoples to implement this Declaration. The rights recognized in this document shall be included in Canadian legislation which can be enforced by Indigenous peoples.

Article 38 Support to Implement

Indigenous peoples have the right to receive financial support from governments to help implement this declaration including the pursuit of their political, economic, social, cultural and spiritual development.

Article 39 Dispute Resolution

Indigenous Peoples have the right to a fair and acceptable dispute resolution process and effective remedies for violations of their rights. Decisions shall consider their customs, traditions, rules and indigenous legal systems.

Article 40 UN Cooperation to Implement

The United Nations shall make its bodies, resources and technical assistance available to ensure the full implementation of this Declaration

Article 41 Special UN Indigenous Body

The United Nations shall create a Special UN Indigenous body to implement this Declaration. Indigenous peoples shall participate directly with this body and all UN bodies will promote the full application of this Declaration.

Article 42 Minimum Standards

The rights recognized in this Declaration are a minimum standard for protecting the rights of Indigenous peoples.

Article 43 Sexual Equality

All rights recognized in this declaration apply equally to men and women.

Article 44 Non Extinguishment

This declaration cannot be used to diminish, extinguish existing or future rights of indigenous peoples.

Article 45 Interpretation

This declaration does not give any right to anyone to do anything contrary to the United Nations Charter.

WORKS CITED

Anaya, S. James. "International Development Regarding Indigenous Peoples." *The Tribal, State, and Federal Judges Conference: Protection of Indigenous People's Human Rights: United States, International, and Comparative Law Perspectives.* Tucson: University of Arizona Press, 2002.

Anaya, S. James. *Indigenous Rights in International Law.* New York: Oxford University Press, 1996.

Briseño Guerrero. "Los Desvaríos del Poder Ante la Autoridad: El Sistema Político del Pueblo Nahua de la Huasteca." Pueblos Indígenas ante el Derecho. Eds. Victoria Chenaut y María Teresa Sierra. México, Centro Frances de Estudios Mexicanos y Centroamericanos, 1995.

Carrigan, Ana. "Chiapas, The First Postmodern Revolution. *Our Word is Our Weapon: Selected Writings* Ed. Juana Ponce de Leon, 2001

Caudillo Félix, Gloria Alicia. El indio en el ensayo mexicano. Guadalajara: Universidad de Guadalajara, 2000.

Cook, Curtis, and Lindeau, Juan D., Eds. *Aboriginal Rights and Self-Government: The Canadian and Mexican Experience in North American Perspective.* Montreal: McGill-Queens Press, 2000. Esteva, Gustavo. "The Revolution of the New Commons." Lindau, Juan D. and Cook, Curtis. "One Continent, Contrasting Styles: The Canadian Experience in North American Perspective." Stavenhagen, Rodolfo. "Indigenous Movements and Politics in Mexico and Latin America."

Downing, Ted. *Development Policy Kiosk. http://www.policykiosk.com/,* 2001.

Draft Declaration on the Rights of Indigenous Peoples. U.N. document 34 I.L.M. 541, 1995.

Falla, Ricardo. *Massacres in the Jungle: Ixcan, Guatemala, 1975–1982.* Boulder: Westview Press, 1994.

Galeano, Jose. *Century of the Wind.* New York: Pantheon Books, 1988.

Garduño Cervantes, Julio. *El fin del silencio: documentos indígenas de México.* México: La Red de Jonas, 1983.

Grimes, Kimberly M. *Crossing Borders: Changing Social Identities in Southern Mexico.* Tucson: University of Arizona, 1998.

González Galván, Jorge Alberto. Panorama del derecho mexicano: Derecho Indígena. México: Universidad Nacional Autónoma de México, 1997.

Haraway, Donna. "The Promises of Monsters: A Regenerative Politics for Inappropriate/d Others." Ed. Laurence Grossberg. *Cultural Studies Reader.* New York: Routledge, 1992.

Instituto Nacional Indigenista (INI). Mexico City, 2000.

Ordóñez Cifuentes, José Rolando. "Constitución y Derechos Étnicos en México." *Derechos Indígenas en la Actualidad.* Ed. José Rolando Ordóñez Cifuentes México: Universidad Nacional Autónoma de México, 1994.

Menchu, Rigoberta. *I, Rigoberta Menchu.* New York: Verso, 1984

Menchú, Rigoberta. *Crossing Borders.* Trans. Ann Wright. London: Verso Books, 1998.

La Feber, Walter. *Inevitable Revolutions: The United States in Central America.* New York: W.W. Norton and Company, 1993.

Robles O., J. Ricardo, y Vallejo, Carlos F., "Los juicios en el pueblo rarámuri." *Tradiciones y costumbres juridicas en comunidades indígenas de México.* Eds. Rosa Isabel Estrada Martinez y Gisela González Guerra. México: Comisión de Derechos Humanos, 1995.

Rubio, Miguel A., y Zolla, Carlos. Estado del desarrollo económico y social de los pueblos indígenas de México, 1996-1997: Primer informe, tomo 1y2. México: Instituto Nacional Indigenista.

Scheper-Hughes, Nancy. *Death Without Weeping: The Violence of Everyday Life in Brazil.* Berkeley: University of California Press, 1992.

Tal, Kali. *Worlds of Hurt: Reading the Literature of Trauma.* Cambridge University Press, 1986.

Tonatierra, *Treaty of Teotihuacan.* Mexico City: Consejo de Organizaciones y Naciones Indigenas del Continente (CONIC). http://www.tonatierra.com/index.html/conic/treaty.htm, 2000.

UC Santa Cruz Native Research and Pacific Research Clusters. Online Posting 2001. "Decolonizing Methodology and Beyond: Constructing Indigenous Methodologies." Four Directions Institute Conferences and Cultural Events. 24 Feb. 2002. http://www.drlamay.com/uc_santa_cruz_native_research.htm.

Vigil, Angel. *The Eagle on the Cactus: Traditional Stories from México.* Englewood, CO: Libraries Unlimited Inc., 2000.

Vio, Victor. *Chitontiquiza: reportaje del silencio mexicano.* Mexico: Grijalba, 1998.

Zion, James. W. "Coming Soon to A Courthouse Near You." *The Tribal, State, and Federal Judges Conference: Protection of Indigenous People's Human Rights: United States, International, and Comparative Law Perspectives.* Tucson: University of Arizona Press, 2002.